ALPINI
ITALIAN MOUNTAIN TROOPS

1872 TO THE **PRESENT**

ALPINI
ITALIAN MOUNTAIN TROOPS

1872 TO THE **PRESENT**

ENRICO FINAZZER

SCHIFFER MILITARY
4880 Lower Valley Road · Atglen, PA 19310

Edited by Ralph Riccio
Designed by Christopher Bower
Cover design by Christopher Bower
Type set in Novecento Sans Wide/Minion Pro

ISBN: 978-0-7643-6654-3
Printed in China

Published by Schiffer Publishing, Ltd.
4880 Lower Valley Road
Atglen, PA 19310
Phone: (610) 593-1777; Fax: (610) 593-2002
Email: Info@schifferbooks.com
Web: www.schifferbooks.com

For our complete selection of fine books on this and related subjects, please visit our website at www.schifferbooks.com. You may also write for a free catalog.

Schiffer Publishing's titles are available at special discounts for bulk purchases for sales promotions or premiums. Special editions, including personalized covers, corporate imprints, and excerpts, can be created in large quantities for special needs. For more information, contact the publisher.

We are always looking for people to write books on new and related subjects. If you have an idea for a book, please contact us at proposals@schifferbooks.com.

FSC
www.fsc.org
MIX
Paper | Supporting
responsible forestry
FSC® C104723

CONTENTS

ACKNOWLEDGMENTS

Many people, organizations, and institutions have offered their cooperation for the successful completion of this book. First, I would like to thank the Museo Nazionale Storico degli Alpini of Trento, my hometown; its former director, General Stefano Basset; and the newly appointed one, Tenente Colonnello Lepore. They and the entire staff have let me research the bulky archives to find documents and pictures, many of which had never been published before. My thanks also go to the Museo Nazionale Storico della Guerra of Rovereto, the largest military museum in Italy, and to the Museo Storico del Trentino, which preserves memories of the Great War.

During my work, I have come into contact with many people who have enthusiastically given their contributions, which include pictures or documents and suggestions for improving the text: Andrea Bianchi, Luigi Carretta, Carlo Cucut, Luigi Manes, Walter Musizza, Roberto Rossini, Pierluigi Scolè, Antonio Tallillo, and David Zambon e Vito Zita. To them I extend my sincerest gratitude.

Pietro Compagni deserves special mention as the creator of the superb uniform drawings.

Last but not least, I would not have succeeded in my work without the help of Ralph Riccio, who has assisted me throughout the entire translation and editing process.

INTRODUCTION

In 2022, the Italian Alpine troops celebrate the 150th year since their foundation within the *Regio Esercito*—the army of the newly established Kingdom of Italy.[1] Since then, every time Italy has fought a war, these soldiers, simply called Alpini, have been at the forefront, giving their tribute in blood, in victory as well as in defeat. They have also often been the first to intervene in the event of natural disasters afflicting the population, both in Italy and abroad. This is probably the reason the Alpini are so popular everywhere in Italy—the black feather they wear on their hats is very well known.

One peculiarity of these troops within the *Regio Esercito* was the local recruitment. From the beginning, the companies were composed of men born in the same villages and valleys, while in the rest of the army, soldiers coming from different regions were mixed and regiments moved rather often from one town to another. This circumstance rendered the Alpine units particularly cohesive. The relationships between soldiers, NCOs, and officers were strong; in general, men felt a deep sense of belonging within this corps.

This book is a tribute to these men, who have had such an important role in the recent history of Italy.

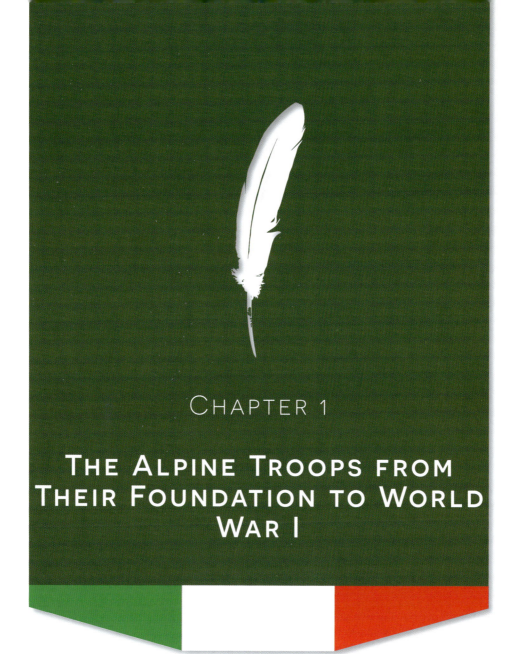

Chapter 1

The Alpine Troops from Their Foundation to World War I

General Cesare Ricotti Magnani, ministry of war, at the time of the foundation of the *Alpini. Museo Nazionale Storico degli Alpini*

General Giuseppe Perrucchetti, traditionally considered the founder of the *Alpini*, as a young officer. *Museo Nazionale Storico degli Alpini*

The existence of special troops dedicated to the defense of mountain areas has been known in Italy since the Roman Empire, which had within its army some *coortes alpinorum* (mountaineers' cohorts). More recently, in the seventeenth century, the militia formed by the Waldensians in the Alps between France and Piedmont fought valiantly against French and Piedmontese troops to defend their freedom and religion. At the same time, the inhabitants of Cadore, a mountain region in the northeast of Italy, kept the armies of the German Empire and, later, of the Austrian Empire at bay several times. These examples from the past were taken into consideration by the higher ranks of the Royal Army after the disastrous war waged in 1866 against the Empire of Austria showed that a reform of the armed forces was called for.[1]

The Kingdom of Italy, which, after centuries, reunited a large part the peninsula south of the Alps under the Savoy dynasty, had been proclaimed only five years before, and its armed forces at the time were the result of a hurried collage of those existing in the old Italian states. During that war, Italy had been defeated on land at Custoza, near Verona, and on sea near the Adriatic island of Lissa— evidence of the limitations of an army and navy that resulted from a union of the professional armed forces of the poorly organized old Italian states. On the other hand, in spite of the disastrous way it had been conducted, the war had won vast territories in the northeast of the peninsula for the Kingdom, causing a great extension of the borders with their traditional enemy, Austria, which needed to be defended.

Last but not least, the short war between Prussia and France in 1870 seemed to demonstrate the superiority of the armies that were organized with the levy of the whole male population. All men were trained during a relatively short military service and then called to arms when needed. They were adopted by the Prussian army, over those armies formed completely of men doing war as a profession; adopted by France but also in Italy and by many other armies throughout Europe.

This generally felt need for renovation led finally to the reform promoted by General Ricotti Magnani,[2] Minister of War from September 1870. By the end of the year, the minister had approved by the parliament his project of an army organized in a so-called "Prussian" way. Italy would be subdivided, for military purposes, into several *Distretti Militari* (military districts), whose officers in charge had the responsibility of registering all the males apt to serve in the army, call them when they reached the prescribed age, and send them to their assignment units. In case of war, the districts handled the general call to arms and mobilization.

The men who were judged to be apt for the army were subdivided into three categories:

- *Esercito permanente*, the standing army formed by soldiers in regular service
- *Milizia mobile*, soldiers recently dismissed, therefore ready to be recalled in case of war and able to serve on the first line like the standing army
- *Milizia territoriale*, formed by older men destined to garrison the rear area

Moreover, each district had a number of standing units at hand, called *compagnie distrettuali permanenti*, always ready to move into action at short notice.

This organization provides the framework for the foundation of the Alpine corps, which is traditionally attributed to an infantry captain named Giuseppe Perrucchetti,[3] who was passionately devoted to the mountains and an expert in mountain warfare. In December 1871, while in service at Verona, he wrote a paper on the defense of the new border and on garrisoning of the Alpine passes, and submitted it to his superior. In his studies, he made a strong proposition that the defense of the Alpine valleys be entrusted to special units formed of mountaineers who had been levied locally, taking advantage of their perfect knowledge of their mountain environment and their attitude about living and fighting in it. Their duty was not intended to be to defeat the enemy, but only to retard its advance and to give the army the time necessary to mobilize and take proper positions. When Minister Ricotti Magnani eventually learned of Captain Perrucchetti's idea, he appreciated it very much and tried to implement it, knowing very well that the political climate was not favorable to new military expenses. However, he was able to take advantage of the need to create new military districts on the territory that had been annexed after the 1866 war. He proposed a further measure to the parliament: to attach a few *compagnie distrettuali permamenti* to some of the districts. These *compagnie distrettuali permamenti* would be entrusted to the defense of the valleys through which an enemy could cross the mountains, formed of men who had been recruited in these same valleys.

This version of the genesis of the Alpini has been questioned in recent years, beginning in the 1980s, when some studies have highlighted[4] how the debate over the best way to defend the Alpine border had already started just after the 1866 war, and others had put forward ideas similar to that of Perrucchetti before him. Therefore, he found a military environment that was already prepared to move in that direction and, most of all, a minster of war who appreciated the value of the mountains and was a climber himself. Be that as it may, the proposal by General Ricotti Magnani was approved, and the Royal Decree n. 1056 was promulgated by the King on October 15, 1872, which has been accepted to be the official date for the founding of the *Alpini*.

Jacket of a corporal dating to the mid-1880s, when the green collar insignia were adopted for the *Alpini*. *Museo Nazionale Storico degli Alpini*

PERSONNEL, ORGANIZATION AND WEAPONS: DEVELOPMENT UNTIL THE GREAT WAR

The new law authorized fifteen companies, soon called *compagnie alpine* (alpine companies), with three officers and 120 Alpini, each company being assigned only a mule with a towed cart, so that during the frequent excursions into the mountains, most of the equipment was borne on the shoulders of the men themselves. The formation took several months; thus, they became operational in March 1873, stationed in the following towns and villages along the Alps:

1ª Compagnia: Borgo San Dalmazzo
2ª Compagnia: Demonte
3ª Compagnia: Venasca
4ª Compagnia: Lucerna San Giovanni
5ª Compagnia: Fenestrelle
6ª Compagnia: Oulx
7ª Compagnia: Susa
8ª Compagnia: Aosta
9ª Compagnia: Bard
10ª Compagnia: Domodossola
11ª Compagnia: Chiavenna
12ª Compagnia: Sondrio
13ª Compagnia: Edolo
14ª Compagnia: Pieve di Cadore
15ª Compagnia: Tolmezzo

In the beginning, the *Alpini* uniform was the one worn by the infantry: light-gray trousers with a red stripe down both sides, a shirt, a dark-blue-gray coat with a red collar insignia and white star, a kepi of the same color, and shoes. The officers wore a blue-gray jacket.

However, very soon the specific role of the Alpini made it necessary to introduce some modifications to distinguish these units from the rest of the army and adapt their equipment to the environment they were meant to live and fight in. First, by 1873, the kepi was replaced by a bowler with a large brim that bore a five-pointed-star badge in front, with the number of the company at its center and on the left side a cockade with the green, white and red colors of the Italian flag. Also making its appearance on the hat was what has become the distinctive feature of the Alpini ever since: a

The bowler adopted in 1873, with the five-pointed star badge bearing the number of the Tenth Company

Side view of the bowler, with the green, white, and red cockade and the feather

The new badge adopted in 1880, representing an eagle with spread wings over a bugle, with two rifles, and an ax and ice ax crossed

The badge of the mountain artillery adopted in 1912, representing the spread-winged eagle over a bugle, with two crossed guns

The Forty-Fifth Company of the Battaglione *Morbegno*, late 1880s, at the Stelvio Pass. The *Alpini* wear a white cover over the bowler. *Museo Nazionale Storico degli Alpini*

crow feather for the enlisted ranks and NCOs and an eagle feather for the officers. In 1874, enlisted ranks and NCOs were issued the blue-gray jacket, while the following year the coat, which was not very comfortable in the mountains, was replaced by a cape of the same color and the shoes by boots. A few years later, in 1880, the badge was replaced by a new style representing an eagle with spread wings over a bugle, with two rifles, an ax crossed with an ice ax in the background, framed by oak leaves. All of these were mounted on a cockade with the Italian colors; the cockade on the left side disappeared and was replaced by a small red tassel; known as *nappina*, which held the feather, was replaced with a black oval patch containing the company number. Soon, the color of the tassel changed according to the number of the battalion within the regiment: white for the First Battalion, red for the Second, green for the Third, and blue for the Fourth. In June 1883, the red collar insignia were replaced by a new green insignia, which was the color that would be, from that moment on, associated with the Alpini. Beginning in 1909, the *Regio Esercito* gradually started to adopt a new gray-green uniform that ensured better camouflage,[5] and the following year the bowler hat was replaced by the characteristic soft felt hat that distinguishes the Alpine troops from every other corps of the Italian army; the badge was also replaced by a less-elaborate one, representing the spread-winged eagle over two crossed rifles and a bugle, without cockade but with the renowned feather on the left side.

The first weapon issued was the single-shot Vetterli M1870 10.35 mm rifle, replaced in 1891 by the 6.5 mm Mannlicher-Carcano M91, with a six-shot magazine, which performed better and became the standard individual weapon of the Italian army until the Second World War. There were two versions: a longer version, with a 30.7-inch barrel, and a short version, with a 17.7-inch barrel, which was known as the *Moschetto mod. 91*, or M91 carbine.

The Alpine companies were such a success that, in September 1873, the number was increased from fifteen to twenty four, with the new units being formed between 1874 and 1875. Furthermore, it was decided to also add twenty-four companies of *Milizia mobile*, ready to be summoned in case they were needed. The direct consequence of this provision was the need to regroup the companies into larger units; thus, in 1875, the first seven battalions were formed, with three or four companies each. In 1878, the number of battalions was increased to ten, with thirty-six companies and the number of personnel doubled because the strength of each company was increased from the original 120 to 250 men, with four officers, commanded by a captain. Only four years later, however, the strength was brought back down to 120 Alpini, splitting each of the thirty-six companies in half, making a total of seventy-two. This again involved the increase in the number of battalions to twenty and, finally, the creation of six regiments regrouping into three battalions each, except for the Sixth Regiment, which had five battalions. For the first time, the battalions were named after

Mountain troops units during a training march in the mountains, in 1907; some *Alpini* wear the cape adopted in 1905 to replace the coat. A couple of years later, the old 1800s uniform would be replaced by the gray-green uniform with the soft felt hat. *Museo Nazionale Storico degli Alpini*

The commanding officers of the first six regiments: 1. Colonel Leone Pelloux, 3° Reggimento. 2. Colonel Giuseppe Ottolenghi, 4° Reggimento. 3. Colonel Nicola Huesch, 6° Reggimento. 4. Colonel Alessandro Tonini, 1° Reggimento. 5. Colonel Federico Queirazza, 2° Reggimento. 6. Colonel Carlo Goggia, 5° Reggimento. *Museo Nazionale Storico degli Alpini*

Mountain artillery marching during the 1866 Third War of Independence, from a contemporary print. *Museo Nazionale Storico degli Alpini*

Alpini of the 7° Reggimento boldly descending a steep slope during an excursion. *Museo Nazionale Storico degli Alpini*

A battery of mountain artillery on a training march a few years after the establishment of the specialty. *Museo Nazionale Storico degli Alpini*

A 65/17 gun adopted in 1910 and assigned to the mountain artillery from 1913, replacing the 70 mm rigidly mounted gun. This was the first piece of artillery entirely designed in Italy with a recoil system, by the *Arsenale Regio Esercito* (the Royal Arsenal) of Turin. *Museo Nazionale Storico degli Alpini*

the town where they had their headquarters, a name that has remained from that moment on. In 1885, a new reorganization entailed the formation of a Seventh Regiment that inherited two battalions from the Sixth, plus two newly formed battalions. Furthermore, a new authority was superimposed over the whole corps, called the *Ispettorato Generale delle Truppe Alpine* (General Inspectorate of the Alpine Troops). In 1902, the regiments were grouped into *Gruppi Alpini*, which in 1910 became brigades. In the meantime, between 1909 and 1910, the number of battalions increased to twenty-six and the companies to seventy-nine.

The following organization, based on three brigades, eight regiments, twenty-six battalions, and seventy-nine companies, remained unchanged until the outbreak of the Great War:

I Brigata Alpina, with headquarters at Cuneo
    1° Reggimento Alpini, with headquarters in Mondovì
        Battaglione *Ceva*
        Battaglione *Pieve di Teco*
        Battaglione *Mondovì*
    2° Reggimento Alpini, with headquarters in Cuneo
        Battaglione *Borgo San Dalmazzo*
        Battaglione *Dronero*
        Battaglione *Saluzzo*
II Brigata Alpina, with headquarters in Torino
    3° Reggimento Alpini, with headquarters in Torino
        Battaglione *Pinerolo*
        Battaglione *Fenestrelle*
        Battaglione *Exillles*
        Battaglione *Susa*
    4° Reggimento Alpini, with headquarters in Ivrea
        Battaglione *Ivrea*
        Battaglione *Aosta*
        Battaglione *Intra*
    5° Reggimento Alpini, with headquarters in Milano
        Battaglione *Morbegno*
        Battaglione *Tirano*
        Battaglione *Edolo*
        Battaglione *Vestone*
III Brigata Alpina, with headquarters in Verona
    6° Reggimento Alpini, with headquarters in Verona
        Battaglione *Verona*
        Battaglione *Vicenza*
        Battaglione *Bassano*
    7° Reggimento Alpini, with headquarters in Belluno
        Battaglione *Feltre*
        Battaglione *Pieve di Cadore*
        Battaglione *Belluno*
    8° Reggimento Alpini, with headquarters in Udine
        Battaglione *Tolmezzo*
        Battaglione *Gemona*
        Battaglione *Cividale*

Meanwhile, a similar evolution was experienced by the mountain artillery, which was born as a branch of the siege artillery in 1861 but progressively grew toward the *Alpini*. Methods to develop pieces of artillery that could be dismounted into lighter packs to be transported on mountains or difficult terrain had been known since the early 1700s, and the Piedmontese army had some of these packs in its arsenals. With the establishment of the *Regio Esercito* in 1861, it was decided that for every regiment of siege artillery (*artiglieria da piazza*, which included all the artillery that did not move with the army in the field), one or two batteries of mountain artillery would be formed, resulting in a total of five batteries. Some of them took part in the aforementioned 1866 war, attached to the volunteer unit led by Giuseppe Garibaldi, the *Cacciatori delle Alpi*, charged with penetrating into what at that time was the Austrian border through the mountains west of Lake Garda, the largest Italian lake, some 150 kilometers east of Milan. Although Garibaldi obtained some remarkable results, one could say that the performance of the mountain batteries was something less than satisfactory, simply because the personnel and the animals assigned to them were not trained to make the best use of each piece. As a result, in 1873, these batteries had artillerymen and mules permanently assigned to them and were therefore able to train for the specific mountain warfare environment. The subsequent development of the mountain artillery was as rapid as that of the Alpine troops: in 1877, the five batteries were grouped in a mountain artillery brigade quartered in Torino, and a sixth battery was formed in 1880. In 1882, when two new batteries were created, the brigade was split in two, with four batteries each, quartered in Torino and Vicenza. In 1887, the batteries became nine, divided in three brigades, under the command of a new mountain artillery regiment. For the first time, this special branch of artillery became independent and formally detached from the siege artillery. In 1895, the force was increased to fifteen batteries and five brigades, with a sixteenth battery attached to the Twenty-Second Field Artillery Regiment, based in Palermo; in 1909, the batteries became twenty-four, grouped in eight brigades, from then on called *gruppi*, which were in turn grouped in two regiments. In 1915, with the Great War in view, a third regiment was formed, so the number of *gruppi* increased to twelve and the number of batteries to thirty-six.

Meanwhile, in 1909, the affiliation between the Alpini and the *Artiglieri da montagna* became official when the three regiments were subordinated to the previously mentioned *Ispettorato Generale delle Truppe Alpine*, which was renamed the "*Ispettorato delle Truppe da Montagna.*" Up until 1910, the mountain artillerymen wore the standard artillery uniform, but in that year, not only did they change to the new gray-green uniform but they adopted the same felt cap of the Alpini with the feather held by a red tassel, the *nappina*, which was changed to a green one in the 1930s. The badge became an eagle with spread wings on a bugle over two crossed guns, which has remained unchanged to the present day.

The first piece adopted by the artiglieria da montagna was the old, bronze, muzzle-loading 3⅓-pound gun, inherited from the previous Piedmontese army and brought to battle by Garibaldi. It was replaced in 1880 by a 75 mm gun, which also had a bronze barrel but had breech loading. It could be disassembled into three loads to be transported on mule's back; this was the gun used during the colonial wars that were fought in the last twenty years of the nineteenth century. At the turn of the twentieth century, in 1904, the use of the 70 mm, steel-barreled gun was adopted; however, although several foreign countries had already turned to pieces provided with a recoil system, the 70 mm was still rigidly mounted, which caused it to be a short-lived model. In fact, by 1913, it began to be replaced by the more efficient 65 mm gun—the well-known 65/17,[6] with a steel barrel and recoil system. It could be disassembled into five packs for mule transport. This was the standard piece of the mountain artillery in the Great War. The standard battery had six guns, divided into two sections of three guns that could be used independently of each other.

At the outbreak of the war, the organizational chart of the mountain artillery was the following:

1° Reggimento
     Gruppo *Torino-Susa*
     Gruppo *Torino-Aosta*
     Gruppo *Torino-Pinerolo*
     Gruppo *Mondovì*
2° Reggimento
     Gruppo *Conegliano*
     Gruppo *Udine*
     Gruppo *Vicenza*
     Gruppo *Belluno*
3° Reggimento
     Gruppo *Oneglia*
     Gruppo *Genova*
     Gruppo *Bergamo*
     Gruppo *Como*

Furthermore, there were three batteries of the Gruppo *Messina*, which had headquarters in that Sicilian town, called "Sicilian batteries."

Alpine troops embark from Naples to Eritrea in the 1890s, from a contemporaneous print. *Museo Nazionale Storico degli Alpini*

ALPINE TROOPS IN ACTION DURING THE COLONIAL WARS

THE FIRST ITALO-ETHIOPIAN WAR

It may come as a surprise that a corps created for the defense of the Italian borders received its baptism of fire not in its own mountains, but in Africa, on the heights of Eritrea.

Italy set foot on African soil officially in 1882, when the government bought the Assab Bay, on the Red Sea, about 150 kilometers north of Djibouti, from the Genoese navigation company Rubattino. The company had acquired the bay in 1869 to use as a docking station for its ships that were en route to the Orient. In 1884, an Italian expedition in search of a new trade route with neighboring Ethiopia was massacred in the region of Dancalia, providing Italy the pretext to retaliate by occupying the Eritrean port of Massaua, which was under Egyptian rule as a mere formality at that time. A small expeditionary corps of 800 men commanded by Colonel Tancredi Saletta landed there in 1885, and in the following months they occupied a number of other surrounding villages, trespassing in parts of the territory that the Ethiopian Ras Alula considered to be his own. In January 1887, Ras Alula's warriors attacked the fort of Saati, which is 25 kilometers west of Massaua, and managed to intercept a rescue party of 500 Italian soldiers and cut it to pieces during the famous clash of Dogali. To retaliate, a strong expeditionary corps reached Massaua in March 1887. Within its units, there was also a special battalion of Alpini that were formed with a company each of the *Gemona*, *Tirano* and *Verona* battalions, commanded by Major Domenico Ciconi. Along with the mountain troops, two sections of mountain artillery were also sent, followed later by two whole batteries. Due to the climate, for this assignment, Alpini and artillerymen wore a new uniform, with trousers and jacket in white canvas and a light helmet made of plant fibers coated in white; it goes without saying that the Alpini added their hallmark feather to the pith helmet. However, these troops did not take part in any fighting, because Italy and Ethiopia reached an agreement. The troops were reimbarked to Italy in April 1888 except for one of the gun batteries. Any casualties were due to Massaua's bad climate, and among them was Major Ciconi himself.

Colonial pith helmet whose writing on the band might mean that the alpino took part in the operations around the village of Adigrat, were an Italian fort was under siege after the defeat at Adua. *Museo Nazionale Storico degli Alpini*

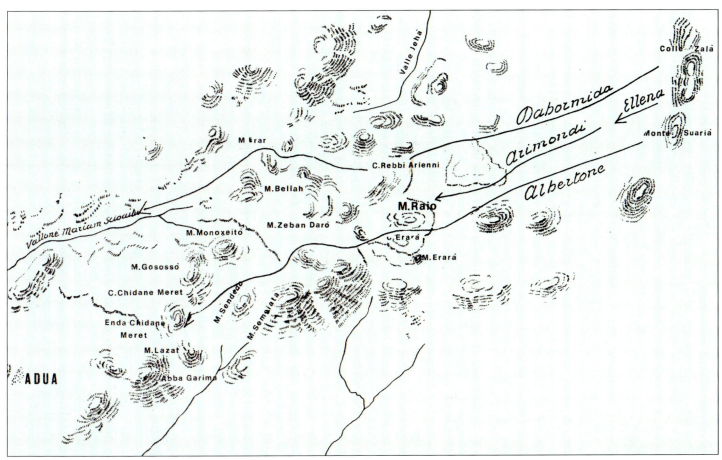

The difficult march of the Italian troops, divided into four brigades, toward the Ethiopian army at Adua, on March 1, 1896. The Alpine troops were attached to the brigade of the General Ellena, in the rearguard.

A battery of mountain artillery in Eritrea, from a contemporaneous print. *Museo Nazionale Storico degli Alpini*

In the following years, the governor of Italian Eritrea would further enlarge the colony at the expense of Ethiopia, taking advantage of the turbulence within that state[7] by occupying vast parts of Eritrea and penetrating deep into the Tigray. Furthermore, following the Italian victory at the battle of Agordat against a Mahdist army in December 1893, the colony was extended a great deal toward Sudan. However, once firmly holding power, the new Negus of Ethiopia, Menelik, decided to retake part of the lost territory and launched an army attack against the Italian garrisons in the Tigray in 1895; in December, the fort at Amba Alagi was attacked, and the nearly 2,500 men defending it were killed.

Lieutenant Colonel Davide Menini, seriously injured, urges on his Alpini during the battle of Adua, in a print from the book *Sul campo di Adua, Marzo Giugno 1896*, by Eduardo Ximenes, published in 1897.

The echo of this serious defeat in Italy was enormous. A new, larger expeditionary corps, which included Alpine troops, was organized on the spot to reinforce the scant forces in Eritrea, which seemed to be in jeopardy itself. The *1° Battaglione Alpini d'Africa*, or First African Alpini Battalion, consisted of four companies, about 950 men, taken from all the existing Alpine units and commanded by Lieutenant Colonel Davide Menini. Once again, new colonial uniforms were distributed: light bronze trousers and jacket and the usual helmet, coated in the same color. Furthermore, for reasons of logistic efficiency, the men exchanged the new M91 rifle for the old Vetterli, which was still in use in Eritrea and whose ammunition was abundant there. Along with the Alpini, four batteries taken from the mountain artillery regiment also landed in Africa.

The governor of Eritrea, General Oreste Baratieri, along with the reinforcements that had arrived from Italy, could muster a corps of four brigades with a force of about 16,000 men and move toward the Ethiopian army, which was more than 100,000 warriors strong. The Alpine troops, attached to the brigade commanded by General Ellena, were part of the reserve, while the mountain batteries, being the bulk of the artillery and the best suited to the task, were distributed among the brigades. The encounter between the two armies, which was rather unexpected, took place on March 1, 1896, near the Ethiopian town of Adua, about 100 kilometers southwest of Massaua. In the ferocious battle that followed, the Italian units were cut to pieces, unable to withstand the sheer number of the enemy; the companies of Alpini were thrown into the fray in bits and pieces. Every place where enemies poured in, there was the need to plug the leak—resulting only in their needless sacrifice. The last men regrouped

around General Baratieri to defend him against a cavalry charge and fought to the very end; Lieutenant Colonel Menini found his death there. Captain Pietro Cella, commander of the Fourth Company, earned the Gold Medal of Valor, the highest decoration in the Italian army and the first such medal awarded to an alpino, although posthumously. The batteries fired until the end of their stocks of shells, then were forced to sabotage the guns before they were captured; not many artillerymen managed to escape death. The total death toll amounted to more than 6,000 men, resulting in the greatest defeat of a European army in a colonial war; the remains of the men would only be recovered thirty years later.

Once again, the Italian government sent reinforcements, two divisions strong and guided by General Antonio Baldissera, to Eritrea. Also sent was a regiment of Alpine troops, with four battalions commanded by Colonel Ettore Troja and two more batteries detached from the mountain artillery regiment. However, these troops did not see action, because a truce had been negotiated followed by a peace treaty, which was signed in Addis Ababa a few months later, in October 1896. The Italian forces were slowly reimbarked to Italy; the last unit of Alpini to leave Eritrea was the Fourth Battalion, which remained until 1897 to take part in some skirmishes against the Dervishes in the north of the colony.

THE CONQUEST OF LIBYA

Far more important was the participation of Alpine troops and mountain artillery in the war declared by Italy against Turkey in 1911. It was fought almost exclusively in Libya, in an environment which was, for the most part, barren. This

Officers of the Battaglione *Ivrea* in Libya, where the unit fought from November 1911 to August 1914. *Andrea Bianchi*

A 149 mm howitzer is being placed into position in a Libyan redoubt built with sandbags; the shield is uncommon for this piece of artillery. *Andrea Bianchi*

environment was even more different from the Alps than it was from the Ethiopian ambas. The occupation of Libya had been a longtime goal of the Italians and was intended to be a sort of compensation for Italy after France had taken possession of Morocco in the spring of that year, although the country was still formally under the rule of the sovereignty of the Ottoman Empire. The presence of Turkish troops was negligible, being no more than 7,000 or 8,000 men that were divided between Tripolitania and Cyrenaica, the two main regions that comprised Libya. Therefore, the conquest seemed rather easy to accomplish; furthermore, Italy counted on the same submissiveness exhibited by Istanbul in previous cases toward France and the United Kingdom.[8] On the contrary, the demeanor of the Turkish government was very firm this time. Worse, the Italian troops found themselves fighting not just against Turkish troops but also against the local Arab population, which amounted to hundreds of very skillful fighters with perfect knowledge of the territory.

The Kingdom of Italy submitted an ultimatum to the Turkish government on September 26, 1911, asking rather straightforwardly to allow Italian troops to occupy Tripolitania and Cyrenaica, giving a twenty-four-hour deadline for the response. War was declared the following day, but, surprisingly enough, nothing happened—simply because the army had not yet prepared the expeditionary corps. The first forces, a few hundred landing troops of the Navy, went ashore at Tripoli on October 3 and at Tobruk on the fourth. The main convoy arrived in the sea before Tripoli on October 11, and troops started to disembark the following day, including five batteries of mountain artillery. A few days later, the first Alpine unit, the Battaglione *Fenestrelle*, also arrived in Tripoli. Meanwhile, the occupation of other cities along the coast

A group of Alpini pull pieces of equipment up a hill in Libya. *Andrea Bianchi*

An Alpini unit in Libya. *Andrea Bianchi*

was proceeding: Derna was taken on the seventeenth, and on the twenty-fifth the Battaglione *Saluzzo* landed there, followed by Benghazi on the nineteenth and Homs on the twenty-first. Progressively, as the Italian government and the army commander in chief realized that conquering Libya was a much more difficult enterprise than anticipated, new troops were sent in. Among them, between November and December 1911, the Battaglione *Mondovì* was sent to Homs, the Battaglione *Ivrea* to Tobruk, the Battaglioni *Edolo* and *Verona* to Derna. Furthermore, three more mountain artillery batteries reached Africa. Throughout 1912, other battalions arrived: *Tolmezzo*, *Feltre*, *Vestone*, and *Susa* as well as two more batteries.

Machine gunners in a Libyan redoubt with a Maxim machine gun. *Andrea Bianchi*

During the war, the Alpini were involved in dozens of actions and fought bravely, particularly in Derna, whose garrison was constantly harassed by a strong party of Arab and Turkish troops under the command of the most valiant Turkish officer in Libya, Enver Bay. Throughout 1912, up to six Alpine battalions and three mountain artillery batteries were concentrated in the town and its fortifications, which, in the summer, were even grouped in a special brigade of two regiments: the First Regiment with battalions *Mondovì*, *Ivrea* and *Edolo*; the Second Regiment with battalions *Saluzzo*, *Fenestrelle* and, later in autumn, *Tolmezzo*. In May 1912, for a few days the Battaglione *Fenestrelle* and three batteries were detached to take part in the landing on the island of Rhodes, a diversion devised to take control of the maritime routes between Turkey and Libya.[9]

The war between Italy and Turkey ended officially on October 18, 1912, with the Treaty of Ouchy, but the fighting in Tripolitania and Cyrenaica did not end at all. On the contrary, part of the Arab population and some of the Turkish officers who did had not followed their troops as they left the country put up an even stronger resistance to the attempts of Italian troops to move from the coastal towns to the interior territory.

To bring Tripolitania into submission, a division was formed in October 1912 and charged to eradicate what was from then on called, rather improperly, the "Arab rebellion," to which was attached a newly created regiment of Alpini. They were the Eighth Alpine Special Regiment, with the Battalions *Tolmezzo*, *Feltre*, *Vestone*, and *Susa*, all under the command of an officer who was to become legendary: Colonel Antonio Cantore. After thorough training in desert operations and a careful preparation of its logistics, the division moved out of Tripoli in

Libya. A picket of honor pays tribute to a fellow alpino fallen in action. *Andrea Bianchi*

December and headed south to the town of Garian, an insurgent stronghold on the slopes of the highland called Gebel Nefara. After marching for three weeks over barren terrain, the Italian troops took the castle of Garian and gained the submission of the local Arab chiefs. The next target was the town of Jefren, about 50 kilometers to the west, but the road was guarded by an Arab encampment near the village of Assaba. A few weeks were spent negotiating the surrender of the insurgents and the bloodless submission of the population, but after failing, the military operations were resumed in March with an attack that was launched on Assaba on the morning of the twenty-second. The Battaglione *Feltre* advanced first, under cover of machine guns and artillery fire, opposed by intense fire from the enemy. Soon it was joined in its movement by the Battaglione *Tolmezzo* on its right flank, while the *Vestone* advanced farther to the right to cover the main column. The *Susa* remained behind as reserve. The Alpini advanced steadily, taking advantage of the terrain, with Colonel Cantore on horseback ahead of them. After the horse was hit, they continued on foot, and once the advance had arrived close to enemy lines, they unleashed very accurate fire that surprised the Arabs and made them disband. At noon the battle was won, and a few days later Jefren was taken also, completing the conquest of Tripolitania.

In those same weeks, military operations against the insurgents were also carried out in Cyrenaica. In April 1913, a division that counted within its units the four Alpine battalions *Saluzzo*, *Ivrea*, *Edolo* and *Fenestrelle* and two mountain artillery batteries landed at the village of Tolmeita. Their goal was to take control of a vast area west of Derna, which had so far been firmly in the hands of the Arabs. The division marched south first and then turned east, moving in a long arc, until it reached the sea again near Cyrene. During two months of military operations, it had engaged in several actions—ensuring, at least temporarily, the continuation of Italian presence by leaving behind some garrisons. However, the situation in Cyrenaica was deteriorating because the supreme religious authority of the region, the Grand Senussi Ahmed Sharif as-Senussi[10] had, after some hesitation, embraced the cause of the insurgency and declared the jihad against the Italians. Furthermore, in a clash south of Derna, the Arabs had defeated an Italian military column for the first time. In an attempt to regain the initiative in the region, the Italian authorities decided to launch a large operation deep into the interior and hit the enemy stronghold of Ettangi. For that purpose, on May 27, the seasoned Eighth Special Alpine Regiment of Colonel Cantore arrived from Tripoli. The regiment had left the Battaglione *Susa* behind to guard what they had recently gained at Garian and Jefren, and they replaced the Battaglione *Susa* with Battaglione *Verona*. The Italian forces moved on June 18, divided into three columns, and the Alpini, reinforced with four mountain artillery batteries, were the right wing of the advance. The men of Cantore faced groups of Arabs from the very beginning, putting them to flight, and they arrived in view of Ettangi before the other columns the following day. They engaged the enemy without delay, obtaining a complete victory and capturing a great booty. This action secured Derna for the time being and allowed the joining of the several areas of Cyrenaica that were under Italian control.

In September and October, the Alpine troops and the mountain artillerymen took part in other fighting, but their time to repatriate had arrived. In October 1913, the Battaglioni *Saluzzo*, *Edolo*, and *Susa* embarked, followed in November by *Tolmezzo*, *Verona*, and *Mondovì*. In the summer of 1914, when Europe was already at war, Battaglioni *Fenestrelle*, *Ivrea*, *Feltre*, and *Vestone*, and most of the mountain artillery batteries, were to be deployed in the Italian Alps in a few months. Only seven batteries remained in the colony, one of which, however, was repatriated in 1916.

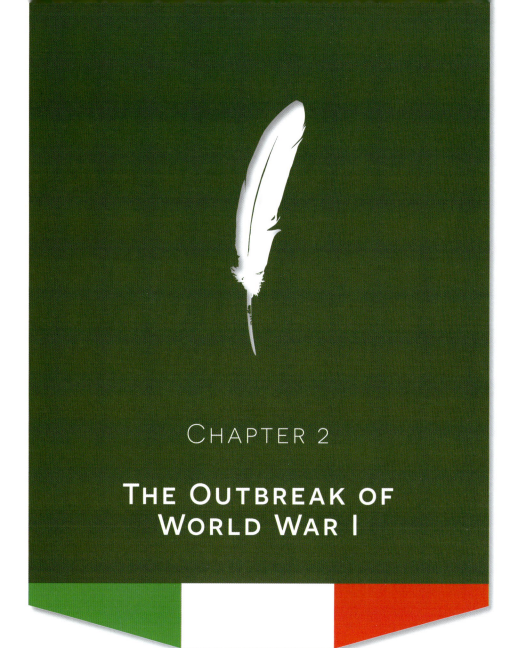

CHAPTER 2

THE OUTBREAK OF WORLD WAR I

POLITICAL AND MILITARY BACKGROUND

On June 28, 1914, a Serbian student, Gavrilo Princip, shot the heir to the Austro-Hungarian throne, Archduke Franz Ferdinand, and Ferdinand's wife, Sophie, to death, setting in motion a dramatic chain of events that, within a few days, led to the Great War.

The Austro-Hungarian Empire's relations with Serbia had been extremely bad for long time, with the Serbians being accused of stirring up Slavic nationalism in the Balkan territories under Austro-Hungarian rule. The opportunity to solve the problem once and for all with the small but troublesome neighbor seemed at hand; this opportunity counted on a small and quick local war like the many others that had bloodied the Balkans for centuries. Unfortunately for the dual monarchy, the events took a different course, due to the complicated system of alliances that divided the European states into two opposing blocks: the Triple Alliance[1] of Germany, Austria-Hungary, and Italy on one side and the Triple Entente[2] of Russia, France, and United Kingdom on the other side. In fact, Russia, protector of Serbia, declared war on Austria-Hungary, giving Germany pretext to declare war on Russia and side with its Austrian ally. France and the UK, after a short delay, declared war on Germany and Austria-Hungary in turn. The Ottoman Empire joined the Triple Alliance in the autumn of 1914, while Italy, for the moment, remained neutral.

One of the forts of Liege, in Belgium, after the shelling by 42 cm German Krupp howitzers, the famous *Dicke Bertha*, and the 30.5 cm Austro-Hungarian Skoda mortars between August 8 and 17, 1914. *Museo Nazionale Storico degli Alpini*

The murder of the Archduke Franz Ferdinand of Austria, heir to the throne of the Austro-Hungarian Empire, and of his wife, Sophie, by the Bosnian Serb nationalist Gavrilo Princip at Sarajevo on June 28, 1914, depicted on the Italian magazine *La Domenica del Corriere* by the famous artist Achille Beltrame.

THE MONTHS OF NEUTRALITY IN ITALY

Although Italy had been part of the Triple Alliance since 1882, it would remain neutral, arguing that the agreement was a purely defensive one, as had been clearly established in its Article 3, whereas Austria-Hungary, attacking Serbia, had been the aggressor. Furthermore, Article 7, with the cynicism typical of the 1800s agreements between powerful nations, declared explicitly that any time Austria-Hungary or Italy proceeded with the occupation of any territories in the Balkans, the other party deserved compensation, while the Austro-Hungarians had declared war on Serbia without consulting Italy or offering something in exchange.

On the other hand, the more time elapsed, the more urgent the requests by powerful Italian political forces to intervene became, but on the Triple Entente side. Those forces were, first of all, the Nationalist Party, which desired to replace Austro-Hungarian influence in the Balkans by Italian influence in the area and, moreover, feared that neutrality would relegate Italy to a role of a second-rank nation in Europe. Secondly, there was the Irredentist movement, which wanted to take the opportunity to reunite the nation's ethnically Italian territories that were still in foreign hands. Trento and Trieste were at the top of the list, which would complete the national unification and so fulfill the long process started in 1800s called *Risorgimento* (the new rising). The Socialist Party was strongly against the

intervention and considered the war to be an expression of purely capitalistic interests and that the proletarians could only lose, whatever the outcome. At the time, the country was led by Antonio Salandra[3] as prime minister and Sidney Sonnino[4] as foreign affairs minister, members of the Liberal Party. But there were several important, prominent politicians, such as Giovanni Giolitti,[5] who opposed this government and were deeply divided amongst themselves. There were those who favored intervention with one or the other side and those who claimed that neutrality was the best option. Their position was not ideological, but they sought a way to obtain the maximum result with minimum effort. The discussion, sometimes ferocious, led to the Treaty of London on April 26, 1915. The treaty was signed with the entente after the refusal of Austria-Hungary to come to terms with and accept the Italian requests; it committed Italy to declaring war within a month with the promise that, in case of victory, it would obtain not only the coveted Trento and Trieste but also a substantial part of Dalmatia, territories in the Balkans, and even in Turkey. War was declared on May 23, 1915, and the following day military operations commenced. However, strangely enough, there had been no declaration of war against Germany, which would not happen until August 1916, even though the *Regio Esercito* had already had the opportunity to face some German units in Trentino.

Two clearly interventionist leaflets. The first calls for a popular referendum to demonstrate the will of the Italians and pushes the government to declare war. The second cites war as the means to complete the reunification of all Italians under the Italian flag.

On the other side of the barricade, a pacifist leaflet that invites the proletariat to refuse to take up arms, as the only purpose would be to advance the interests of the bourgeoisie.

As was commonly known, the opposing armies on the western front at the time were already dealing with bitter trench warfare, with lines strongly protected by barbed wire and manned with hundreds of machine guns. Great attacks, led by thousands of men, led to advances of a few hundred meters with very high losses: the situation had reached a stalemate. The entente genuinely hoped that the new southern front could contribute to breaking the equilibrium and rapidly win the war. Unfortunately, as had happened rather often in the past, the Italian army was far from a well-oiled instrument of war in May 1915: the availability of the very deadly machine guns was limited to a few dozen American Maxim M1911s, and many months were necessary to raise availability to a barely acceptable number, importing hundreds of French Saint-Étienne machine guns from France. Artillery was scarce as well and lacked the howitzers and pieces with a high angle of fire that had been shown to be so useful against trenches and barbwire. The Italian soldiers had no steel helmets, the first being imported from France. Furthermore, and most importantly, it was widely known that the army needed six weeks to mobilize, but the chief of staff was notified of the Treaty of London only after its conclusion and could start to mobilize only at the beginning of May, with three weeks to meet the deadline set in the negotiations for the declaration of war, not to mention the necessity to change all the war plans, which had so far been focused on war against France. All in all, in May 1915, the *Regio Esercito* numbered fewer than 900,000 men, divided between thirty-five infantry divisions, one *bersaglieri*[6] division, four cavalry divisions and 26 Alpini battalions; the artillery counted 467 batteries of all calibers, with about 2,000 pieces. It was commanded by Supreme Commander General Luigi Cadorna.[7]

A satirical poster depicting the armies of the Austro-Hungarian, German, and Ottoman Empires fearing the arrival of the Italian army, here represented by a giant advancing *bersaglieri*.

A battery of powerful 305 mm Italian howitzers in the Dogna Valley, a valley not far from the border between Italy and Austria, entrusted to the responsibility of the Zona Carnia. The 305 mm howitzer was originally designed for coastal defense, adapted to the ground role with the adoption of different types of carriages as a gap-filling piece of artillery. *Museo Nazionale Storico degli Alpini*

General Luigi Cadorna, chief of the general staff of the Italian army since July 27, 1914, then supreme commander until his dismissal in November 1917

Field Marshal Konrad von Hötzendorf, at the beginning of the war chief of the general staff of the Austro-Hungarian army

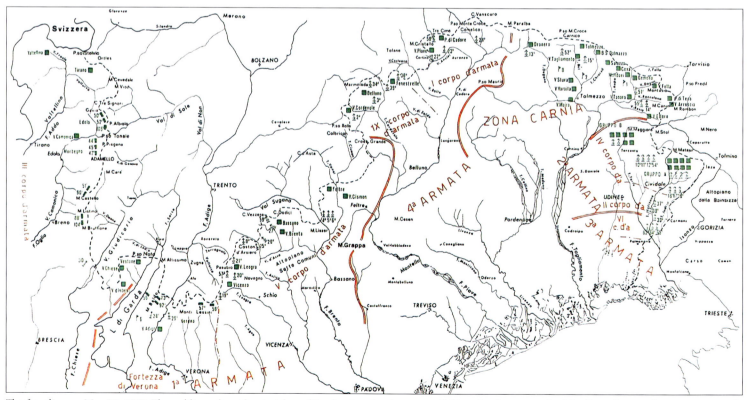

The frontline on May 24, 1915. The red lines show the stretches of the front under the responsibility of each army and of the Zona Carnia: the preeminent role of the Second Army and the Third Army, deployed along the Isonzo River, emerges clearly. The map highlights the position of the Alpine battalions (*green squares*) and of the Alpine artillery batteries (*green arrows*).

The long front was subdivided into five zones: two in the Trentino salient, with the First Army west of the Monte Grappa massif and the Fourth Army east of it; two more along the Isonzo River Valley, with the Second Army in the high valley and the Third Army in the lower part of it; they were linked by the what was known as the "*Zona Carnia,*" or Carnia Area, in the northern part Friuli, entrusted to the *Comando Zona Carnia,* later renamed "XII Army Corps."

On the opposite side, the Austro-Hungarian army, although it had faced tremendous losses on the eastern front against the Russians, was at its best after almost a year of warfare, with millions of men and a first-class military industry. Furthermore, it could rely on its border with Italy, which was naturally defended by high mountains and an effective chain of fortifications prepared during peacetime. After the severe crisis of the first few days, when the whole line was garrisoned by just 100,000 soldiers, many of them old men left behind to guard the home front, the high command led by General Conrad von Hötzendorf[8] would take the necessary countermeasures and keep the Italians at bay with relatively limited forces.

The new war plan, developed hurriedly by the Italian Supreme Command, was to take a defensive posture along the long salient of Trentino; a strong attack to the east to ford the Isonzo River; and, once over the mountains, a maneuver to the heart of enemy territory after reaching the plain of Ljubljana. A secondary direction of attack was considered and would force its way through the Puster Valley to the town of Brixen in order to cut the previously mentioned salient at its root and, turning north, push on to Innsbruck, endangering the whole Tyrol area or, turning south, threaten the rear of the Austro-Hungarian forces in Trentino. The belief was that these results could be obtained in a few weeks against weak forces. Instead, due to the slowness in the mobilization of the army and the lack of initiative of the commanders, the advance was performed very cautiously, giving the enemy the time necessary to send in reinforcements. The meager results obtained in those days were more the outcome of the spontaneous withdrawal of the Austro-Hungarians to better defensible positions than that of a well-planned and victorious advance of the *Regio Esercito.* Today, it is a common and documented opinion that more audacious conduct of the operations in the first few days would have spared the Italian soldiers many months of bloody assaults. As a result, the advance to Ljubljana or through the Puster Valley to chase the enemy remained a chimera, and soon the war turned into a series of great offensives, overall, along the Isonzo River valley, throwing into the fray division after division with no results more often than not.

THE ALPINE TROOPS PREPARE FOR WAR

In August 1914, the last units were back from Libya; therefore, all twenty-six battalions of Alpini, a total of seventy-nine companies, were battle-ready. Every battalion had two machine guns assigned to it, a *sezione,* which were soon increased to four weapons divided between two *sezioni.* In the autumn of 1914, when Italy was still neutral, the mobilization of the

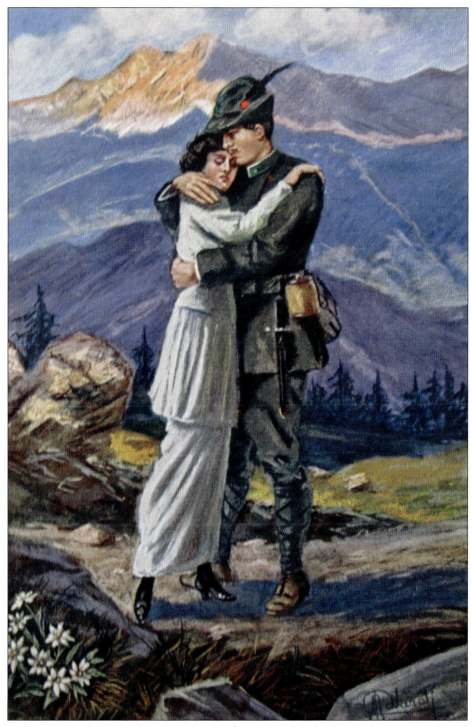

In this propaganda postcard, an alpino hugs his fiancée or wife before leaving for war, where he will be entrusted with the defense of his mountains, which stand out in the background. *Giuseppe Rossini*

thirty-eight *Milizia Mobile* companies began. The companies were named after famous valleys, while the sixty-three companies of the *Milizia Territoriale*, named after famous mountains, followed at the beginning of 1915, thus increasing the total number of battalions to fifty-two. In May 1915, these troops were rapidly deployed to the mountains along the border. Since the very beginning, the brigades and the regiments ceased to exist as permanent units and remained simply as framework commands, also called *Gruppo Alpino* (Alpine group) or *Comando di Settore* (area command), created as the occasion warranted for specific tasks or given responsibility for a specific part of the front—but always formed with battalions assigned specifically and temporarily for the task. It is correct to say that the only organic unit within the Alpini was the battalion, used very flexibly wherever necessary and assigned to whatever higher unit needed it.

In 1915, some units of volunteers were also formed, which, during the war, were either incorporated into regular battalions or were eventually disbanded and the men reassigned. The following units are counted in detail: *1ª Compagnia volontari*, formed in the town of Morbegno; *2ª Compagnia volontari*, formed in Milan; *3ª Compagnia volontari Val Camonica* (a valley in the northeast of Lombardy, bordering what was at the time Austrian Trentino); *Compagnia volontari Feltre*; *Compagnia volontari Cadore* (a mountain area in the north of Veneto); *Compagnia volontari Alpini Gemona-Cividale, Reparto volontari Vestone*; *Compagnia volontari Chieti-l'Aquila*.

During the same period in which the deployment of the mountain artillery was also completed, eleven batteries of *Milizia Mobile* were mobilized and added to the existing thirty-nine batteries. In May 1915, there was a total of fourteen Gruppi, composed of three batteries of four 65/17 pieces each, plus eight independent batteries. Seven more batteries remained temporarily in Libya and were still armed with the old 70 mm rigidly mounted gun.

Apart from the mountain artillery, it must be borne in mind that from 1914, when it became clear that the war would be fought in the mountains, several field artillery regiments started to organize batteries that could accompany the infantry units, partially equipped with mules and armed with the old 70 mm rigidly mounted gun, called *someggiate* (mule packed). However, only the guns and an allocation of ammunition for immediate use were carried by a pack mule, while the rest of the equipment was towed on carts; thus, these batteries had less logistic autonomy in comparison with the mountain artillery batteries. This difference would progressively fade, until in 1918, the two specialties would be merged.

A 65 mm mountain gun with its crew. *Museo Nazionale Storico degli Alpini*

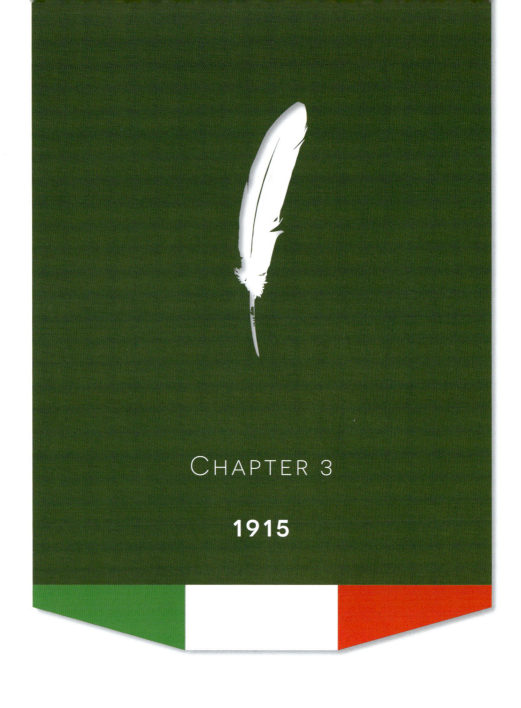

CHAPTER 3

1915

EARLY ACTIONS IN THE UPPER ISONZO VALLEY AND THE CONQUEST OF THE MONTE NERO RIDGE

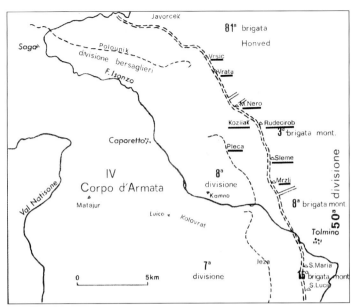

The theater of war of the high Isonzo Valley, showing the stronghold of Tolmino, partially on the right bank of the river, and the ridge of peaks culminating with Monte Nero

In the first weeks of warfare, while the bulk of the army was busy with the complex mobilization, one of the few noteworthy military operations carried out by Alpine troops was the conquest of the important position of Monte Nero, 2,245 meters (7,365 feet) above MSL. It is the most important peak of a mountain chain that runs on the left side of the Isonzo River, with a roughly northeast/southwest course, almost parallel to the river itself. There are other important peaks to the north of Monte Nero, such as Monte Vršič, Monte Vrata and Mount Potoce; to the south, one can encounter Monte Rosso, Mount Rudecirob, Mount Sleme, Mount Mrzli, and Mount Vhodil. Not far to the west, as a buttress, stood Mount Pleca and Mount

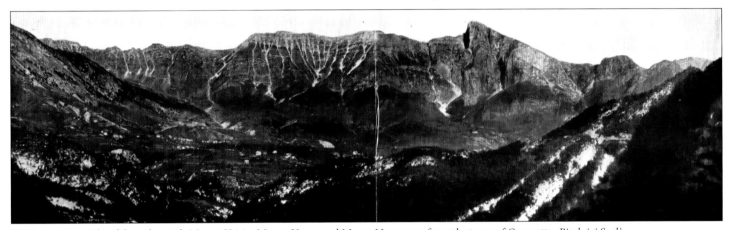

The impressive sight of the ridge with Mount Vrisic, Mount Vrata, and Monte Nero, seen from the town of Caporetto. *Pierluigi Scolè*

A unit of Alpini advancing along a mule track in the early hours of May 24, 1915. *Pierluigi Scolè*

The Eighty-Fifth Company of the Battaglione *Susa*, the unit that took part in the conquest of Mount Vrata and Mount Vršič on May 25, and of Mount Potoce on June 16. *Pierluigi Scolè*

Il monumento agli alpini caduti sul Monte Nero, che venne profanato dagli slavi ed è stato ora ricostruito.

The monument erected, in 1922, to the memory of the Italian soldiers fallen on Monte Nero. *Pierluigi Scolè*

Second Lieutenant Alberto Picco, here depicted in ceremonial uniform

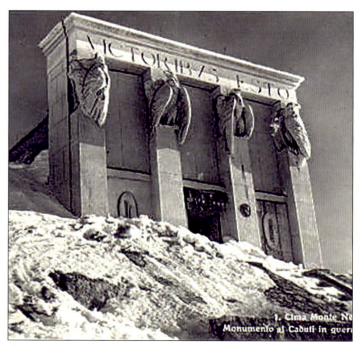

The monumental hut built on Monte Nero in 1928 and dedicated to Alberto Picco, with its unusual neoclassical façade. It was demolished at the beginning of the 1950s by the Alpine society of Nova Gorica (Yugoslavia), to be replaced with another hut. *Pierluigi Scolè*

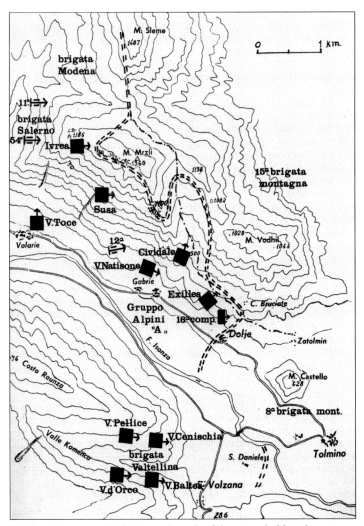

The frontline around Tolmino and north of the stronghold in the autumn of 1915

Kozliak. From its heights this massif dominates the basin of Plezzo to the north and the basin of Tolmino to the south, which gave access to the valley of the Drava River and the coveted Ljubljana plain. Being extremely important for both the Italian Supreme Command and, for opposite reasons, for the Austro-Hungarian general staff, those mountains would be ferociously fought over for more than two years.

The Supreme Command released the order of operations for this area of paramount significance on May 16 and expected a rapid advance by the left wing of the Second Army. This was in order to ford the Isonzo River and come into contact with the enemy stronghold of Tolmino. Its IV Army Corps was in charge of the conquest of the massif that defended the northern side of Tolmino, to outflank the stronghold. The army corps relied on fourteen battalions of Alpini and six mountain artillery batteries, divided into two groups: the Gruppo Alpini "A," with Battalions *Ivrea, Aosta, Intra, Cividale, Val d'Orco, Val Baltea, Val Toce* and *Val Natisone*, with four batteries of the Gruppo *Bergamo* on the right; the Gruppo Alpini "B," with Battalions *Pinerolo, Exilles, Susa, Val Pellice, Val Cenischia* and *Val Dora*, with two batteries of the Gruppo *Torino-Pinerolo* on the left. On the morning of May 24, on the opposite side of the front, stood not much more than a single enemy battalion. Just after midnight of the twenty-fourth, the Alpini moved forward, got the better of the weak forces guarding the border and, in a few hours, reached the town of Caporetto, in view of the mountains that were their target, which, however, was occupied by a unit of *bersaglieri* just the following day. Once having forded the Isonzo River, the Alpini would easily take control of the weakly garrisoned Mount Pleca and Mount Kozliak. Quite surprisingly, the headquarters of the IV Army Corps did not push farther on until the deployment of its units was complete, therefore, nothing happened for three precious days, apart from a few replacements of first line units. Unfortunately, the information about the strength of the enemy was scarce, and nobody wanted to risk the smallest setback; but it is clear that these few hours gave the new Austro-Hungarian commander of the Isonzo front, General Svetovar Borojević, the opportunity to rush in a whole mountain brigade, miraculously closing the gap. Finally, on the twenty-ninth, everything seemed to be ready for a new advance, led this time by the *bersaglieri*, but their attempt was frustrated by the accurate fire of the newly deployed machine guns, and they were forced back. From then on, every new attack needed to be better planned.

The following day, the Battaglione *Susa* was ordered to take Mount Vršič and Mount Vrata. The Alpini approached the enemy lines during the night, and at dawn of the thirty-first, they were—unseen—positioned very close to them. At first light the troops launched the attack, and after a brief fight, they overcame the defenders with little loss, capturing numerous prisoners and some machine guns; a counterattack was repelled a few hours later. The result of a similar action aimed at the conquest of Mount Sleme was not as good. It was entrusted to the Battaglione *Intra*, who were assisted by infantrymen of the *Modena* Brigade, and Mount Mirzli, targeted by the Battaglione *Pinerolo* and by units of the *Salerno* Brigade. Artillery support was provided by some batteries of the Gruppo *Torino-Pinerolo* and Gruppo *Mondovì*. On the afternoon of June 1, the Italian troops attacked bravely, but this time they met the firm resistance of an enemy that was now completely deployed and, due also to the scarce support of the few pieces of artillery assigned to the action, did not achieve any relevant result, despite heavy losses. On the other hand, a counterattack by the Austro-Hungarian troops, which was aimed at regaining the positions lost in the previous days on Mount Vršič, Vrata, and Kozliak, was broken off. A small but important success was achieved by a small party of thirty-one Alpini, who volunteered for the assault against an enemy stronghold positioned on a saddle between Vrata and Potoce, at a height of 2,102 meters (6,896 feet) above MSL. The volunteers climbed a 700-meter slope and swooped down unexpectedly on the Austro-Hungarians, forcing them to flee. Thus, the front line was secured, and the movements of the troops became easier. This action was of paramount importance because it demonstrated that, in the mountains, a surprise attack conducted by a small, well-trained, and motivated unit could often obtain better results than a larger-scale frontal attack; unfortunately, the lesson was neither well understood nor always applied by Italian commanders in the following years. However, after this period of intense military activity, some days of calm followed, which were used by the Alpini to better prepare for future actions and by Austro-Hungarians to further fortify their positions.

The crucial action to take Monte Nero was organized and it was planned to take place at dawn of June 16. The action was entrusted to the Battaglione *Exilles*, which had to move from Mount Kozliak; furthermore, it was decided that the Battaglione *Susa* would carry out a contemporaneous attack on Mount Potoce, moving from its positions on MonteVrata to take the entire northern ridge. To support the assault, the Seventh Battery and the Ninth Battery were deployed in order to be able to hit the enemy trenches and the approaches that possible reinforcements could take. At 4:00 a.m., the Thirty-First and Eighty-Fourth Companies of the Battaglione *Exilles* were ready to attack; they were preceded by a platoon of fifty selected Alpini, which in turn had, as a point element, a squad of only five volunteers armed with a great number of grenades. They were led by Second Lieutenant Alberto Picco. The approach had been made in perfect silence; thus, the enemy sentinels did not notice the attackers until they were already on them. After only forty-five minutes of fighting, the peak of Monte Nero was in Italian hands with losses limited to three dead and nine injured. Meanwhile, the attack on the Potoce had succeeded as well, securing the whole northern part of the mountain ridge. At 5:00 a.m., the enemy launched an immediate counterattack to prevent the Alpini from consolidating their new positions, but it was driven back with severe losses. The Italians entrenched themselves deeply into these mountains, and the guns of the Seventh Battery were transported on the artillerymen's shoulders to reinforce the lines.

As brilliant as the action had been—and as severe a blow as it had been for the Austro-Hungarians—the victory did not completely resolve the situation because the enemy positions of Tolmino could not be outflanked yet. For these reasons, military operations were resumed on July 3 and, by coincidence, while the first of many offensives launched in the Isonzo Valley were carried out.[1] The aim of these new attacks was to complete the conquest of the mountain ridge, taking the peaks south of Monte Nero that were still in enemy hands—Monte Rosso, Mount Rudecirob and Mount Sleme—with the view of completing the movement around the stronghold of Tolmino and forcing the Austro-Hungarians to evacuate it. The action was to be supported by a direct frontal attack on Tolmino itself. Four Alpini battalions were chosen for the assault. From north to south: Battaglione *Exilles* was to move from Monte Nero to Monte Rosso, while the *Val Toce* had to aim at the Rudecirob from its positions on Mount Kozliak; the attack against the enemy positions between Rudecirob and Sleme was entrusted to the Battaglione *Intra*, thus indirectly aiding the action of the *Val Toce*; while the Battaglione *Aosta*'s task was to carry out the assault on Mount Sleme itself. Artillery support was provided by six batteries of mountain artillery, including the Seventh Battery deployed on the top of Monte Nero. The four columns moved at 3:00 a.m., but were soon detected by Austro-Hungarian sentries and stopped in their advance by heavy and precise fire; furthermore, the enemy lines were now defended by kilometers of barbed wire that had not been damaged by artillery fire. The Alpini attacked bravely, suffering heavy losses, but could not advance any farther; the Seventh Battery

was located and targeted by counter-battery fire, almost being annihilated. Finally, the attackers were forced to retreat. No better results were achieved by the following attacks against Monte Rosso on the sixth and on the nineteenth of July. The peak was finally taken on the twenty-first by the Battaglioni *Intra* and *Val d'Orco*, supported by two batteries, although with a severe death toll. However, faced with the strong resistance of the Austro-Hungarian units, contemporaneous attacks launched by Battaglioni *Aosta* and *Susa* to take the last enemy positions north and west of Monte Nero failed.

The conquest of Monte Nero had seemed to be a decisive move in the beginning, but the realization had soon emerged that it was neither sufficient to threaten the stronghold of Tolmino nor to break through the mountains and reach the Ljubljana plain. In fact, although the ridge was almost entirely in Italian hands, to the south the enemy positions resisted tenaciously on Mount Sleme, Mount Mrzli, and Mount Vhodil, which closed the way to Tolmino, and to the east lesser—but no less impervious—peaks faced Monte Nero. The Austro-Hungarians had had enough time to provide them with lines of barbed wire, impossible to pass without appropriate tools, deep trenches with shelters dug into the rock, and a good number of pieces of artillery of a better quality compared to the Italian ones. The illusion of an easy victory was gone.

New strong attacks against the mountain ridge were organized in autumn, in October and November, in the framework of the Third and the Fourth Battle of the Isonzo, with the view of pushing farther south toward Tolmino. On October 21, the Battaglioni *Susa* and *Val Toce* moved against Mount Mirzli while *Exilles* and *Val Natisone* assaulted Mount Vhodil; the Battaglione *Cevedale* had to attack the saddle between the two peaks, covering the flanks of the main attacks. The first two days' progress was rather modest, until a company of the Battaglione *Exilles* was able to penetrate a portion of the last entrenchment that protected the peak of Mount Vhodil on the twenty-third; however, during the night, an Austro-Hungarian counterattack dislodged the Alpini. With the support of the guns of the Thirty-Second Battery, the attack was resumed on the twenty-seventh by several companies of the Battaglioni *Exilles*, *Val Natisone* and *Cevedale*, and they succeeded in the conquest of some lower enemy trenches. In the following days, the Italian troops were counterattacked several times but held firmly, though their positions were dominated from above by those of the enemy. From November 26, aided by two infantry companies, Mount Mrzli was attacked again by the Battaglione *Intra* and, later, by the Battaglione *Ivrea*. But enemy artillery fire was too heavy to advance much in the open ground, and the few results achieved were lost due to counterattacks. The peak of Mount Vhodil was assaulted by the Battaglioni *Exilles*, *Susa* and *Cividale*, but it was not possible to make any progress, due to heavy fire. The Austro-Hungarians were now firmly rooted on these mountains and aware that there was not much room behind them to retreat farther; therefore, every advance by the Italians was immediately counterattacked. These were the last operations in the Monte Nero-Tolmino area for 1915: the weather forced both contenders to dig into their respective positions and organize the lines to face a fierce winter in the high mountains.

MILITARY OPERATIONS IN THE ZONA CARNIA

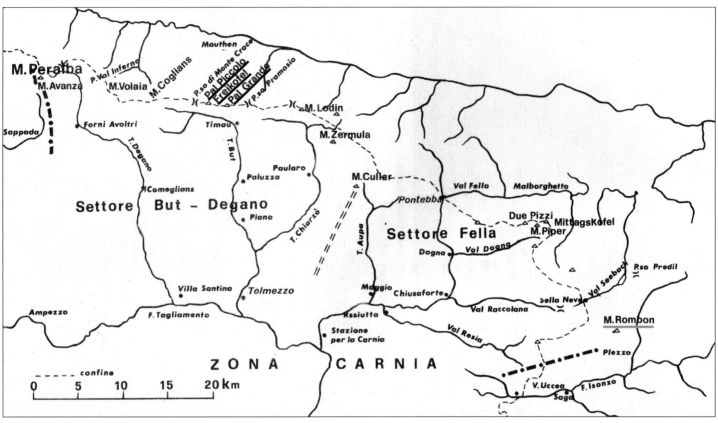

The theater of war in the Zona Carnia

Mule baggage column near the village of Timau, to the rear front of Monte Pal Grande and Monte Pal Piccolo. *Museo Nazionale Storico degli Alpini*

A 149 mm gun in firing position in the Dogna Valley. *Museo Nazionale Storico degli Alpini*

Outpost of the Alpini on Monte Pal Piccolo. *Museo Nazionale Storico degli Alpini*

In this area, where the Carnic Alps border the Austrian territory directly, unlike along the rest of the front, from the first days of war the enemy showed an active attitude: the Austro-Hungarians were determined not to retreat. The same day, May 24, they conquered Monte Pal Piccolo, garrisoned by a small unit of Alpini of the Battaglione *Tolmezzo*, but a counterattack by two platoons detached by *Tolmezzo* and *Val Tagliamento* regained the lost position. Another action on the twenty-eighth against the Pal Piccolo and the Pal Grande was unsuccessful, but a few days later the Austro-Hungarians managed to occupy Monte Freikofel, giving them the ability to harass the Italian lines. The mountain was retaken on June 10, by Alpini of the Battaglione *Tolmezzo*, but the Pal Piccolo was lost again on the fourteenth, and the attacks launched to retake it in June and July did not succeed. Austro-Hungarian attacks against the Italian positions continued during the autumn, without any relevant result, until the operations were suspended to prepare for winter because of the worsening weather conditions.

Conversely, the eastern part of Zona Carnia that coincides with the north side of the Plezzo Basin remained calm for weeks, until the Italians took the initiative, focused on the conquest of the massif that stands on the right side of the Isonzo River Valley. The valley is dominated by Mount Rombon, 2,208 meters (7,244 feet) above MSL high and comprising Mount Palica and Mount Cuckla. It was a wild environment, even lacking the smallest pathways, rendering troops' movement extremely difficult.

Two battalions of Alpini, the *Val Ellero*, which also comprised a company of the *Mondovì*, and the Battaglione Speciale *Bes*, composed of two companies of the *Ceva* and one of the *Pieve di Teco*, were commanded by Captain Bes. They moved southeast from Sella Prevala on August 14, amid forbidding weather conditions; the advance was hindered more by climate and terrain than by the enemy, which was deployed farther east. On the twenty-third, the Battaglione *Bes*, supported by the Fifty-First Battery, was able to take the Palica and the Cuckla, which were lightly defended, by surprise and hold on to the new positions under heavy artillery fire that lasted twenty-four hours. Four days later the Alpini, with the support of the Fifty-First Battery, tried to conquer the Rombon itself, but the Austro-Hungarians were very well positioned, and the opportunity for surprise was already gone; after a whole day of bloody fighting, the Italian troops were forced to retreat under cover of darkness, leaving behind dozens of casualties.

New units of Alpini were sent to the area; in particular, three companies detached from the Battaglioni *Pieve di Teco*; *Mondovì* and *Saluzzo* assembled in a battalion renamed "*Piazza*" after the name of its commander; and a new unit, called "*Comando Truppe Monte Rombon*," was created, comprising all the Alpini companies employed therein. A new action was launched on September 11 with the Battaglioni *Bes* and *Piazza* on the first line. They were supported by the Fifty-First Battery, which had the Rombon as their target; units of *bersaglieri* that flanked the attack along the basin below, aiming at Plezzo; and the Battaglioni *Aosta* and *Pinerolo*, with the Seventh and Tenth Battery, in a coordinated, south-to-north attack from Mount Vršič on the south side of the basin. Eight days of fighting were not enough to unhinge the solid, deeply entrenched Austro-Hungarian defenses—and, as would become typical, they were supported by excellent artillery. These were the last relevant actions in this area, which remained calm in the following months; the *Bes* and *Piazza* battalions were disbanded, and the companies reattached to their respective units.

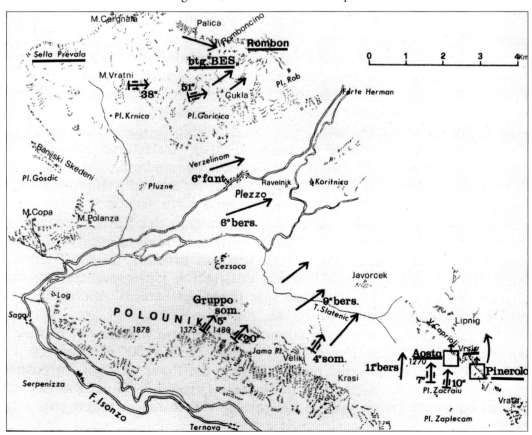

Military operations in the upper Isonzo Valley and in the Rombon massif between August and September 1915

THE WAR IN THE DOLOMITES

The Dolomites occupy the area that runs along the northeastern part of the Trentino salient, featured by a continuous ridge of high mountains that run all along what is now the border between Trentino and Veneto, in northern Italy, but what was then the border between the Kingdom of Italy and the Austro-Hungarian Empire. From south to north, they go from the Marmolada, whose highest peak, Punta Penia, is 3,343 meters (10,968 feet) above MSL, to the Tre Cime di Lavaredo (or "Drei Zinnen" in German), 2,999 meters (9,839 feet) above MSL. Between them, there is a series of peaks, like Col di Lana, Sass di Stria, Lagazuoi Piccolo, Cima Falzarego, and Cima Bois. There is the Tofane massif, with its three peaks of Tofana di Rozes (3,225 meters/10,581 feet above MSL), Tofana di Mezzo (3,244 meters / 10,643 feet above MSL), and Tofana di Dentro (3,238 meters / 10,623 feet above MSL). There are Monte Cristallo and Monte Piana, and, behind the Tofane, crossing a deep valley called Travenazes Valley, one encounters another ridge, which includes Lagazuoi Grande, Punta Fanes, Monte Cavallo, Monte Castello, and Vallon Bianco. This impressive mountain wall, which is several hundred kilometers long, is navigable through only a few passes, such as Falzarego Pass and Valparola Pass.

Since the end of 1800s, the Austro-Hungarians were very concerned that an Italian offensive through the Puster Valley or the Fassa Valley could cut the salient, isolate the troops deployed to the south, and leave the western part of Austria at the mercy of the enemy. Therefore, they had provided the border with strong defenses that could take advantage of these high mountains. During the first weeks of the war, due to the lack of troops to deploy there, the Austro-Hungarian high command obtained the help of its renowned *Alpenkorps*, a corps specializing in mountain warfare, from its ally, Germany.

The area was the responsibility of the Italian Fourth Army, which had six Alpini battalions and nine mountain artillery batteries at its disposal at the beginning of the war. In the first weeks of war, the army remained very cautious and, in general, did not take any initiative to take advantage of the precarious state of the enemy garrisons. The reasons were that the Italians did not fully know the situation and that the heavy artillery was still on its way and could not be

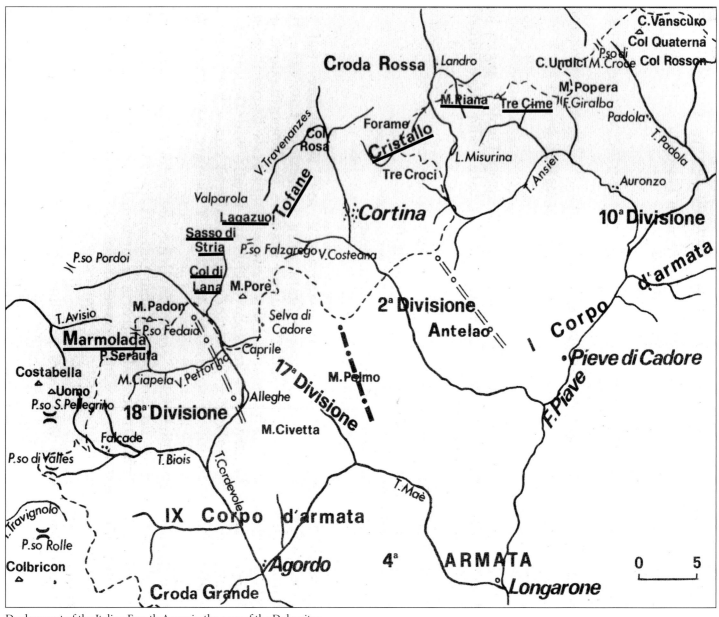

Deployment of the Italian Fourth Army in the area of the Dolomites

used for an offensive. However, some audacious actions were carried out by the Alpine troops. On June 8, a company of the Battaglione *Belluno* occupied the two important passes of Ombretta and Ombrettola, to the south of the Marmolada massif, while on June 16, the Battaglione *Val Chisone* completely surprised the Austro-Hungarian defenses on the Sass di Stria with a brilliant assault, almost conquering the mountain. Unfortunately, the enemy managed to maintain the extreme top of it, and after few days, the Italian command ordered the Alpini to leave the positions, a decision that was much regretted in the following months. In June, the Battaglione *Fenestrelle* advanced again along the eastern slopes of the Tofana di Dentro and clashed with the Germans of the *Alpenkorps*, causing them losses and capturing prisoners, at a time when Italy and Germany were not yet formally at war. It is certain that, had the Fourth Army been more active, it could have reached important targets that later remained out of its reach in short time, notwithstanding bloody efforts.

Images from the Marmolada massif: an Italian sentry on the Ombrettola Pass; Alpini in a trench on the Ombretta Pass; shelters on the Cima Ombretta di Mezzo, 2,893 meters (9,491 feet) above MSL. *Museo Nazionale Storico degli Alpini*

The gun crew of a 65/17 mountain gun on the Cima Ombretta di Mezzo. *Museo Nazionale Storico degli Alpini*

In the foreground is the Tofana di Mezzo, with the Tofana di Rozes in the background; at the base of the Tofana di Mezzo, one is able to notice a few lines of barbed wire. *Museo Nazionale Storico degli Alpini*

A 149 mm gun is towed on a road covered with snow in the mountains around Cortina d'Ampezzo, in the Dolomites. *Andrea Bianchi*

An Italian 210 mm howitzer aimed at the Austro-Hungarian positions on the Col di Lana. *Andrea Bianchi*

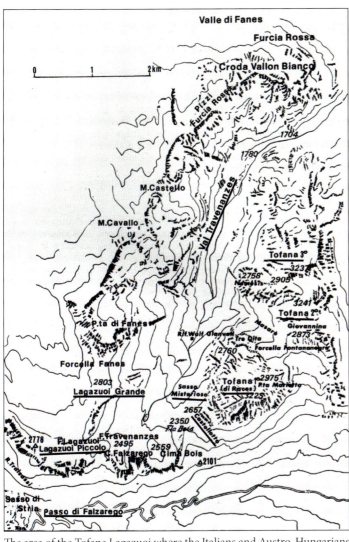

The area of the Tofane Lagazuoi where the Italians and Austro-Hungarians fought bravely for more than two years

Finally, in July, all the heavy artillery was in place; thus, the army went on the offensive. Beginning in July 7, the Battaglione *Val Chisone* renewed its attacks on the Sass di Stria after the mountain had been shelled for two whole days. Twice, the Alpini reached the upmost enemy entrenchment, but they were repelled by heavy artillery fire and a violent counterattack. The Battaglione *Belluno* assaulted Cima Bois, conquering the lower saddle and the top of the mountain, but could not proceed any farther, due to the heavy fire from the Lagazuoi and from a very strong Austro-Hungarian stronghold called *Castelletto* (little castle), dug into the rock close to the Tofana di Roces. On July 8, a brilliant action was almost able to open a breach in the Austro-Hungarian line—two companies of the *Fenestrelle*, with infantrymen of the Twenty-Third Regiment, got around the northern side of the Tofana di Dentro and penetrated the Val Travenazes, taking an enemy unit by surprise. The Alpini crossed the valley and climbed the opposite slopes, taking the Furcia Rossa and the Vallon Bianco, but the forces were too weak to push farther. The Austro-Hungarians were able to stop any further advance along Val Travenazes and organized a quick counterattack that forced the Italians to retreat, lest they be cut off from their lines. A great opportunity had been lost, and another action was organized on July 15, with even greater failures. A company of the *Fenestrelle* and one of infantrymen attacked the entrance of Val Travenazes pushed south, while units of the *Val Chisone* and *Belluno* attacked the south side of the valley coming from Col di Bois and pushed north. At the same time, infantrymen attacked a narrow saddle between Tofana di Rozes and Tofana di Mezzo, called Forcella di Fontananegra, trying to break into the middle of the valley. Four days of hard fighting did not produce any notable result and only cost heavy losses to both contenders. Another furious

On the Tofane in 1915, there were German units as well: the famous *Alpenkorps*, before Italy and Germany were formally at war. Here, German mountain troops are in position on a small saddle between two peaks. *Museo Nazionale Storico degli Alpini*

Unsettling view of the *Castelletto*, with the Tofana di Rozes in the background. *Museo Nazionale Storico degli Alpini*

The Travenazes Valley, viewed from the Austro-Hungarian positions of its north side; on the left is the Tofana di Rozes with the Castelletto; on the right, the Torre di Fanes; and in the center, the silhouette of the Col di Bois. *Museo Nazionale Storico degli Alpini*

attack followed on the thirty-first, when two companies of the Battaglione *Belluno* and two infantry companies moved from Cima di Bois against Punta Falzarego and Forcella Travenazes, while Alpini of the same battalion and infantrymen tried again to take the Forcella di Fontananegra. Only the last action was finally successful on August 2, with the capture of many German soldiers of the *Alpenkorps*, but, as is often experienced during the war, it did not have any decisive affect since the enemy line was able to be rebuilt a few hundred meters behind the lost one. On September 18, a great success was scored by the *Compagnia Volontari Alpini Feltre*, which managed to conquer the peak of the Tofana di Rozes. About a hundred volunteers moved from the Italian outpost at 2,975 meters (9,760 feet) above MSL and after a silent march of three hours reached the enemy positions, which were promptly assaulted and conquered. The Alpini were targeted for days with heavy artillery fire and counterattacked several times but held on to the new positions, succeeding in time to clean up the whole Tofana di Rozes of enemy presence. Italian troops could not progress any further in the Tofane area, due to the *Castelletto* stronghold. With its 2,657-meter (8,717 foot) height, they controlled any access to the lower part of Val Travenzes and had a perfect line of fire along the whole valley. A few hundred meters to the north, another stronghold, called Sasso Misterioso (Mysterious Rock) by the Italians, acted as a counterfort, covering the *Castelletto* with its fire and being covered in turn by fire from the latter. The attacks launched by the Alpini of the Battaglioni *Belluno* and *Val Chisone,* and by the *Compagnia Volontari* Alpini *Feltre,* failed against these tremendous fortifications on September 24 and October 17 with a white blanket of snow that covered everything. The season made it advisable to stop operations and prepare for the incoming winter, but on October 18, an action was attempted against the Piccolo Lagazuoi and Cima Falzarego by the infantrymen of the Forty-Fifth Regiment and the exhausted Alpini of the *Val Chisone,* who had barely recovered after the previous day's attacks. Punta Falzarego was finally conquered by the infantry, while the Alpini did not manage to climb the Lagazuoi to the top but set foot on the eastern peak of the massif, later named "*Punta Berrino*" (Berrino's Peak), after Captain Berrino, commander of the 230th Company of the *Val Chisone.* The next day, they installed themselves precariously on a lower ledge, later called *Cengia Martini* (Martini's Ledge), after the commander of the *Val Chisone*, Major Martini. These two positions, although exposed to enemy fire coming from various directions, not least the upper trenches of the Lagazuoi itself, allowed the Italians to in turn seriously harass some key Austro-Hungarian positions in Val Travenazes on one side and on the Valparola Pass on the other side. Therefore, from the very first days, they contended with heavy artillery fire and continuous counter-attacks, always beaten back by the occupants, and at a high price. In the following months, the Lagazuoi would also be the theater of a ferocious war of mines, with several attempts to blow up the opposite positions, the first attempt was by the Austro-Hungarians on the New Years Eve of 1915. The Italians did manage to cling to those rocks for more than two years, although they could not move any farther in that direction.

Italian barracks clinging to the rock on the Tofane. *Museo Nazionale Storico degli Alpini*

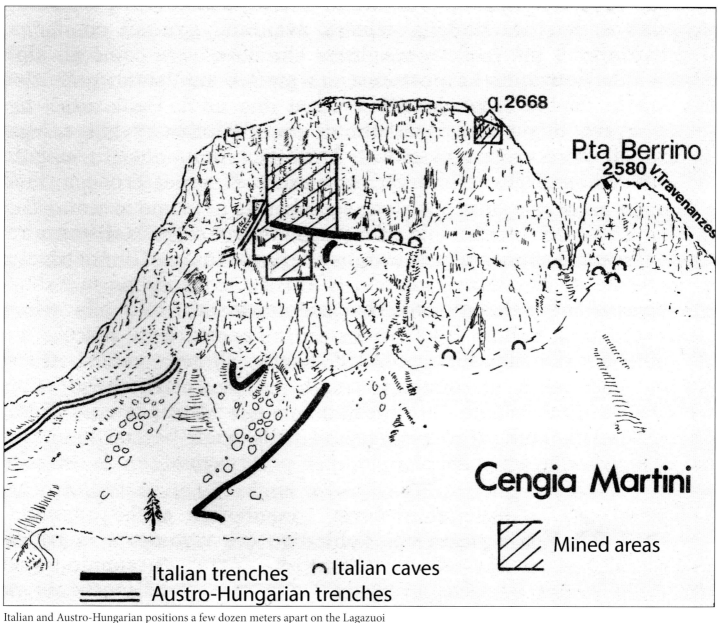

Italian and Austro-Hungarian positions a few dozen meters apart on the Lagazuoi

Italian barracks in the area of Monte Piana. *Andrea Bianchi*

More to the north, in the area between Monte Piana and Tre Cime di Lavaredo, the Austro-Hungarians took the initiative from the very beginning, trying to drive the Italians from some positions that formed a sort of salient into their lines and threatened the Val di Landro, a direct access to the vulnerable Puster Valley. On May 26, the Alpini of the Battaglione *Pieve di Cadore* and *Val Piave* faced an enemy attack with success and, while counterattacking, managed to conquer Monte Paterno; between July and August, the two battalions engaged the enemy several times and finally took hold of the whole plateau of the Tre Cime di Lavaredo but were stopped farther to the west by the strong defenses of Monte Piana. In July, a company of the Battaglione *Cadore* succeeded in setting foot on the southern slope of Monte Cristallo, near Cortina d'Ampezzo, trying to get around the Monte Piana from the south and reach the Val di Landro. In the following weeks, Alpini of the *Pieve di Cadore* and *Fenestrelle*, infantrymen and artillerymen of the Thirty-Fifth Battery tried to extend the conquest, but they clashed against solid and well garrisoned defenses, notwithstanding great effort. Military operations subsided in autumn, when the weather worsened and the temperatures dropped dramatically.

Italian soldiers pulling equipment on a sledge up a snowy valley near Monte Cristallo. *Andrea Bianchi*

THE ADVANCE IN THE SOUTHERN TRENTINO

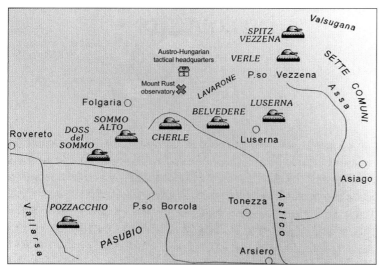

The powerful chain of forts built by the Austro-Hungarians on the south border of the Trentino salient

Forte Luserna, or Werk Lusern, after the heavy shelling by Italian artillery between May 25 and 28, 1915, when the garrison was about to surrender. *Museo Nazionale Storico degli Alpini*

Forte Verle under artillery fire. *Museo Nazionale Storico degli Alpini*

The area between the southern Trentino, east of the Adige River, and the northern Veneto, once the border between Italy and Austria-Hungary, is occupied by some plateaus—Folgaria, Lavarone, Tonezza, and Asiago—the latter is the widest of them, known also as Sette Comuni, in reference to the seven municipalities located on the territory. To the northeast, the of Plateau of Asiago extends into the vast mountain area of the Lagorai, separated from the latter by the valley of the Brenta Torrent, the Valsugana. While the Lagorai is characterized by wilderness and barren peaks over 2,500 MSL, the plateaus are in comparison easier to cross. This is the reason why the Austro-Hungarian High Command had worked hard for many years before the war to fortify them with a strong chain of modern fortifications dug in solid rock and protected with several meters of concrete. At the outbreak of the war, the Austro-Hungarians decided to leave the more exposed portion of their territory and retreat behind the forts. The Italian High Command had entrusted this part of the front to the First Army, which was requested to conduct aggressive activity, in order to prevent the enemy to move units from this area to the more crucial eastern front, without conducting great offensives; Italian forces assigned to the army were, therefore, relatively scarce. On the plateaus, from the first hours of war the contenders started to exchange heavy artillery fire,[2] and the Alpini of the Battaglione *Bassano* tried an assault on Cima Vezzena, an important peak of the region with its height of 1,903 meters (6,243 feet) above MSL. They aimed to make a surprise attack on the fort built on top of it, Vezzena Fort, or Werk Spitz Verle for the Austro-Hungarians, which offered a complete view on the Austro-Hungarian lines in the Valsugana. However, the position was already heavily defended, and the attack failed. Other attacks were launched from mid-August until October, without any appreciable result. In August, the Italian troops that comprised the mountain troops battalions *Feltre* and *Val Cismon*, also started the advance on the region of Lagorai; they achieved some initial successes, pushing the enemy some kilometers to the west, but soon the resistance stiffened, and winter came, imposing a stop to military operations.

To the west of the River Adige and around Lake Garda, the Italians could advance almost without opposition since the enemy carried out a deep retreat to reach better defensible positions. On May 25, the Battaglione *Val d'Adige* would advance on the Monte Baldo massif, between the valley of the Adige River and Lake Garda, and arrive on Monte Altissimo, 2,079 meters (6,829 feet) above MSL, which allowed a perfect view of the enemy positions on both sides. On the opposite side of the valley, on the twenty-ninth the Battaglione *Verona* conquered Monte Zugna, where a fort was under construction, and on July 5 it was able to advance further north to Monte Zugna Torta that dominated the town of Rovereto: the Austro-Hungarians would pay dearly these losses the following year, when the defenders of the Zugna would be able to stop their offensive for weeks. Farther to the east, the Battaglioni *Vicenza* and *Val Leogra* managed to occupy the Pasubio massif, which would be heavily contended for in 1916.

Austro-Hungarian positions on the Colbricon and on Cima di Cece, on the northeast side of the Lagorai. *Museo Nazionale Storico degli Alpini*

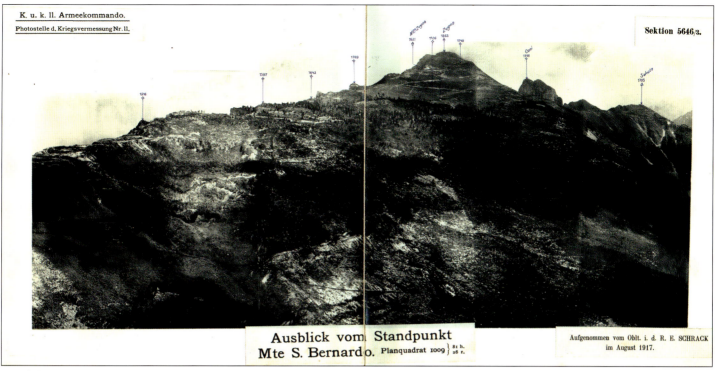

Detailed photographic map of Monte Zugna, produced for the Headquarters of the Austro-Hungarian Eleventh Army. *Museo Nazionale Storico degli Alpini*

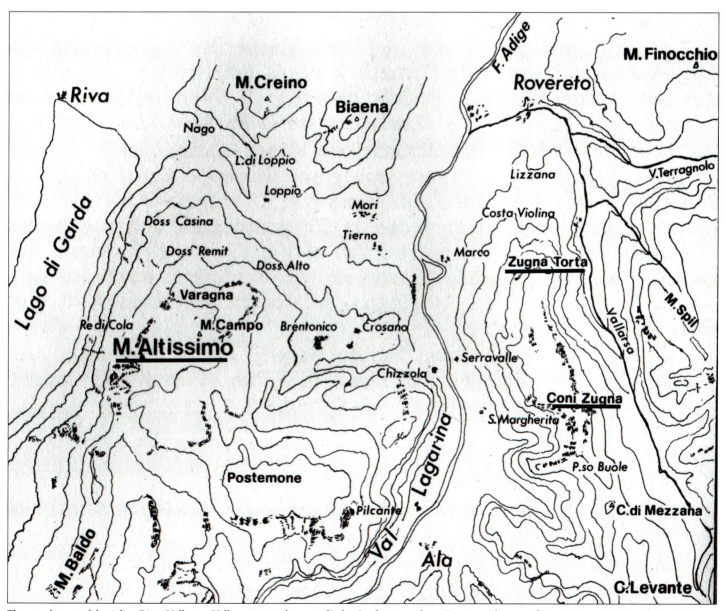

The war theater of the Adige River Valley, or Vallagarina, to the east of Lake Garda, in southern Trentino. The area of Monte Zugna Torta and Monte Zugna, with the Buole Pass in the rear, would be intensely fought over in the following years.

COMBAT ACTIONS IN EXTREME CONDITIONS ON THE ADAMELLO

Along the western border of Trentino with Lombardy run a series of mountain ranges with peaks beyond the height of 3,000 meters (9,843 feet) above MSL, covered in snow and beaten by blizzards even in the summer, with numerous glaciers, where it seemed impossible for men to live, let alone fight. The northern range is the Ortles-Cevedale that runs from the Stelvio Pass to the north and the Tonale Pass to the south; south of it extends the Adamello-Presanella, formed by several parallel ridges that run roughly in a north-south direction. In the Ortles-Cevedale area during 1915 only patrol activity was carried out by the belligerents, with some limited attacks against the enemy supply lines. Not until the end of October was an action planned to take the peak of Monte Cevedale, at a height of 3,769 MSL. A company from each of the Battaglione *Tirano* and *Valtellina*, with volunteers detached from various battalions and grouped for some weeks in a special unit called *Centuria*[21] *Valtellina*, moved during the night in the high snow but could not advance very far, stopped not by the Austro-Hungarians

The Cevedale Pass, in the Ortles-Cevedale mountain range, protected by a deep strip of barbed wire. *Museo Nazionale Storico degli Alpini*

An old 70 mm, rigidly mounted gun positioned on Monte Ortles. *Museo Nazionale Storico degli Alpini*

The western border of the Trentino salient, with the Ortles-Cevedale and the Adamello-Presanella mountain ranges.

The Garibaldi Hut at the beginning of the war. *Museo Nazionale Storico degli Alpini*

but by the terrain itself. After this failure, the troops prepared for the winter.

The behavior of the Italians was more active on the Adamello where, very soon, a unit of the Battaglione *Morbegno* occupied the important position of the Garibaldi Hut, taking control of the mountain passes of Venerocolo, Brizio and Garibaldi. Meanwhile, the Austro-Hungarians installed themselves in the Mandrone Hut, some 6 kilometers to the northeast. The first action in this area was organized at the beginning of June, aimed at the conquest of the northern ridge of the range, known as the Monticelli, to control the southern side of the Tonale Pass. Unfortunately, the action turned out to be badly planned: due to poor reconnaissance, the Alpini of the *Morbegno* marched long hours to reach their target with inadequate artillery support. Furthermore, the troops were still wearing the gray-green uniforms, not having yet received the white camouflage uniforms; therefore, they were easily spotted on the white background and hit by enemy fire. On top of everything, the Austro-Hungarians were able to counterattack with units of skiers, who were much more mobile than the troops who were on foot. On July 15, the Austro-Hungarians organized an action against the Venerocolo, Brizio, and Garibaldi passes, which were poorly defended by small units of the *Morbegno* that had been detached from the Garibaldi Hut. The Alpini, although outnumbered, resisted bravely, forcing the attackers to retreat. But it was clear that the Italian line was too weak and not deep enough to be effective. More forces were assigned to the

The Centuria Valtellina lined up, awaiting the visit of King Vittorio Emanuele III in September 1915, at S. Caterina, in Valtellina, a valley on the border between Lombardia and Trentino. It would be disbanded a few weeks later. *Museo Nazionale Storico degli Alpini*

Garibaldi Hut, new barracks were built, and regular labor gangs transported supplies to this position, which became the headquarters of a very well-organized and strong special Alpine unit. In time, the hut would be connected with the valley below by a cableway. On the other hand, any attempt to drive the enemy away from some of its positions failed. The Monticelli, considered of paramount importance for the development of any action against the Tonale Pass, were attacked several times: by the Battaglione *Morbegno* at the end of August; by the same battalion with the support of companies of the Battaglioni *Val d'Intelvi*, *Valcamonica*, and volunteers grouped in the *Centuria Valtellina*, on September 13 and 14; and at the end of October, just before the winter pause, by *Morbegno*, *Edolo*, *Valtellina*, and *Val d'Intelvi*, but all the assaults were repelled.

On the Adamello during the long winter months, the delivery of supplies to the outposts was ensured, thanks to dozens of sledge dogs. *Museo Nazionale Storico degli Alpini*

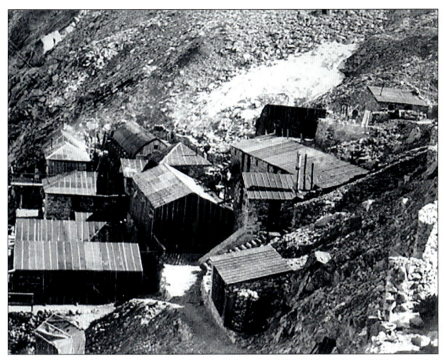

Barracks near Monte Corno di Lagoscuro, 3,166 meters (10,387 feet) above MSL, some 8 kilometers to the northeast of the Garibaldi Hut. *Museo Nazionale Storico degli Alpini*

A unit of Alpini at the Brizio Pass.
Museo Nazionale Storico degli Alpini

Cableways on the Adamello massif; the cableways were of paramount importance for both the Italians and the Austro-Hungarians to be able to deliver supplies and, sometimes, move ill and injured soldiers to the higher positions that were not reachable by roads. *Museo Nazionale Storico degli Alpini*

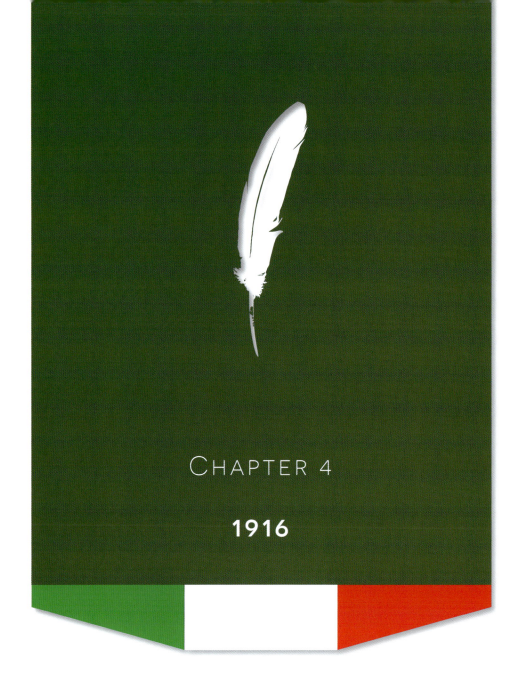

CHAPTER 4

1916

A column of trucks on a newly built road in the Dolomites. *Andrea Bianchi*

Machine gunners lurking on a high peak; the machine gun is a war-booty Austro-Hungarian Schwarzlose m. 07/12. *Museo Nazionale Storico degli Alpini*

The Alpini become heroes in the propaganda movies; in this case, the mythological character of "Maciste the Mighty," created by Gabriele D'Annunzio at the beginning of the 1900s, enlists in the Alpini and, using his strength, leads the Italian troops to victory. Movie by Itala Film, 1916.

During the winter between 1915 and 1916, military operations subsided for many months along the whole Italian front due to the forbidding weather conditions and to the need to ensure the subsistence of millions of soldiers in a situation never experienced before in the history of mankind. Until that time, war had been fought predominantly between spring and autumn, and the troops were, for the most part, demobilized during the long winter months, when battles were rare. For the first time, it became necessary to provide everything to millions of men-at-arms, who were often deployed into impenetrable areas. The priority changed from gaining a trench or fort to building shelters on the front line, building barracks in the rear, and expanding the road system to be able to send supplies to every point of the front. In the mountains, shelters needed to be dug in solid rock, and many pathways and trails had to be hacked out; in many areas, cableways that were able to bring supplies to the most distant places were built. This titanic operation was hampered by the exceptional snowfalls that caused many avalanches that winter, resulting in more casualties than the war itself had. In brief, the struggle for survival became more important than combat against the enemy.

During the winter months, the *Regio Esercito* mobilized the Alpini battalions of the *milizia territoriale*, named after the mountains. But instead of using them in territorial duty, as had been expected, the Army sent them to the front line, where they, like their younger fellow soldiers, fought bravely. With these twenty-six new battalions, the mountain troops corps completed its organizational chart, with a total of seventy-eight battalions that encompassed 225 companies. During 1916, the number of machine guns finally started to increase due to the faster production of FIAT M1914 and the import of a great number of Saint-Étienne machine guns from France. Thus, between 1916 and part of 1917, every battalion had an assigned machine gun company with six weapons. In the spring of 1916, many battalions also received a section of two exemplars of the Villar Perosa M1915 submachine gun, a practical, portable automatic firearm, derived from an aircraft weapon. During the same period, sixteen new mountain artillery batteries were formed: twelve with the standard 65/17 gun and four that were armed with war-booty Austro-Hungarian 7.5 cm M15 mountain howitzers. The total number of batteries therefore increased to sixty-six, grouped into twenty-one battalions.[1]

Operations in 1916 were characterized by the great Austro-Hungarian offensive launched in the spring through the southern Trentino, in the area of the plateaus, continuing well into the summer, and by the subsequent Italian counteroffensive. Alpine troops played a primary role, both in the defensive and in the offensive. As a consequence, actions on other parts of the front were comparatively limited, but the Alpini scored some remarkable results.

COMBAT ACTIVITY IN THE UPPER ISONZO VALLEY

In the Mount Rombon area, the year opened with a checkmate for the Italians: Mount Cuckla, guarded by the Alpini of the Battaglione *Pieve di Teco bis*, which was a temporary unit formed of companies of other battalions, was lost on February 12, and hasty counterattacks mounted the following day could not reconquer it. A well-planned action conducted by companies of the four battalions *Ceva*,

Machine gunners in the upper Isonzo Valley with a Maxim machine gun; near the foot of the alpino on the forefront appears the water tank to cool the weapon, while on the right is the ammunition box. *Pierluigi Scolè*

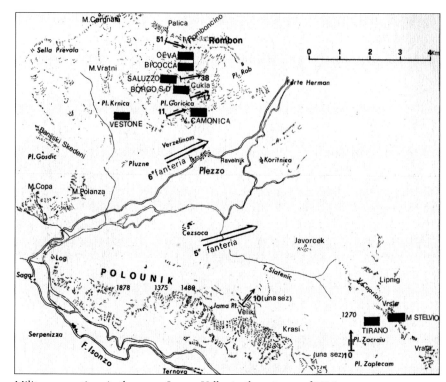

Military operations in the upper Isonzo Valley in the autumn of 1916

Alpini of the Battaglione *Ceva. Museo Nazionale Storico degli Alpini*

A mule train climbs the slopes of Monte Nero.

La guerra sulle cime nevose: come i pezzi da montagna giungono sulle posizioni più difficili.
(Disegno di A. Beltrame).

The illustrated magazine *La Domenica del Corriere* of March 12, 1916, shows the artillerymen carrying a mountain gun up to the frontline on their shoulders to help their fellow Alpini during the action.

Borgo San Dalmazzo, Saluzzo and *Val Camonica*, with the close support of the Thirty-Eighth Mountain Artillery Battery, did not finally succeed until May 10. Exploiting the momentum, the Alpini also captured other surrounding peaks, which were later held against the usual enemy counterattacks. In the area of Monte Nero as well, the Austro-Hungarians launched an assault in the spring against Mounts Potoce and Vršič, defended by small units of the battalions *Monte Spluga* and *Monte Stelvio*. The Vršič temporarily fell but was soon retaken by the Alpini. In the whole upper Isonzo Valley, the operations were interrupted during the Austro-Hungarian spring offensive, to be resumed only in mid-September. An important action was planned that involved the whole area of the Rombon massif, aimed at the conquest of Rombon itself. This action was flanked by an action in the northern area of Monte Nero against some residual positions that were still held by the enemy on Mount Vršič and, to the north of it, against Mount Javorcek. On September 16, the Battaglione *Ceva* attacked Mount Rombon frontally, supported by the Fifty-First Battery, while the *Bicocca*, with one piece of the Thirty-Eighth Battery, tried to climb the southern slopes of the mountain. At the same time, the Battaglioni *Borgo San Dalmazzo* and *Saluzzo*, with two pieces of the same Thirty-Eighth Battery, moved from Mount Cukcla and tried to assault the enemy trenches on a lower saddle while the *Val Camonica*, with the Seventeenth Battery, assaulted the peak located to the south of the saddle. The flanking action was carried out by the Battaglione *Monte Stelvio* against Mount Vršič and by the *Tirano* against Mount Javorcek with the support of infantry units. The fighting flared up during the whole day, and the Alpini came very close to their targets on several occasions. But the artillery bombardment had been rather ineffective, so the main Austro-Hungarian positions held firm. Finally, under cover of darkness, all of the battalions retreated to their earlier positions, leaving many casualties on the terrain.

THE USE OF COMMANDO TACTICS: THE CONQUEST OF THE SENTINELLA PASS

Italo Lunelli. *Fondazione Museo Storico del Trentino Photographic Archive*

The planner of the exploit at the Sentinella Pass, Giovanni Sala. *Biblioteca Storica Cadorina, via W. Musizza and G. De Donà*

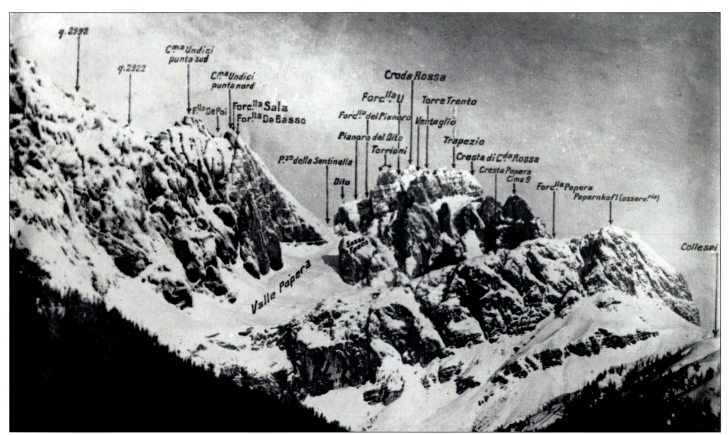

The area of the Sentinella Pass and the surrounding peaks. *Biblioteca Storica Cadorina, via W. Musizza and G. De Donà*

April 1916, Captain Sala and his Alpini are resting at a hut close to Cima Undici. *Biblioteca Storica Cadorina, via W. Musizza and G. De Donà*

The western side of Cima Undici with the Szgismondj Hut. *Museo Nazionale Storico degli Alpini*

View of the impenetrable area of the Croda Rossa. *Museo Nazionale Storico degli Alpini*

Sandbag wall put in place by the Italians on the Sentinella Pass. *Biblioteca Storica Cadorina, via W. Musizza and G. De Donà*

The action against the Sentinella Pass is certainly one of the most remarkable actions carried out by the Alpini during the Great War. It was conducted, using infiltration tactics, in a territory and season that seemed impossible for human beings to live in. The attempts to penetrate the Puster Valley through the Val di Landro had failed since they faced the strong defenses of Monte Piana (see above). Therefore, the Italians decided to try another route: through a small valley located to the east of the latter, the Val Fiscalina. The access to the valley was dominated by the Sentinella Pass, 2,717 meters (8,914 feet) above MSL, whose possession would also permit a good view of the Austro-Hungarian positions in the Puster Valley, with the possibility to precisely direct the artillery fire, thus interrupting the military traffic on its road, which was the quickest way for the enemy to move troops from the Trentino to the Isonzo Valley and vice versa. Until July 1915, no one had thought to occupy the pass nor the peaks that surrounded it, but at the beginning of the month, the Austro-Hungarians positioned a small garrison on the pass and on nearby Monte Croda Rossa. Alpini of the Battaglione *Fenestrelle* had tried to assault the positions several times in the following weeks but had been unsuccessful. It had become clear that a frontal attack would never reach the goal, and a surprise action was necessary.

At the beginning of winter, an incredible plan was devised that proposed taking the pass from above, occupying first the peaks that dominated its southern side, the main one being Cima Undici, 3,092 meters (10,144 feet) above MSL. The Austro-Hungarians had not yet occupied it, as they were sure that there was no way to survive up there. The most impressive part of the plan was that this occupation needed to be started during the winter in order to be ready to launch the attack at the first possible opportunity in the spring. The action was entrusted to a group of expert alpinists chosen from within the Alpini of the Battaglioni *Fenestrelle* and *Pieve di Cadore*. They were led by an officer who was a first-class alpinist and knew the places very well, Captain Giovanni Sala. A small group of climbers were among these men, who were guided by another renowned alpinist, Italo Lunelli. They were charged with the task of literally opening the path with spikes and ropes and then rendering it secure enough for the passage of the other men with supplies and materials. The small party set off on January 30, with meters of snow and temperatures well below zero, which caused several cases of frostbite. In something less than a month, the way through those mountains was open, with ropes, ladders, small barracks, and stores for military supplies; the party also discovered some small forks that gave free view to the pass below and prepared them to install machine guns and small mortars.

The plan was to include, first of all, a frontal attack launched by a platoon of Alpini, two companies of infantrymen and one of *bersaglieri*, supported by guns positioned on the peaks in front of the pass. A 65/17 gun was even hoisted at a height of almost 3,000 meters (9,843 feet) above MSL to be able to engage the enemy positions on the Croda Rossa and prevent their participation in the defense of the pass below. Secondly, two companies of the Battaglione *Fenestrelle* had to climb and position themselves on a wide ledge at the foot of the Croda Rossa, on the northern side of the pass, called Pianoro del Dito (finger plateau) after a rock spire that, from below, resembled a finger. From there, they had to target the Austro-Hungarians with their fire and then proceed with the conquest of the Croda Rossa itself. But the main role was played by the Alpini under the command of Sala and Lunelli. From their dominant positions directly over the pass, they could fire on the garrison to force the enemy to take cover. This would allow them to descend from Cima Undici with ropes and swoop down on the enemy trenches without opposition.

The action started during the night between April 15th and 16th in 1916, when the Alpini set foot on the Pianoro del Dito. At first light of the sixteenth, both the artillery and the Alpini from the Pianoro opened fire and, overall, the men of Sala and Lunelli started to fire down on the Austro-Hungarians from Cima Undici, forcing them to flee or to take cover in a shelter nearby. At 11:00 a.m., the main attack party started to climb along the gully that led to the pass from below, without being disturbed by enemy fire: at the top they found the trenches empty and seven of the defenders still in the shelter, who were taken prisoners. At the same time, other men descended from Cima Undici. At 1:45 p.m., the position was firmly in Italian hands, with only five Alpini injured. The enemy, taken completely by surprise, was unable to mount a strong reaction or a counterattack but could only begin a light barrage on the pass. At the same time, reinforcements were sent on the Croda Rossa, which resisted the attacks of the *Fenestrelle*. All in all, the action had been a great success, and the Italian artillery could start to shell the Puster Valley; on the other hand, as often happened in the Great War, it was not a decisive victory since the Austro-Hungarians fortified some other peaks a few hundred meters behind, keeping the Val Fiscalina closed.

In Action over 3,000 Meters!

In the Dolomiti theater, combat operations resumed as soon as weather conditions improved enough. On the Marmolada massif, the Austro-Hungarians preceded the Italians on the important Forcella Serauta (Serauta Fork), which dominated the access to the wide glacier below. Thus, it was necessary to mount an action to drive the enemy off and take the position entrusted to a special unit of only twelve Alpini of the 206th Company of the Battaglione *Val Cordevole.* They moved on April 6 up a large gully, called Vallone di Antermoia, and reached the saddle after fourteen hours of marching and climbing, achieving a completely surprise attack; they conquered Forcella Serauta and, pursuing the enemy, were also able to occupy Monte Serauta, 3,069 meters (10,069 feet) above MSL, which faced the saddle. Some reinforcements were moved in, which on April 15 were able to expand the occupied area by also taking the small ridge to the right of the saddle that ends with Punta Serauta, 2,962 meters (9,718 feet) above MSL, and even the peak farther west of Monte Serauta, 3,153 meters (10,344) above MSL, called Quota 3,153 (Hill 3,153).

The Austro-Hungarians, on the other hand, managed to hold out in a deep, steep fork between Monte Serauta and Hill 3,153, digging two galleries that could not be attacked from above into solid rock, called by the Italians from then on, the *Forcella a "V"* ("V"-shaped fork). A few days later, a terrible blizzard forced the Italians to abandon their positions still exposed to the bad weather and once more the Austro-Hungarians were quicker in reoccupying them after the snowstorm subsided. A new attack was mounted on April 30, by two platoons of Alpini of the Battaglione *Val Cordevole* and a company of infantry that led to the reconquest of the Serauta Fork and of the Serauta Peak, but not of Hill 3,153 and the *Forcella a "V."* To be able to supply these extreme positions, the Austro-Hungarians dug an intricate system

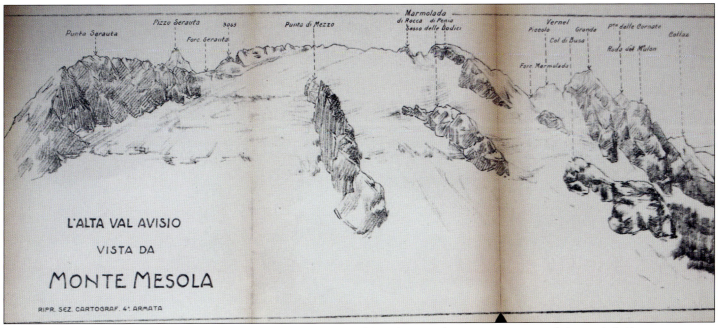

The Marmolada massif in a drawing produced by the Cartographic Section of the Italian Fourth Army. *Museo Nazionale Storico degli Alpini*

of more than 10 kilometers of tunnels under the ice of the Marmolada Glacier, where supplies and materials could be stored in wide caves carved into the ice as well. They called it the *Eisstadt*, the Ice City. This part of the front was not active during the rest of the year, due both to the extreme environmental conditions, where men had to think of survival rather than combat, and to the previously mentioned spring Austro-Hungarian offensive, which drained forces in favor of other sectors of the lines.

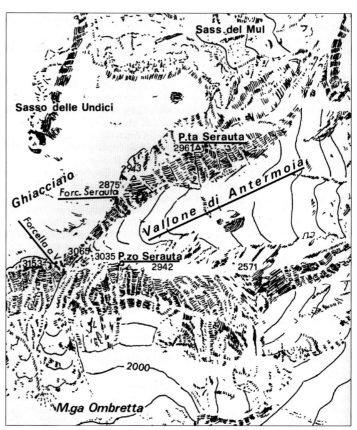

Two Alpini of the 206th Company of the Battaglione *Val Cordevole* are on the lookout on the Marmolada. *Museo Nazionale Storico degli Alpini*

The Italian positions on the Serauta, Marmolada massif, in the spring of 1916. Behind the Serauta, the Vallone di Antermoia and a little further the *Forcella a "V."*

Austro-Hungarian positions overlooking the Marmolada Glacier; opposite, the Italian positions on the Forcella Serauta and Hill 3,153. *Museo Nazionale Storico degli Alpini*

A corvée of Alpini descends the Vallone di Antermoia coming from Punta Serauta. *Museo Nazionale Storico degli Alpini*

The lower part of the Vallone di Antermoia, protected by stone walls and sandbags. *Andrea Bianchi*

The Italian positions between Forcella Serauta and Punta Serauta. *Museo Nazionale Storico degli Alpini*

THE FALL OF THE CASTELLETTO

A squad of skiers on the Tofane. In the background is the arrival of a cableway. *Museo Nazionale Storico degli Alpini*

The extreme ways to ascend to the Italian positions overlooking the Castelletto. *Andrea Bianchi*

Italian shelters at the Forcella di Fontananegra. *Museo Nazionale Storico degli Alpini*

The terrific effects of a mine's explosion. *Museo Nazionale Storico degli Alpini*

Second Lieutenant Eugenio Tissi

The pit left by the explosion of the Castelletto mine, with some remains of the Austro-Hungarian defenses, is being occupied by Italian soldiers. *Museo Nazionale Storico degli Alpini*

The hardest fighting in these first months of 1916 was carried out in the area of the Tofane and Monte Falzarego, particularly directed at tearing down the *Castelletto*, which had, for months now, prevented any Italian progress in Val Travenazes and against the ridge on the west side of the valley. After the useless attacks of the previous year, the Italian command now took into consideration the proposal made in November 1915 by a young officer, Second Lieutenant Eugenio Tissi, an alpino of the Battaglione *Belluno*, who had been employed in the mining sector before the war. His project was to dig a long tunnel under the enemy stronghold and then blow it up with a large quantity of explosives. Once his plan had been approved in January, Tissi, aided by another officer and civilian engineer, Second Lieutenant Luigi Malvezzi, promptly began the excavations by organizing a party of 120 Alpini. They worked around the clock in groups of forty, with six-hour shifts each, using simple hand tools in the beginning. Not until March was

it possible to obtain two gasoline-powered jackhammers, enabling work on the tunnel to proceed with considerably more speed. Meanwhile, units of Alpini tried to find locations on the slopes of the Tofana di Rozes that were suitable for marksmen who could harass the Austro-Hungarian positions from above. Eventually, in September 1915, a machine gun was positioned on a small rock spur, barely large enough for the weapon, some sandbags, and a trench shield, which was named—not casually—"*Lo Scudo*" (the shield). The ascent to *Lo Scudo* was ensured by a rope ladder of no fewer than 380 rungs! A small party of volunteers of the *Compagnia Volontari Alpini Feltre* occupied an even higher position, at 2,900 meters (9,514 feet) above MSL, where it could target the *Castelletto* with their rifles. These preparations needed to remain secret, so both the machine gun and the riflemen had orders to remain inactive until the very day of the attack. The excavations went on during the whole spring and part of the summer, and it goes without saying that the Austro-Hungarians could not fail to notice these preparations for very long: the jackhammers were too noisy to go unheard, and too much debris was discharged to remain unseen; they started, therefore, to hastily dig a countermine tunnel, endangering the whole operation. However, at the beginning of July, the Italian tunnel, about 500 meters long, was ready. The chamber under the *Castelletto* was filled with 35 tons of explosives, and the explosion was scheduled for July 11. The plan was that, after the explosion, units of the Battaglioni *Belluno* and *Monte Pelmo* would attack the *Castelletto* frontally while other Alpini penetrated the enemy positions using the tunnel itself. At the same time, small arms fire would rain onto the defenders from *Lo Scudo* and the Tofana. Unfortunately, the plan did not work out as expected. The explosion took place at 3:30 a.m. on July 11 and had the terrific effect of blowing up more than half of the *Castelletto*. However, a score of the defenders was still combat effective and took positions as soon as the smoke cleared. On the other side, the frontal attack was hindered by the massive stones and the debris thrown into the valley by the explosion itself, and the Alpini in the tunnel could not move in because they had almost asphyxiated: the side effects of the mine's destruction had been underestimated. The machine gun from *Lo Scudo* and the riflemen started their fire, forcing the defenders to take cover, but it was not enough. July 12 passed without further attacks, but with intense shelling by both parties; however, the activity did not stop. Another machine gun was hoisted on the Tofana di Roces and a few men of the *Compagnia Volontari Alpini Feltre* managed to descend with ropes from the side of the Tofana itself down near the *Castelletto* and take cover, although some of them were injured in the process. At midnight, they were joined by seventeen Alpini of the Battaglioni *Belluno* and *Monte Pelmo*, who had been able to climb the slopes of the *Castelletto*. On the morning of the thirteenth, thanks to the cover of fire offered by the machine guns and the riflemen, they were able to enter the stronghold and force the surviving defenders to surrender. In the following weeks, the Italians managed to sweep away all other residual enemy resistance on the Tofane and achieve complete possession of the whole ridge on the right side of Val Travenazes, although all attempts carried out during the rest of the year to position themselves on the opposite side failed.

Battle on the Adamello

On the western side of the Trentino salient, in environmental conditions not too dissimilar to those of the Marmolada, the Adamello massif was heavily contended for by the Italians and Austro-Hungarians in 1916. As mentioned, some peaks had already been occupied by the Alpini in the summer of 1915, but the local command decided it was necessary to press forward and deepen the lines, which were now too thin and weak to resist an enemy offensive. Furthermore, if successful, the progress could even enable the Italian troops to gain access to the valleys on the eastern side of the massif. The Garibaldi Hut was designated as the hub of the offensive; thus, men and supplies were amassed there for weeks. Over a period of months, the small party of about 300 men that had first occupied the

Garibaldi Hut, soon named the "*Compagnia Autonoma Garibaldi*," had become a larger unit of about 800 soldiers; in April 1916, it was transformed into a ski battalion consisting of three companies, named "Battaglione *Autonomo*" at first but renamed "Battaglione *Monte Mandrone*" in September. At the beginning of March, patrols of Alpini reached the Monte Fumo, 3,419 meters (11,217 feet) above MSL, to the southeast. And they reached some of the farther peaks, such as the Crozzon di Lares, which is 3,354 meters (11,004 feet) above MSL, and the Fargorida Pass, and found that they were still unguarded and could be permanently garrisoned by Italian troops. However, once more, the Austro-Hungarians moved faster and managed to settle on the range of peaks directly opposite the Garibaldi Hut, occupying Monte Fumo, the Dosson di Genova, the Cresta della Croce, and the Lobbia Alta, thus trying to block every line of advance per the Alpini: they needed to move quickly, before the enemy could consolidate its positions.

The action was planned for the beginning of April and was entrusted to the *Compagnia Autonoma*, which had been formed from a ski unit and a snowshoe unit with machine guns. Similarly, the Battaglione *Edolo* provided a ski platoon with two machine guns, while another platoon was formed by the *Val d'Intelvi*, and a third unit was formed from Alpini who were detached from several other battalions; a section of two

Operations on the Adamello massif in the spring of 1916

Alpini skiers on the Mandrone Glacier. *Museo Nazionale Storico degli Alpini*

In the foreground are the Lobbia Bassa and the Lobbia Alta; in the background, the Cresta della Croce. *Museo Nazionale Storico degli Alpini*

View of the Mandrone Glacier seen from the north; on the left of the glacier there are the Lobbia Bassa and Alta and the Cresta della Croce, while in the background on the left the Corno di Cavento stands out. *Museo Nazionale Storico degli Alpini*

A 65 mm mountain gun positioned by its crew on the Cresta della Croce just after the peak has been conquered by the Alpini. *Museo Nazionale Storico degli Alpini*

machine guns was taken from the Battaglione *Val Baltea*. This entire special unit was commanded by Captain Nino Calvi, commander of the *Compagnia Autonoma* and a seasoned veteran of the Adamello war theater. The plan involved an attack split into three columns: the first one against the Dosson di Genova, the second against the Cresta della Croce, and the third against the Lobbia Bassa Pass. A flanking attack was mounted against Monte Fumo by the *3ª Compagnia Volontari*, which moved from the valley below.

On the evening of April 11, the columns started to approach their targets, and on the following morning, after a night of marching in a snowstorm, they were positioned for the attack. At 6:30 a.m., the Alpini moved out of cover and assaulted the enemy strongholds. The first positions to fall were the Lobbia Alta with the lower Lobbia Pass, which were taken at 9:00 a.m. At 11:00 a.m., the Cresta della Croce was captured as well, and some of the men turned right to support the attack against the Dosson di Genova, which surrendered at 12:00 noon. They spent the rest of the day and the following night getting rid of the last pockets of resistance, but in the morning the whole ridge was firmly in Italian hands. Once more, an action conducted by a small number of well-trained, well-equipped men had obtained a brilliant success, with limited casualties. The only failure of the day was the attack at Monte Fumo, because the *3ª Compagnia Volontari* was unable to advance from the valley in the intense snowstorm. However, the position was now too isolated and exposed, so the Austro-Hungarians decided to give it up and retreat, leaving a company of the Battaglione *Val Baltea* to occupy it without opposition.

Still not satisfied with this achievement, a couple of weeks later, the Alpini were again on the attack, targeting the peaks in the range farther east of the one just conquered, with the Crozzon di Fargorida, the Crozzon di Lares, and the Corno di Cavento, including the several high passes between them. The action was to be conducted by the newly renamed "Battaglione *Autonomo*" with its skiers and the support of a unit of cadets, and the Battaglioni *Val d'Intelvi* and *Val Baltea* as reinforcements in case they were needed. The Battaglione *Edolo* was charged with a diversion to the north, to pin down enemy units. As artillery support, the Alpini could rely on several 70 mm and 75 mm pieces, and even on a 149 mm gun,[2] nicknamed "*Ippopotamo*" (hippopotamus), positioned at the Venerocolo Pass, over 3,000 meters (9,842 feet) above MSL. At first light on April 29, three columns moved to assault their targets, and at 8:00 a.m., the column on the right had already conquered the Crozzon di Lares, the Lares Pass below, and the Cavento Pass while the left column, formed of only twenty volunteers, had set foot on the Crozzon di Fargorida and on the nearby Punta

dell'Orco, occupied just ahead of an enemy unit. However, the central column had encountered heavy opposition and could not reach its objectives, the Fargorida Pass and the Topete Pass. An attempt to support the attacks by moving a 70 mm gun forward failed because the gun overturned after two shots and was damaged. After a few days of hard fighting, a unit of the Battaglione *Val d'Intelvi*, moving from the Crozzon di Lares, succeeded in conquering the Diavolo Pass, creating a wedge in the Austro-Hungarian line that threatened the rear of the Fargorida and Topete Passes; thus, the enemy command was forced to pull its units to a rear line. However, for the moment, the Austro-Hungarians managed to maintain their positions on the southern Corno di Cavento. After these doubtless brilliant operations, the front remained relatively calm, with both parts busy in consolidating their new lines.

The famous 149 mm gun, Ippopotamo, on the Adamello in a contemporary, although somewhat dark, image. *Museo Nazionale Storico degli Alpini*, and in another picture taken recently at Cresta della Croce. *Nicola Larentis*

THE AUSTRO-HUNGARIAN FRÜJAHROFFENSIVE

Deployment of the Austro-Hungarian and Italian units along the south Trentino at the beginning of the spring offensive.

In the spring of 1916, the Austro-Hungarian Empire decided that the moment had arrived to strike back on the Italian front. The plan had been devised already in its general lines by the High Commander of the Imperial-Royal Army, General Conrad von Hotzendorf, in 1908. It was named "*Früjahroffensive*" (spring offensive) but was soon given the nickname "*Straffexpedition*" by the Austro-Hungarian troops—"the punitive expedition." It planned an attack through the southern part of the Trentino salient, with a thrust directed roughly from northwest to southeast, aiming at the vast plain of Veneto. Once there, the main part of the Italian army, deployed on the eastern part of the front, could be enveloped and attacked from behind, ending, in the mind of the high command, the war.

To obtain this decisive result, the Eleventh Army was amassed in the area of the Folgaria Plateau, behind the chain of the forts, charged to attack on a front between Monte Zugna, on the right side of the Vallagarina; the lower part of the Adige River Valley in the Trentino; and the valley of the Astico Torrent, the Val d'Astico. Another narrow valley, the Vallarsa, which lay to the south between the two, was of paramount importance. Another army, the Third, deployed to the east of the latter, was to move between the Val d'Astico and the Valsugana, taking control of the Asiago Plateau. The two armies consisted of fourteen divisions and three mountain brigades. Along the front of the offensive, which measured 70 kilometers, a huge number of artillery pieces were deployed, including the fearsome, large guns produced by the Škoda Werke of Pilsen, one of the largest producers of armaments worldwide. These guns, which ranged from 30.5 cm to 42 cm caliber, were capable of demolishing even concrete fortifications. This array of forces could have

A 30.5 cm Austro-Hungarian siege mortar is positioned for the impending offensive. *Museo Nazionale Storico degli Alpini*

Field Marshal Conrad von Hötzendorf observes the development of the offensive with his staff. *Museo Nazionale Storico degli Alpini*

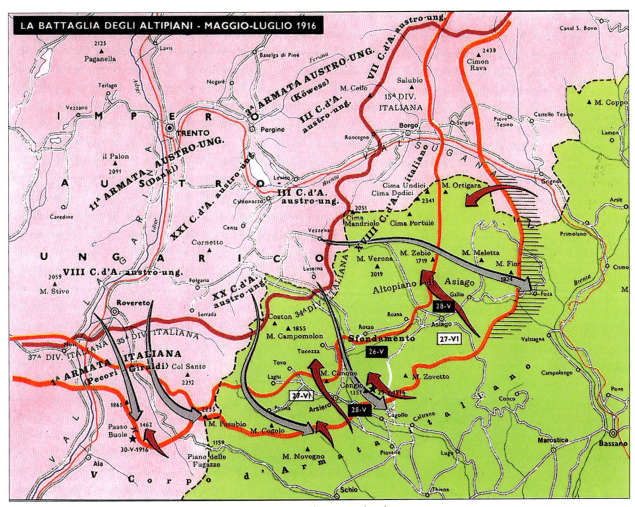

The Austro-Hungarian spring offensive and the Italian counteroffensive on the Plateaus

been even greater, had Germany conceded some of its good divisions. But the Imperial High Command, led by General von Falkenhayn, considered the southern front a secondary one and refused to divert forces from the western front, which in its view was decisive.

The *Regio Esercito* deployed scarce forces in the area. From west to east: the Thirty-Seventh Division between the eastern shore of the Lake Garda to the Vallarsa, involved only with its right wing, including the Alpine Battaglione *Val d'Adige* within its subordinate units; the *Sbarramento Agno-Posina*, comprising the *Battaglione Val Leogra*, the *Battaglione Monte Berico* and the XVII Gruppo of mountain artillery, and the flanking 35th Division, with the *Battaglione Vicenza* and the XVII Gruppo of mountain artillery, both faced the Folgaria Plateau; the Thirty-Fourth Division, with the Battaglione *Adamello*, and the IX Gruppo of mountain artillery was on the Asiago Plateau.

It goes without saying that the preparations for such an offensive could not go unnoticed, but the Italian Supreme Command was convinced that the Austro-Hungarian army was not in any condition to launch a vast offensive anywhere in Italy, after the terrific losses suffered in two years of war. The forces deployed in that part of the front were judged sufficient for the task entrusted to them. However, to be on the safe side, some reinforcements were sent in, and a number of divisions were concentrated in Veneto and grouped in a new Fifth Army. Just behind the Asiago Plateau, a force of nine Alpini battalions and six mountain artillery batteries was concentrated, named "Gruppo Alpini 'E' ": it comprised the Battaglioni *Cividale, Val Natisone, Monte Clapier, Monte Mercatour, Monte Matajur, Exilles, Monte Levanna, Monte Cervino, Monte Suello.* Furthermore, Supreme Commander General Cadorna, inspecting the lines few days before the

enemy offensive, had noted that, contravening his orders, the First Army had a definitely offensive deployment instead of maintaining an active defense, with the troops massed on the first line, without an organized rear line of resistance, and with the artillery very close behind the troops, as in preparation for an attack. The army commander was dismissed on the spot and replaced, but it was too late to move hundreds of pieces of artillery and thousands of men into a more suitable deployment.

The Austro-Hungarian Spring Offensive, which the Italians called the Battle of the Plateaus, can be divided into four phases:

First phase: from May 15 to May 19, when the Eleventh Army attacks first
Second phase: from May 20 to May 28, when the Third Army moves in as well
Third phase: from May 28 to June 10, both Armies advance, but the Italian resistance stiffens
Fourth phase: from June 11 to June 18, the last Austro-Hungarian effort concentrated in a narrow area across the Astico Torrent, in the Val d'Astico

THE FIRST PHASE: THE ELEVENTH ARMY THRUSTS FORWARD

At 5:00 a.m. on May 15, 350 pieces of artillery began to shell the Italian lines between the Vallagarina and the Val d'Astico, and after four hours of fire, two Austro-Hungarian army corps moved to attack. On the extreme right of the advance, they conquered the Zugna Torta on the seventeenth, but could not proceed

Italian soldiers in a trench on Monte Zugna, near the Zugna Hut. *Fondazione Museo Storico del Trentino Archivio Fotografico*

farther, because the Alpini of the Battaglione *Val d'Adige*, deployed in the area only the previous day, stopped them on Monte Zugna. Over the following weeks, the Austro-Hungarians would furiously assault this mountain that hindered the passage of men, artillery, and supplies along the route of the Vallarsa, without any success. Farther east, on the steep southern slopes of the Folgaria Plateau, crossed by the Leno Torrent, the Battaglioni *Monte Berico* and *Val Leogra* were the most exposed and among the first troops to be involved in the fighting; they held on to their position during the fifteenth and the sixteenth, but then they were forced to retreat in order not to be surrounded. From that moment on, they were pushed south with heavy losses, making the Austo-Hungarians pay for every inch of terrain, until they reached more-defensible positions on the Pasubio massif and on the Borcola Pass. In this area they were joined by the Battaglioni *Monte Suello, Exilles, Monte Cervino*, and *Monte Levanna* that were able to slow the enemy advance for a while. However, after a few days, with the companies intermixed because of the confused and hard fighting, they were forced to withdraw deeper into the Pasubio massif.

On the Tonezza Plateau that faced the eastern slopes of the Folgaria Plateau, part of the Italian line, which was flanked by the Val d'Astico, ceded under the attacks, and the Alpini of the *Vicenza* were ordered to counterattack to close the gap. During the action, the battalion lost one of its companies, and the remaining two companies were forced to retreat and redeploy along a rear makeshift line, where they held out doggedly for several days. Finally, the few survivors were able to retreat farther east. In those same several days, the batteries of VII and XVII Gruppo, being deployed very close to the front lines, were directly involved in the fighting, and in the first three days, two batteries had already been lost.

Italian trenches on the Pasubio massif, still covered in snow, in May 1916. *Fondazione Museo Storico del Trentino Fondo Pietro Calamandrei*

Starting on May 18, when the seriousness of the situation had been fully appreciated by the Supreme Command, several reserve units were sent to this stretch of the front to cover the retreat of the Thirty-Fifth Division: among the first reinforcements were the Battaglioni *Cividale, Monte Matajur, Monte Clapier*, and *Monte Mercatour*, with the XVI Gruppo of mountain artillery. In the following four days, these units bore the full weight of the Austro-Hungarian attacks, contesting every meter of terrain, until they reached the area in front of the town of Arsiero. A last stand was organized on Monte Cimone, north of the town, but they were pushed back on the twenty-sixth, and the town was occupied by the enemy the day after. The Alpine battalions were so worn out in just a week of fighting that they had to be withdrawn from the line to be re-formed with new recruits.

THE SECOND PHASE: THE THIRD ARMY MOVES IN

On the sixth day of the offensive, May 20, when the Austro-Hungarian High Command thought that the Italian reserves had been engaged by the Eleventh Army, the Third Army launched its attack against the Italian Thirty-Fourth Division, advancing on the Asiago Plateau. The Battaglione *Monte Adamello* with some batteries of the IX Gruppo of mountain artillery occupied some positions on the extreme left of the division, opposite the Austro-Hungarian stronghold of Werk Spitz Verle. They were involved in the general retreat of the division toward Asiago, occupied by the enemy on May 28. This was the deepest point reached by the attackers in this phase,

Aerial view of the narrow Val d'Astico. *Museo Nazionale Storico degli Alpini*

The town of Asiago nearly razed to the ground during the offensive, in a picture taken just after the war. *Museo Nazionale Storico degli Alpini*

because they were finally stopped in the mountains just behind Asiago by the Italian reserves hastily deployed in the area. In particular, the Battaglioni *Monviso*, *Val Maira*, *Monte Argentera*, and *Morbegno* were moved east of Asiago from the upper Isonzo front to defend some peaks known as the Melette, including the Monte Fior, Castelgomberto, and Tondarecar mountains. Here, they dug in and resisted the attacks over the following days.

The result of the first two phases of the offensive was a deep penetration into the plateau's front, but the hoped-for breach in the Italian front line to reach the Veneto plain had not been achieved. A new Italian line rested on Monte Zugna on its extreme left, where the Battaglione *Val d'Adige* still stubbornly resisted, supported by two batteries of mountain artillery plus other units hastily sent to help. It passed through the Pasubio massif, guarded by the worn-out battalions *Monte Levanna*, *Monte Suello*, *Monte Cervino*, and *Exilles*, among others, with some batteries of the III, XVII and XX Gruppi of mountain artillery. Monte Novegno, to the south of the town of Arsiero, was guarded by the Alpini of the Battaglioni *Monte Clapier* and *Cividale*, with three batteries. Monte Cengio, southwest of Asiago, in the Val d'Astico, on whose slopes were deployed the *Monte Mercatour*, *Monte Matajur*, and *Val Natisone*, was guarded by the *Granatieri di Sardegna* Brigade. Its right wing was on the Melette, with its peaks Monte Fior, Castelgomberto, and Tondarecar, firmly held by the Battaglioni *Monviso*, *Val Maira*, *Motne Argentera*, and *Morbegno*.

THE THIRD PHASE: THE AUSTRO-HUNGARIANS THROW IN THEIR RESERVES

Once the Austro-Hungarian High Command realized that the Italian lines were still holding but that its troops were as far forward as the last low mountains before the plain, it decided it was worth persisting, even at the cost of its reserves. From May 28, new divisions were sent in to help, and sometimes to replace, the ones that had been on the lines for days, and attacks were launched along the whole front. The fighting was particularly hard on the Monte Zugna because that position kept the whole right wing of the Austro-Hungarians in check, preventing the free use of the Vallarsa, which was a vital route for allowing reinforcements, artillery and supplies to reach the Pasubio area. On June 9, what remained of the Battaglione *Val d'Adige* was replaced by the *Aosta*. Since the frontal attacks across the narrow ridge of the mountain had so far been unsuccessful due to the determined opposition of the Alpini, the enemy tried to outflank their positions with an action from the Vallarsa to the Buole Pass, some kilometers to the rear, but were driven back by the infantrymen of the *Taro* and *Sicilia* Brigades. This failure probably also affected the fighting on the Pasubio, where the Alpini could limit the enemy advance to a minimum because

A view of Monte Novegno, scene of fierce fighting during the spring offensive

it was not supported by enough artillery, which had fallen behind. To the southeast, Monte Novegno was furiously attacked, because of the awareness that it was the last stand for the Italians, and no other mountains lay between it and the plain; however, the Italians were also well aware of it; thus, the Alpini fought desperately, counterattacking every time a trench was lost. Farther east, the *Granatieri*, which had been heavily attacked, were finally driven off Monte Cengio on June 3, and the Austro-Hungarians were able to see the Veneto plain. It seemed to them that success was at hand. However, their attacks against the last Italian strongholds were unsuccessful in the following days. In particular, on the extreme western slopes of the mountain, the last ledges before the valley floor were defended effectively by the last Alpini of the Battaglioni *Monte Matajur* and *Monte Mercatour*, supported by the guns of the XVI Gruppo, with the *Val Natisone* in the rear, until they were replaced by infantry units on June 5. The enemy had come so close to the objective but had been stopped in time.

The Melette area was the theater of the last attempts of this phase to dislodge the Italians from their last-ditch positions. On the late afternoon of June 5, after a shelling that lasted for the whole day, an Austro-Hungarian brigade moved to attack the Alpini positions. Monte Fior was defended by the *Monte Argentera* and the *Morbegno*. The *Val Maira* was deployed on the Castelgomberto and the *Monviso* on the Tondarecar, supported by the Twenty-Seventh Battery of mountain artillery and units of the *Sassari* Brigade. The furious fighting caused heavy losses for both parties, but the Italian lines remained intact. On the sixth, the front was calm since the Austro-Hungarians needed to reorganize. But on the seventh, they attacked again with fresh forces, concentrating on Monte Fior. Here, the remains of the Battaglione *Morbegno* yielded momentarily, but the Alpini found the strength to counterattack once again, guided by an NCO, since all the officers had been hit, and pushed the enemy back. This was the last attack in the area because the Austro-Hungarians thought they were facing superior forces and desisted.

Italian troops encamped on the slopes of Monte Novegno in the summer of 1916. *Fondazione Museo Storico del Trentino Fondo Pietro Calamandrei*

The Austro-Hungarian attacks on Monte Novegno between June 12 and 13, 1916

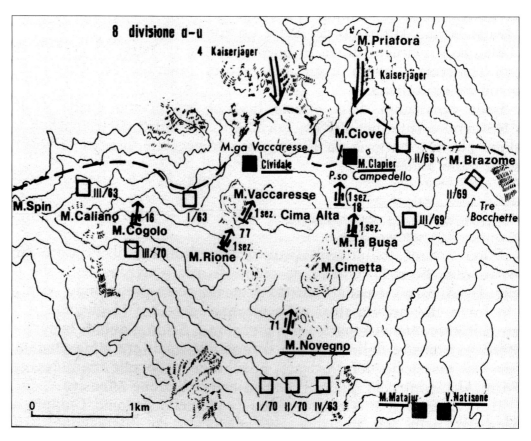

THE FOURTH PHASE: LAST ATTEMPT TO BREAK THROUGH

By June 10, it was clear to the Austro-Hungarian High Command that its forces were no longer in any condition to continue the offensive along the entire front and that if a final effort had to be made, it was necessary to carefully choose a weaker point in the Italian line and strike there with the last reserves at hand. The selected area was the one across the Astico Torrent, particularly Monte Novegno, the last obstacle on the way to the town of Schio. The positions were defended by the *Ancona* Infantry Brigade and the Alpini of the Battaglioni *Cividale* and *Monte Clapier*, supported by four batteries of mountain artillery. The enemy artillery barrage started at 8:00 a.m. of June 12, but when the infantry advanced, instead of finding disrupted trenches and dazed men, they found a solid resistance that lasted the whole day and forced the enemy to retreat to its starting line. During the night, the two Alpini battalions were replaced by the relatively rested *Val Natisone* and *Monte Matajur*—that for hours bore the enemy shelling—thereby announcing that a new attack was imminent. At 10:00 a.m., the Austro-Hungarian infantry made its very last attempt to dislodge the Italians from the Novegno, but after nine hours of furious assaults, the attackers had barely reached the barbed wire that protected the trenches. At 7:00 p.m., the attack subsided, and with it the great offensive that had failed to punish the Italians. Local fighting went on for a few more days, but the Italian counteroffensive was already beginning to move. Furthermore, on June 4, the Russians had launched their offensive that forced the Austro-Hungarian High Command to move forces from the Italian front to the eastern front.

THE ITALIAN COUNTEROFFENSIVE

The echo of the battle on Monte Novegno was still in the air when the Italian Supreme Command launched a major counteroffensive along the entire front that now formed a large salient, potentially still dangerous because it was very close to the Veneto plain. It had been becoming clear for days now that the momentum of the Austro-Hungarian offensive was running out. Therefore, the deployment of the Italian forces had been progressively more modified to be able to counterattack as soon as possible in order to retake the lost terrain before the enemy could consolidate its hold. Deployment would also send the message to both Austro-Hungary and its ally that Italy was still alive

and capable of fighting back. The first blow was delivered on the east side of the salient, to the north of the Melette, with an action carried out by the *Bari* Infantry Brigade, units of *bersaglieri*, and the Alpine battalions *Monte Saccarello*, *Val Cenischia*, *Bassano*, and *Sette Comuni*. Also included were a mountain artillery battery, striking from the Valsugana, and the weary Battaglioni *Val Maira*, *Monte Argentera*, *Monviso*, and *Morbegno*, which were attached to the reserves for the moment. The attack, launched on June 16, was successful, producing an immediate breach of the Austro-Hungarian line, which was forced to retreat. The gap was filled later by moving a new mountain brigade into it. But the Austro-Hungarian High Command had perceived that the defense of the whole

The Ortigara massif and the surrounding peaks. *Andrea Bianchi*

Austro-Hungarian barracks clinging to the western slopes of the Corno di Campoverde, a mountain to the southeast of Monte Ortigara. *Fondazione Museo Storico del Trentino Fondo Pietro Calamandrei*

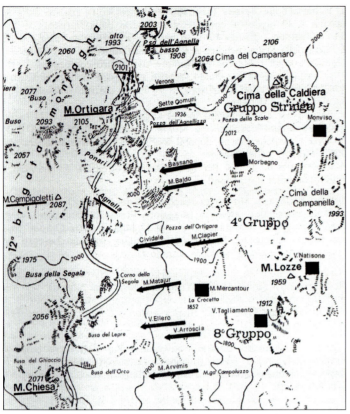

The last phase, between July 22 and 23, of the First Battle of the Ortigara

The weekly magazine *La Domenica del Corriere* on August 6, 1916, dedicates its first page to the assault of Monte Campigoletti by the Battaglione *Bassano*.

salient, given the scarcity of any available troops, was simply not feasible. The decision was therefore made to break contact with the advancing Italians and retreat to positions that were more defensible and which leaned on Monte Zugna Torta to the west, crossed the Pasubio massif and the Borcola Pass, and reached Monte Ortigara, giving up a good portion of the recently conquered plateaus of Tonezza and Asiago. The retreat occurred in the night between June 24 and 25, undisturbed by the Italians, who became aware of the withdrawal only the following morning. They moved in pursuit of the enemy with no great decision; thus, it took them several days to come into contact with the new Austro-Hungarian positions.

On the eastern side of the salient, the Italian troops pursued the enemy up to Monte Ortigara (a mountain with a bare and somewhat round summit), which was first assaulted by the Battaglione *Bassano* on June 30, without success. The new positions occupied by the Austro-Hungarians in this area were naturally strong. Apart from the Ortigara itself, 2,106 meters (6,909 feet) above MSL, they rested to the south on Monte Campigoletti and to the north on two peaks, which the Italians named "Hill 2,101" and "Hill 2,003," traversed by the Agnella Pass, which led directly to the Valsugana. To the south of Monte Campigoletti, the line continued with Monte Chiesa and Monte Forno, preventing any attempt to outflank the main positions. Furthermore, to attack these peaks, the Italian troops needed to descend into two deep, barren gorges, which were exposed to the fire of the artillery and machine guns that were deployed opposite them, called Agnelizza Gorge and Agnella Gorge. These positions served to defend the access to the Valsugana from the south. Therefore, the Austro-Hungarians were prepared to hold onto them stubbornly. On the other hand, the Italian Supreme Command considered the conquest of the area to be of paramount importance because it saw it as a good starting base for future enemy offensives. Therefore, it planned a new assault, entrusting it to no fewer than eighteen Alpini battalions and eight batteries of mountain artillery. The action, known as the First Battle of the Ortigara, was launched on July 6. The battalions mentioned above, which were already in the frontline by June 30, were joined by the Battaglioni *Monte Mercatour*, *Cividale*, *Monte Clapier*, *Monte Matajur*, and *Val Natisone*, which had been replenished after the battles on Monte Novegno of few weeks before. At the beginning of July, then, they were joined also by the Battaglioni *Val Tagliamento*, *Monte Arvenis*, *Val d'Arroscia*, and *Val Ellero*. Finally, when the attack was already in progress, the Battaglioni *Verona* and *Monte Baldo* arrived from the Vallagarina.

On the morning of July 6, the Battaglione *Val Cenischia* moved toward Hill 2,101, and the *Monte Argentera* and the *Morbegno* led a frontal assault against the Ortigara itself. The *Bassano* attacked Monte Campigoletti and, to the south, the *Cividale* aimed for Monte Forno. No unit managed to engage the enemy positions; they were stopped by heavy fire and barbed wire. Further attacks launched on the seventh and eighth yielded no better results, although the Battaglioni *Val d'Arroscia* and *Monte Arvenis* had moved in. Thus, the offensive was interrupted for the moment. In the following days, with the arrival of the Battaglioni *Verona* and *Monte Baldo*, the *Monte Saccarello*, *Monte Argentera*, *Val Cenischia*, and *Val Maira* were withdrawn and sent to the rear for an overdue period of rest and reorganization after a month on the line. The offensive resumed on July 22, with a new plan to outflank Monte Campigoletti from the south, with a diversion against the Ortigara and another against Monte Forno to pin down the enemy troops. The main attack, led by the Battaglioni *Cividale*, *Monte Clapier*, *Monte Matajur*, and *Val Ellero*, was able to make very little progress, and nowhere did it manage to get through the line of barbed wire. Meanwhile, the diversion against the Ortigara, entrusted to the *Verona*, *Sette Comuni*, *Bassano*, and *Monte Baldo*, ended in a bloody failure since the *alpine*, once they had left their positions and descended in the gorges below, could not move farther and remained almost without cover under the uninterrupted fire of guns and machine

A column of Austro-Hungarian prisoners escorted to the Italian rear line. *Museo Nazionale Storico degli Alpini*

An Italian military cemetery. *Museo Nazionale Storico degli Alpini*

guns. The following day new assaults were mounted, but after hours of fighting the Austro-Hungarian trenches and strongpoints were still far. On the evening of July 23, the offensive was definitively called off and the exhausted survivors retreated to their lines.

Toward the western side of the salient, around Monte Zugna and in Vallarsa, where the enemy withdrawal was of more limited extent, the Italian counteroffensive started on June 27 and initially seemed successful. The Alpini of the Battaglione *Val Leogra* and *Monte Berico*, with a section of mountain artillery, advanced along the valley and conquered the stronghold of Matassone. But the subsequent attacks against Monte Zugna Torta by the same battalions and by the *Aosta* that moved from Monte Zugna

were repelled. The Battaglione *Vicenza* tried to set foot on Monte Corno on the eastern flank of the valley, but it was heavily counterattacked and nearly annihilated by the Austro-Hungarians, and survivors were taken prisoners.[3]

To the southeast, in the area of the Pasubio, the Italian troops started to move forward on June 27 as well, aiming for the Borcola Pass. The Battaglioni *Monte Cervino, Monte Suello, Monte Levanna,* and *Exilles* reached the new Austro-Hungarian line protecting the pass after a few days of marching but were stopped by the enemy, who was resolved not to retreat farther back. A hurried assault was launched on July 12 by *Monte Cervino* and *Exilles,* supported by a flanking attack mounted by the *Monte Berico,*

A small town of Italian military barracks on the Pasubio. *Museo Nazionale Storico degli Alpini*

A section of two 149 mm Italian guns in the area called "Forni Alti," on the Pasubio. *Museo Nazionale Storico degli Alpini*

which was moving up from the Vallarsa. After hard and bloody fighting, the Alpini had been able to conquer some stretches of the first line of the enemy trenches but were inextricably stuck there, unable to advance. After a few days, it was necessary to withdraw them from the line due to their exhaustion, replacing them with fresh troops; however, the positions that had been taken with such effort were soon lost. As in the case of the Ortigara, the action had been ill conceived in their hope that the enemy would continue its retreat, and it had cost them heavy losses.

THE ITALIAN OFFENSIVE ON THE PASUBIO MASSIF

In this narrative of the Austro-Hungarian Spring Offensive and the Italian counteroffensive, the Pasubio massif has been mentioned several times but needs to be described in more detail since it was to be the theater of furious, and basically useless, fighting for months. The massif extends in a roughly northwest-to-southeast course across the territories of southern Trentino and northern Veneto. The northern part is a sort of corrugated plateau, about 2,000 meters (6,562 feet) above MSL, covered with pasture, but proceeding south, it changes dramatically to stony ground, crossed by many deep gorges, and dotted with peaks. The southern slopes literally overhang the plain below. The main peak of the massif is Monte Palon, 2,235 meters (7,333 feet) above MSL, and the ridge that is farther to the south of that has peaks of over 2,200 meters (7,218 feet) above MSL and also includes Monte Roite and Monte Col Santo. A bit detached from those and to the west, overlooking the Vallarsa, stands the Monte Corno, mentioned above.

During the Spring Offensive, the Pasubio massif had been invested by the Austro-Hungarian Eleventh Army, which had easily conquered the northern and central part, but had been stopped by the stubborn resistance of the Italian troops in the southern part. The respective lines passed between two peaks of Monte Palon, no more than 50 meters apart, named the "*Dente Italiano*" (Italian tooth), to the south, and the *Dente Austrico* (Austrian tooth), to the north. When the Austro-Hungarian high command called off the offensive and broke contact with the Italian lines, there was no retreat on the Pasubio; on the contrary, it was to become one of the main strongholds of the new defensive line, and the Austro-Hungarian troops tried to maintain the initiative there, mounting new attacks throughout the months of June and July. Although it

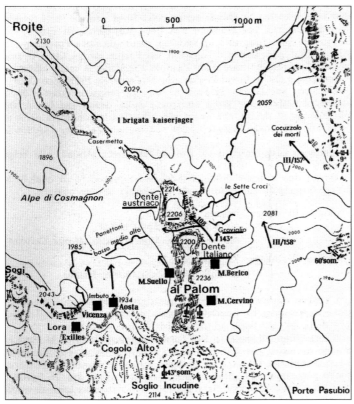

The Italian attacks to the Dente Austriaco in September 1916

An injured Italian soldier is evacuated with a stretcher. *Museo Nazionale Storico degli Alpini*

A ski unit patrolling an area of the Pasubio

The Dente Austriaco, seen from the Italian positions on the Dente Italiano. *Fondazione Museo Storico del Trentino Fondo Paolo Oss Mazzurana*

seemed clear that the Imperial-Royal Army had very little capability to mount another great offensive at the moment, the Italian Supreme Command judged that the lines of the *Regio Esercito* on the Pasubio lacked the necessary depth and were definitively too close to the plain to be able to maneuver in case of new attempts by the enemy to break through. Therefore, an offensive was planned that aimed to gain some terrain.

For the main action, the Battaglioni *Aosta, Exilles, Vicenza, Monte Berico, Monte Suello*, and *Monte Cervino*, grouped in the 6° Gruppo Alpini for this offensive, together with infantry units of the *Ancona* and *Puglie* Brigades, were gathered close to Monte Palon, while the *Val Toce* and the *Monte Adamello* took position in the Vallarsa. The close artillery support was provided by three batteries of mountain artillery. The plan was to attack from the right and the left side of the *Dente Italiano*, aiming to set foot on the *Dente Austriaco* and, farther north, on Monte Roite, with flanking attacks to the west against Monte Corno from the Vallarsa, and to the east by infantry units. The secondary actions were launched on the morning of September 10, but both the Alpini and the infantrymen were able to make very little progress because they were opposed by stiff enemy resistance from well-prepared positions. The main assault started in the afternoon. But, due to the persistent fog, the preliminary artillery barrage was rather ineffective and did not cause much damage to the barbed wire, and the results were very modest. Only the Battaglione

Monte Berico, to the right of the *Dente Italiano*, succeeded in setting foot on a small portion of the *Dente Austriaco*. It tried to dig in and resist the furious enemy reaction but, due to the failure of the other units, was forced to retreat after suffering heavy losses. During the night, all the battered battalions were withdrawn to their previous positions.

The action was repeated in October, with better weather conditions and an artillery preparation time of eight hours that resulted in more effective results. The Battaglioni *Val Toce, Monte Adamello, Exilles*, and *Monte Berico*, having *Monte Suello, Monte Cervino*, and *Aosta* as reserves and six batteries of mountain artillery as close support, moved out of their trenches on the ninth and, exploiting the momentum, managed to conquer some peaks right and left of the *Dente Austriaco*. Later, the *Monte Berico* even managed to take a small peak, named "Hill 2,206," of the same *Dente Austriaco*. The Austro-Hungarian reaction was, as usual, very determined: heavy shelling poured onto the lost positions, and before the Alpini could consolidate their conquest, several counterattacks threw them back, except for on Hill 2,206, where the survivors of the *Monte Berico* held steady for the whole night. On the tenth, the attacks by the Battaglione *Aosta* and infantry units enabled the Italian troops to retake some positions to the west of the *Dente Austriaco*; this time, there were no counterattacks, because the Austro-Hungarians, as weary as the Italians, preferred to

Pasubio massif: artillerymen with a section of two 70 mm mountain guns deployed on a ledge. *Fondazione Museo Storico del Trentino Fondo Paolo Oss Mazzurana*

retreat to other strongholds on Monte Roite. On Hill 2,206, the situation was desperate for both contenders, but the fighting went on the whole day. Finally, on the night between October 10 and 11, the *Monte Berico* was replaced by the *Monte Suello*, and the few Alpini who remained were able to enjoy some rest. The eleventh was a relatively calm day because the fog prevented any action, but during the night, the Battaglione *Aosta* attempted a surprise attack without artillery preparation against the northern slopes of the *Dente Austriaco*. They were, however, driven off by immediate enemy counterattacks. On the afternoon of October 12, an artillery shell hit the entrance to the cave of the headquarters of the 6° Gruppo Alpini, killing many officers and the commander himself. Consequently, a few days of inaction followed as replacements were put in place. On the seventeenth, the Alpini were on the attack again, this time with the Battaglione *Aosta* directly engaged on the *Dente Austriaco*, moving from Hill 2,206 toward the northern peak, 2,214 meters (7,264 feet) above MSL, while the *Monte Cervino* attacked the right flank of the *Dente* itself, clashing against enemy positions named, rather evocatively, "*Il Groviglio*," (the tangle). The *Val d'Adige*, *Val Maira*, and *Exilles* supported the action by assaulting the left flank and trying to advance toward Monte Roite. As in the previous cases, the Alpini could not go farther than the barbed-wire lines, and only the Battaglione *Aosta* managed to advance some meters toward

Hill 2,214 of the *Dente Austriaco*. The situation did not change in the following four days, when the Battaglioni *Monte Adamello* and *Val Toce* also joined the offensive. On the contrary, the important position on Hill 2,206 was lost by the *Aosta*, which sacrificed itself almost completely on its barren rock; it was temporarily retaken by the *Monte Suello*, but then it was definitively lost. Finally, the offensive ceased, due also to the worsening of weather conditions. Weeks of sacrifice and blood had gone without any significant success, except for the attrition felt by the Austro-Hungarian forces. However, the game was not over but was just postponed for the following year.

Two images of the Monte Cauriol, in the Lagorai: an Italian observatory on the slopes of the mountain and at the top of it. *Museo Nazionale Storico degli Alpini*

On the Attack Again on the Lagorai Massif

The previously mentioned area of the Lagorai, lying to the north of the Valsugana, had been rather calm so far during 1916, as both parties were completely absorbed with the hard fighting on the plateau and on the Pasubio massif. Although this part of the front had an essentially defensive role, the operations were resumed in August with an action planned to conquer two peaks. The command intended for this to result in gaining access to the Fiemme Valley, which was one way to reach Trento. Units of infantry and *bersaglieri* with the Alpini of the Battaglioni *Val Brenta*, *Feltre*, and *Monte Rosa*, with the close support of the First, Fourth, and Fifth Batteries of mountain artillery, were entrusted with the actions. On August 23, the *Val Brenta* moved against Cima di Cece, 2,754 meters (9,035 feet) above MSL, and again on the twenty-fifth and twenty-sixth, but failed to conquer it.

On the contrary, the assault launched by the *Feltre* on the twenty-fifth against Monte Cauriol, 2,494 meters (8,182 feet) above MSL, enabled the Alpini, who were followed closely by the artillerymen of the Fifth Battery, to reach the top and entrench themselves after two days of hard fighting up the slopes of the mountain. The constant, terrible enemy artillery barrage decimated the battalion, which had to be relieved by the *Val Brenta* after few days. It is reported that Monte Cauriol's height decreased by 6 meters due to the hard shelling. However, a counterattack to retake the peak was beaten back. In mid-September, another offensive was launched from the newly acquired positions to take the last ridge before the Fiemme Valley, and the opportunity seemed so tangible that a few more mountain troop battalions were sent in: *Cividale*, *Val Natisone*, *Val Tagliamento*, *Monte Matajur*, and *Monte Arvenis*. However, notwithstanding their efforts through to the end of October, forward progress was infrequent, and the Fiemme Valley remained out of reach until military activity was suspended due to the arrival of the bad season.

On *La Domenica del Corriere* of October 1, 1916, the Alpini are climbing the steep walls of Monte Cauriol.

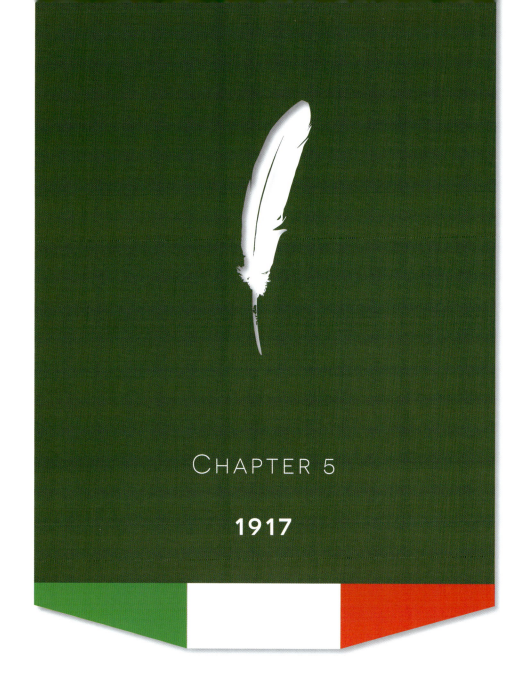

CHAPTER 5

1917

All sources agree in reporting the winter between 1916 and 1917 as one of the coldest and snowiest of the century, and it forced the belligerents to suspend the military operations for months. However, cold and snow caused thousands of casualties, either by freezing and frostbite or by avalanches, the latter especially when temperatures started to rise slowly in the spring. Apart from a few rare local actions, operations were not resumed until May and often showed attempts to prevail over the enemy by using different techniques from those that had proven themselves useless before. For example, the use of mines to blow up enemy positions that had so far resisted every attack was intensified. The Regio Esercito was able to enjoy the increase of industrial output in Italy to improve the equipment of its units, which now had a far greater number of machine guns than before and could count on a greater number of mortars, howitzers, and guns of a variety of calibers.

The Italian Supreme Command strategic guidelines for 1917 did not deviate from those adopted in 1915 (repeated offensives on the Isonzo River front, in a search for an illusory breakthrough). The rest of the front was to remain on the defensive except for local offensives that were dictated by the need to improve positions deemed to be precarious, as would happen in the unfortunate new battle on Monte Ortigara. Therefore, the bulk of the army and supplies was concentrated on the eastern part of the front. The turning point of the year was the joint October Austro-Hungarian and German offensive at Caporetto, which, in a couple of days, achieved what had not been achieved in more than two years. Using infiltration techniques developed by the Germans, the Italian line was broken, and the enemy was able to pour into the rear of three Italian armies and threaten to annihilate them. During the 150-kilometer retreat, the Alpini units were often in the rearguard, and due to their toughness, none fled their positions.

A comical propaganda postcard that intends to represent the Alpini's strong will to march on Trento and defeat the Austro-Hungarians, depicted as hangers of Italian patriots

In this image, which is, unfortunately, a bit blurred, the sad search for fellow soldiers buried under a snow avalanche, as happened rather often during the winter months in high mountains. *Museo Nazionale Storico degli Alpini*

Trenches and Frisian horses in the snow. *Museo Nazionale Storico degli Alpini*

An alpino on sentry service just outside a cave excavated in the ice. *Andrea Bianchi*

As far as the Alpini are concerned, during the winter of 1916–17, twenty-six ski companies were created, which were grouped into seven new battalions in the spring: *Cuneo, Courmayeur, Pallanza, Monte Tonale, Monte Pasubio, Monte Marmolada*, and *Monte Nero*. With respect to the equipment, it was finally possible to assign a machine gun company to every battalion and significantly increase the number of Villar Perosa M1915 submachine guns, with a section of two weapons assigned to every company. The mountain artillery saw a great increase of its batteries from 75 to 93 during the year, grouped into thirty-one Gruppi, some of whom were deployed in the Balkans.

MINE WARFARE ON THE PICCOLO LAGAZUOI

The *Cengia Martini*, on Monte Piccolo Lagazuoi, was conquered in October 1915 and had been doggedly defended and strengthened throughout all of 1916. The small rock spur of a year and a half ago was now a position dug in a cave and protected by an entrenchment of solid rock that penetrated the mountain, with tunnels provided with loopholes that enabled the Italians to hit the enemy positions in the Valparola Valley below. The ledge was still defended by the Alpini of the Battaglione *Val Chisone*. After the attempt with the mine on January 1, 1916, the Austro-Hungarians had tried using all possible means to expel the Italians with continuous shelling, machine gun fire, and asphyxiating gas, with no result. Therefore, they decided to make another attempt with a new mine. The works for the mine tunnel started in the autumn of 1916, but soon the Italian observers noticed the activity and understood that the target would be the entrenchment; the solution was to dig a countermine tunnel that would disperse the force of the explosion into another direction. The Austro-Hungarian mine blew up on January 14, 1917, but, as had been calculated by the Italian engineers, the

countermine tunnel absorbed the greatest part of its force; thus, the trenches above did not suffer great damage. The Austro-Hungarians realized this as soon as the smoke of the explosion dissipated and, accordingly, cancelled the infantry attack that was to follow. However, still convinced that there was no other way to get rid of the Italians, they started a new mine tunnel in February. This time, the excavations were kept more discreet, and the Alpini noticed them only a few weeks later. Once it was clear that the countermine tunnel would not be ready in time, Italian headquarters decided to leave the entrenchment temporarily but reoccupy it immediately after the explosion in order to forestall an anticipated enemy move. On May 22, 24 tons of explosive blew up the entrenchment, making the whole mountain tremble. Immediately afterward, the Austro-Hungarian artillery started a terrific barrage. However, the Alpini were quick to leave the cover of the caves and occupy the ruins of their positions, which were now—paradoxically—even more inaccessible to the enemy than before due to the huge pile of amassed debris. At the same time, the Italian artillery immediately started to shell the enemy trenches, de facto preventing the Austro-Hungarian infantry from launching its attack. In brief, the action had been a complete failure, and to underline the defeat of the enemy, the battalion's brass band played an Alpine song, which was heard by all of the troops deployed on the surrounding mountains! After three attempts by the enemy, it was the Italians' turn to attempt to blow up the Austro-Hungarian positions with a mine; in particular, the target of the explosion would be a peak above the *Cengia Martini* named "Hill 2,668," where a small gun was harassing the trenches on the ledge itself. For this purpose, a tunnel that was 1 kilometer long was excavated under the peak, entrusted once more to Lieutenant Malvezzi. He was aided by Lieutenant Mario Cadorin, and the explosion was scheduled for June 20. The works had been detected by the enemy, who had deserted the position with the intention of reoccupying it after the explosion, just as the Alpini had done a few weeks before.

Columns of Alpini skiers on a glacier. *Museo Nazionale Storico degli Alpini*

The Lagazuoi, seen from the Italian positions to the east of it, with the pass below closed with multiple lines of barbed wire. *Museo Nazionale Storico degli Alpini*

On the Lagazuoi, the Alpini dig the countermine tunnel to prevent the Austro-Hungarians from blowing up their positions. *Museo Nazionale Storico degli Alpini*

An Italian encampment on the Lagazuoi. *Andrea Bianchi*

However, the coordination between the artillery and the Alpini allowed a unit of the *Pieve di Cadore* to arrive first on the shattered trenches, while the barrage prevented the enemy to leave their cover, scoring an important success in that grinding war. A final attempt by the Austro-Hungarians was made on September 16, but once more, the countermine tunnel dug by the Alpini dispersed most of the force of the explosion and the attack failed. However, notwithstanding many strenuous efforts, the *Cengia Martini* as well as the whole eastern side of the Trentino salient had to be abandoned a few weeks later due to the break of the front at Caporetto.

THE SECOND BATTLE OF MONTE ORTIGARA

Monte Ortigara had been the theater of a bloody battle in the summer of 1916. But, in the end, the Austro-Hungarians had maintained the control of that mountain and of the surrounding ones. The Italian Supreme Command had not given up the idea of conquering it, considering it to be a real danger for the Asiago Plateau if there were a new offensive from the south Trentino, as with the one launched in the spring of the previous year. The subordinate commands were less convinced about the importance of that mountain, down to the divisional command that was directly charged with the attack, which it was opposed to. It knew very well that Monte Ortigara, Monte Campigoletti, and

the other peaks that had so bravely resisted a year before had become even more formidably defended by thousands of men from the best Austro-Hungarian units, hundreds of machine guns, and kilometers of barbed wire in several lines that were fixed with poles directly into the rock. The shelters were dug into solid rock and were clearly capable of withstanding intense bombardment; the enemy artillery covered every approach very effectively. Furthermore, it was known that the terrain offered

Italian artillery shells the top of Monte Ortigara on June 10, 1917. *Museo Nazionale Storico degli Alpini*

General Montuori, *center*, commander of the XX Army Corps, inspects the Italian troops during the battle. *Andrea Bianchi*

Italian soldiers attend the holy service before one of the many assaults on Monte Ortigara. *Andrea Bianchi*

Italian entrenchments on Cima della Caldiera, opposite Monte Ortigara. *Andrea Bianchi*

Italian barracks at the Pozzo della Scala, at the foot of the Cima del Campanaro. *Andrea Bianchi*

Alpini at work on the Cima del Campanaro to improve the shelters against enemy shelling. *Andrea Bianchi*

An Italian encampment with tents and barracks in the area of Monte Ortigara. *Andrea Bianchi*

no cover for the attackers, who were forced to cross certain points such as the notorious Agnella and Agnelizza Gorges, which could easily be hit by machine gun and artillery fire. Needless to say, the Supreme Command did not budge an inch, and the preparations for the offensive started with a great number of men and weapons involved to ensure its success. The final plan entrusted the main attack to an entire army corps, the XX, consisting of two divisions: the Fifty-Second, composed entirely of mountain troops who were to attack Monte Ortigara and Monte Campigoletti directly; and the Twenty-Ninth, which was to move against Monte Forno. To the south, an action was mounted by the XXII Army Corps against the Monte Zebio-Monte Interrotto line, while flanking attacks, aimed at pinning down the Austro-Hungarians and prevent movements of reinforcements from one sector to the other, were planned both to the north and to the south. Artillery support was ramped up to the maximum level possible, with 1,150 pieces of artillery of various calibers and almost 600 bombards, representing power considered to be enough, in and of itself, to demolish any enemy position. As mentioned, the direct attack against Monte Ortigara and Monte Campigoletti was assigned to the Fifty-Second Division, which had been formed specifically for this action by joining two *raggruppamenti* with a total of eighteen Alpini battalions—the greatest concentration of Alpine troop units that had been assembled so far in the war. The organizational chart of the Fifty-Second Division was as follows:

IV Raggruppamento Alpini, consisting of:
8° Gruppo Alpini, with the Battaglioni *Val Ellero*, *Val Arroscia*, *Monte Mercantour*, and *Monte Clapier*
9° Gruppo Alpini, with the Battaglioni *Verona*, *Bassano*, *Monte Baldo*, and *Sette Comuni*
XXII Gruppo of mountain artillery

I Raggruppamento Alpini, consisting of:
1° Gruppo Alpini, with the Battaglioni *Tirano*, *Vestone*, *Monte Spluga*, *Monte Stelvio*, and *Valtellina*
2° Gruppo Alpini, with the Battaglioni *Ceva*, *Mondovì*, *Bicocca*, *Val Tanaro*, and *Val Stura*
XIII Gruppo mule pack artillery.
10° Raggruppamento of mountain artillery consisting of XXIII e XIV Gruppo plus five batteries of mule pack artillery
The division also counted two infantry brigades, five regiments in total, a field artillery regiment, an engineer battalion, and the XIII Raggruppamento of bombards. Other Alpine battalions were in the reserve, and were moved in later on: *Monte Saccarello*, *Val Dora*, *Cuneo*, and *Monte Marmolada*.

The date of the attack had been set for June 9, but due to the extremely bad weather, it was postponed until the tenth. At quarter past 5:00 a.m., the artillery barrage started, including gas shells, but at quarter past 2:00 p.m., when the *Alpini* were supposed to move to make the assault, a heavy fog prevented proper observation of the battlefield. The patrols sent to check on the effects of the artillery fire reported that most of the barbed wire lines were still in place and that no passage had been created. Nevertheless, the attack was confirmed, only to be postponed

for forty-five minutes before resuming the shelling. At 3:00 p.m., the men left their cover and started to advance, surrounded by fog and soaked by the heavy rain, while the Italian artillery extended its fire to the Austro-Hungarian second line, trying to prevent the movement of troops forward. The Battaglioni *Bassano* and *Sette Comuni*, closely followed by the Battaglioni *Monte Baldo* and *Verona*, moved against the Agnella Pass, the peaks to the right and left of the pass—Hill 2,003 and Hill 2,101, and the top of the Monte Ortigara, at 2,105 meters (6,096 feet) above MSL—but after just a few minutes they were targeted by furious artillery and machine gun fire that, notwithstanding the fog, was able to aim blindly at the spots where the *Alpini* were forced to pass, thus causing a great number of casualties. In the late afternoon, the Battaglioni *Bassano* and *Monte Baldo*, against all odds, were able to set foot on the Agnella Pass and seize the two side peaks but could not move farther, due to heavy artillery fire. On the other hand, the *Verona* and *Sette Comuni* could do nothing against the defenses of Monte Ortigara and were forced to retreat, leaving behind many fellow Alpini. Farther south, the action against Monte Campigoletti was no more successful; the Battaglioni *Vestone* and *Mondovì*, supported by *Bicocca* and *Ceva*, managed to occupy only a few stretches of the first-line trenches but were completely pinned down and could move neither forward nor backward. The first day ended with very few results: only on the right front of attack had some success been achieved. In the center and on the left, the Austro-Hungarians had held firmly. The offensive to the south and the flanking attacks both to the north and to the south had been a failure. The offensive was momentarily suspended, except for the action to the north, where two fresh battalions, *Valle Ellero* and *Monte Clapier*, replaced the exhausted *Bassano* and *Monte Baldo* and were charged to attack from the newly conquered Agnella Pass toward the Val Caldiera Pass, just behind the latter, while the *Verona* and *Sette Comuni* resumed the assault on Monte Ortigara. Unfortunately, on the eleventh, the weather conditions remained very bad; thus, the artillery preparation was once again ineffective. Therefore, when the attack started, the *Alpini* were stopped immediately. The Forty-Seventh Mountain Artillery Battery advanced its guns very bravely to the line of the fighting to support the attack, but to no avail. In the following days, the Italians remained inactive on the precarious lines occupied so far, but even this inactivity cost heavy casualties because the positions were improvised and offered little shelter against enemy fire that could target the men from above. On the other hand, some counterattacks launched by the Austro-Hungarians on the night of June 14 and 15 were repelled, with heavy casualties for both contenders. On June 15, 16, and 17, the operations were suspended by both sides, who tried to reorganize their forces for a new effort. The Italians managed to strike before the enemy, mounting an attack that had been planned following the same guidelines of the June 10 attack. The guidelines included the Battaglioni *Val Dora* and *Val Stura*, an infantry battalion, and a *bersaglieri* battalion; with the Forty-Seventh Battery for close artillery support, charged to take the Val Caldiera Pass; and the Battaglioni *Verona*, *Monte Baldo*, *Bassano*, and *Sette Comuni*, who were to converge on Monte Ortigara from the center; and *Valtellina*, *Monte Saccarello*, and *Monte Stelvio*, who were to converge on Monte Ortigara from the left. The flanking attacks to the north and to the south were also renewed.

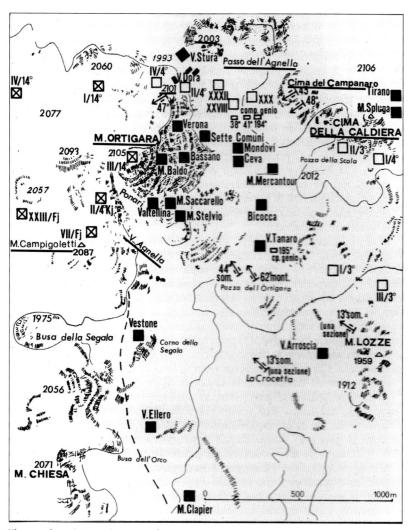

The attack on Monte Ortigara of June 19, 1917

Austro-Hungarian prisoners led away from the battlefield on June 20, 1917

A machine gun section on Monte Ortigara. *Fondazione Museo Storico del Trentino Archivio Fotografico*

The huge artillery preparation started at 7:00 a.m. on June 18, and lasted until 6:00 a.m. the following day, and this time it was extremely effective, neutralizing many enemy strongholds and opening large gaps in the barbed wire. There was almost no opposition when the Alpini moved to attack, and Monte Ortigara was conquered in about one hour with the capture of about a thousand prisoners, who were still bewildered by the violence of the bombardment. It is reported that the first unit to set foot on the top was the 137th Company of the Battaglione *Monte Stelvio*, but due to the chaotic mixing of the battalions, other units have claimed this distinction. Unfortunately, the other actions had failed. Therefore, Monte Ortigara had now become a sort of salient wedged into the Austro-Hungarian lines, with little to shelter the Alpini against the enemy artillery, which immediately started to shell the whole mountain. The battalions tried their best to dig some improvised defenses, move the injured men back, and reorganize, all under enemy fire. They even relieved some units that were particularly worn out, but by the end of that day, the casualties amounted to almost 4,000 men. The following days were terrible for the occupants because, although with hard work the positions were improved a little and three batteries were brought up and deployed close to the first trenches, the Austro-Hungarian artillery went on taking its daily toll of dead and injured.

Needless to say, the Austro-Hungarian High Command was not ready to give up Monte Ortigara. Therefore, it ordered an assault entrusted to the best troops it had at its disposal in that sector of the front. On the night between June 24 and 25, the Austro-Hungarian assault troops attacked after only ten minutes of artillery preparation, also armed with flame throwers, and were able to overwhelm the Italian positions, which were still weak. Every peak that had been conquered in the past days, with great effort, was lost in a relatively short time, and the Austro-Hungarians managed to redeploy their units on the Ortigara and on the Agnella Pass. The confusion was at its peak in the Italian camp, where the commanders were slow to realize how serious the situation had become. A counterattack was hastily mounted, sending in all the battalions at hand, even if worn out and tired. *Ceva, Val Tanaro, Val Stura, Monte Stelvio, Monte Baldo, Vestone, Bassano, Val d'Arroscia, Bicocca, Monte Spluga,* and *Tirano,* mixed with infantry and *bersaglieri* units, attacked bravely, but the only result was the addition of 6,000 more casualties to the already high toll. During the night, the troops started to withdraw to the positions they had occupied before the beginning of the battle. On June 29, a final enemy counterattack repelled the Alpini from the last trenches still held in the Agnella Pass area, and the battle was definitively over. After twenty days of hard and bloody battle, the battle that had seen the greatest participation of Alpini in the whole Great War came to an end, with more than 25,000 casualties—of which over 12,000 were among the mountain troops—without reaching any result.

WAR ON HIGH PEAKS: THE CONQUEST OF MONTE CORNO DI CAVENTO AND OF THE FORCELLA A "V"

The daring actions carried out by the Alpini during 1916 on the Adamello massif had only left the last eastern ridge of peaks in the hands of the Austro-Hungarians. Their line extended along an arc anchored to the north to Cima Presena, 3,059 meters (10,036 feet) above MSL, and to the south to Corno di Cavento, 3,402 meters (11,161 feet) above MSL, with the Monte Carè Alto, 3,462 meters (11,358 feet) above MSL, a little to the rear. So far, in 1917, the operations on that front had been at a standstill, the contenders being absorbed elsewhere; therefore, the Austro-Hungarians had used the time to strengthen their strongholds and secure their supply lines. New machine guns had been brought in and positioned at dominant points to cover every possible approach, and a long tunnel in the ice had been excavated to connect the positions on the Corno di Cavento with the cableway that carried ammunition and supplies. Thus, the supply troops could perform their duty in relative security. On the other side of the front, the Corno di Cavento was considered by the Italians to be of paramount importance in consolidating the right side of their line. Therefore, they planned an action that was assigned to units of the Battaglione *Val Baltea*, supported by four ski companies, thirty volunteers of the Battaglione *Monte Mandrone*, and a unit of cadets. Artillery support was provided in part by a battery of mountain artillery and by the well-known 149 mm gun, Ippopotamo, now positioned at Cresta della Croce.

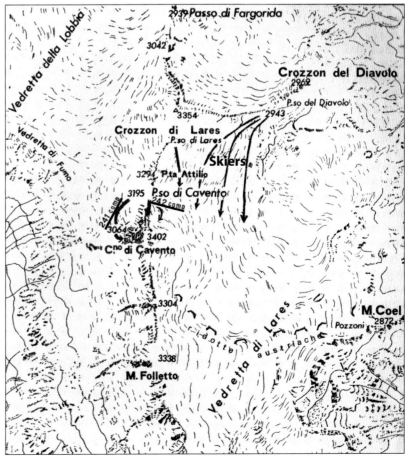

The action of June 1917 on the Corno di Cavento

Italian artillery shelling the top of the Corno di Cavento on June 15, 1917. *Museo Nazionale Storico degli Alpini*

Alpini are climbing the slopes of the Corno di Cavento. *Museo Nazionale Storico degli Alpini*

Alpini take some rest in a trench on the Corno di Cavento, in the summer of 1917. *Museo Nazionale Storico degli Alpini*

During the spring of 1917, some patrols carefully reconnoitered the sites, trying to identify new routes of access to deceive the enemy and determine its defenses as precisely as possible. At the same time, large quantities of ammunition, supplies, and medicines were amassed close to the first line, without raising the suspicion of the Austro-Hungarians.

The plan was for the ski companies to engage the enemy positions on the glacier below the mountain as a diversion while the 242nd Company of the *Val Baltea* attacked the Corno di Cavento directly, moving from the Cavento Pass along the ridge, with the volunteers on the *Monte Mandrone* as vanguard. The 241st Company of the same battalion was charged with outflanking the mountain to the west and climb the southwestern side of it, with the cadets as the vanguard. The action started on June 15 at half past 4:00 a.m. with the usual artillery preparation on the enemy positions; at half past 9:00 a.m., the skiers attacked across the glacier, engaging the machine gun nests, while the Alpine platoons started to climb the steep slopes of the Corno di Cavento. After three hours of ascent, exposed to enemy fire, the Alpini reached the top of the mountain, where they managed to overcome the defenders and take the position. The skiers managed to withdraw during the night, having accomplished their duty. Significantly, the Austro-Hungarians did not attempt any counterattack for the moment. This was the last important action on the Adamello massif for the year 1917, a significant success for the Italians. In the summer, excavation started for a long tunnel in the glacier, more than 5 kilometers long, at a depth of between 5 to 10 meters, to ensure the connection between the Garibaldi Hut and the advanced strongholds—regardless of weather conditions and without enemy disturbance. The tunnel, which was completed and then opened to the passage of the supply troops in December, was named "*Galleria azzurra*" (light-blue tunnel) due to the color of the reflection in the tunnel's ice.

At the other end of the long Trentino salient, on the Marmolada massif, a daring action was planned in the spring of 1917. It aimed to conquer Hill 3,153 and the *Forcella a "V"* below, which endangered the Italian hold on the area between Pizzo Serauta and Punta Serauta being as they were in enemy hands. After having discarded other ideas,[1] it was decided to dig a tunnel with an entrance at about 3,000 meters (9,842 feet) of altitude that emerged directly over the fork. The action was entrusted to the infantrymen of the 51° Regiment of the *Alpi* Brigade, who were supported both during the excavations and in the assault by the Alpini of the Battaglione *Val Cordevole*. The tunnel was completed on September 20, and the attack was planned for the following night. After two days of extremely confused fighting in the bowels of the mountain, the *Forcella a "V"* was finally conquered, and enemy counterattacks failed. On the thirty-first, Hill 3,153 was finally taken by a handful of volunteers of the 206th Company of the Battaglione *Val Cordevole*, who managed to climb a sheer wall of the peak and escape enemy observation. The small Austro-Hungarian garrison was taken completely by surprise, rapidly overwhelmed, and captured. It was the last act of bravery of the Alpini in that area because a few days later, due to the break of the front at Caporetto, the whole Marmolada had to be rapidly evacuated.

An Italian shelter almost buried in snow on the Marmolada massif. *Museo Nazionale Storico degli Alpini*

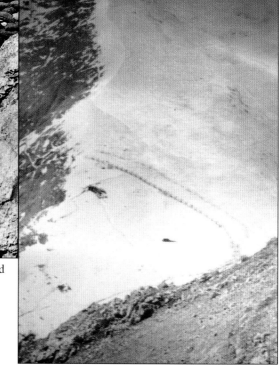

August 1917, the area of Forcella Serauta fortified by the Italian soldiers with sandbag walls and lines of barbed wire. In the background, the Forcella a "V." *Andrea Bianchi*

A better view of the Forcella a "V" seen from the Italian positions on the Serauta. *Andrea Bianchi*

A 65 mm mountain gun with its crew in position on Forcella Serauta. *Museo Nazionale Storico degli Alpini*

IN ACTION AGAIN ON THE EASTERN FRONT

After the failed offensive against Monte Ortigara, the Italian Supreme Command decided to regain the initiative with a new offensive along the Isonzo Valley. The plan of the Eleventh Isonzo Battle, fought from August 17 to 31, did not differ substantially from the previous ten offensives. As usual, the aim was to eliminate the stronghold of Tolmino, which stubbornly resisted for more than two years, and conquer the Bainsizza Plateau and the Tarnova Plateau, to the south of it; this duty was entrusted to the Second Army. Moreover, the Third Army had to mount an offensive to reach Trieste, the large Austro-Hungarian port on the Adriatic Sea, capturing the extreme enemy defenses on Mount Hermada (more of a hill than a real mountain, with its mere 323 meters [1,059 feet] above MSL), and on the Come Plateau. For the attack against the Bainsizza Plateau, the Second Army could count on two army corps: the XVII Army Corps, charged to penetrate the region between the stronghold of Tolmino and the northern side of the Plateau; and the XXIV Army Corps, entrusted with the frontal assault. The XXVII Army Corps had assigned to it the Alpine battalions *Pieve di Cadore, Monte Pelmo, Monte Antelao, Monte Albergian, Val Chisone,* and *Belluno,* which were grouped for the action in the V Raggruppamento Alpini, as well as the I, XXIV, XXX Groups and the Nineteenth Battery of mountain artillery; the XXIV Army Corps could depend on the Battaglioni *Monte Pasubio*

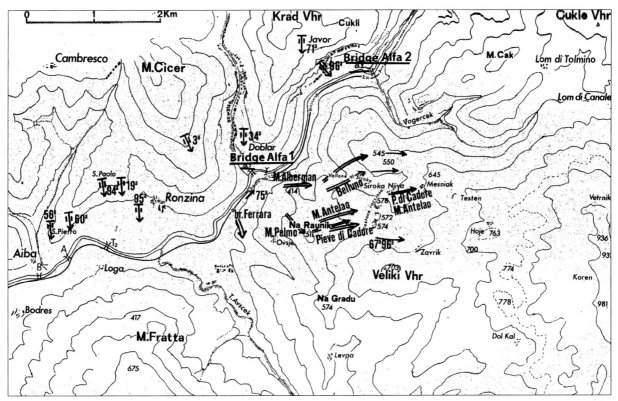

The action of the Alpini battalions during the Eleventh Isonzo Battle, or Battle of the Bainsizza, in August 1917. The positions of the "Alfa1" and "Alfa2" bridges are highlighted.

and *Monte Tonale* together with the VII and XXIX Groups of mountain artillery. The first wave of attack had to cross the Isonzo River, which was particularly narrow in that stretch, over several pontoon bridges that had been built during the nights that preceded the action. In particular, the Alpini of the V Raggruppamento had to cross the river on a bridge named "Alfa2," but the *Monte Pelmo* was to cross on another bridge, named "Alfa1," along with the infantrymen of the *Ferrara* Brigade. Quite obviously, the operations had not gone unobserved by the enemy, which did its best to prevent the bridges from being completed. It was aided in this task by the nature of the river itself, which was characterized by high and steep banks in that area. Furthermore, the eastern bank was heavily defended by strongholds dug into solid rock, which could also take advantage of some railway galleries that run parallel to the river itself.

The offensive was launched on August 19 after the usual long artillery preparation, but the battle did not begin as the Italians had hoped. First of all, the pontoon bridge "Alfa2" turned out to be impossible to build due to some short rounds of the Italian artillery that hit part of the building material, unfortunately, thus rendering it necessary for the Alpini to move south to the "Alfa1" bridge. Using this latter bridge, the Battaglione *Monte Pelmo* managed to set foot on the eastern bank, followed by four infantry companies of the *Ferrara* Brigade; the Battaglione *Monte Albergian* managed to cross the river as well, but then accurate Austro-Hungarian artillery fire interrupted the passage, and the bridge was first partially damaged and then completely destroyed. The Italian units that had already crossed the river moved immediately against the enemy positions, trying to enlarge the bridgehead, with the direct support of the guns of the I Gruppo, which fired from the western bank. It was not until the morning of August 20 that other units were able cross the river on the newly built bridge, among them the Battaglioni *Belluno*, *Pieve di Cadore*, and *Monte Antelao*, as well as a gun of the Thirty-

Fourth Battery of mountain artillery. The hold on the eastern bank of the Isonzo River could now be considered strong enough; however, the V Raggruppamento had been able to cross the river much more to the south of the Tolmino stronghold, which was its target, but which was now too far and extremely difficult to reach. Furthermore, after two days of fighting, the barren nature of the battleground, completely devoid of water, had already weakened the men. Everything, including the large quantities of water what were necessary due to the hot weather, had to be transported from the rear line by long supply lines, which needed to cross the river, though it was still partially under enemy fire. Notwithstanding these difficulties, the advance continued during the twentieth and the twenty-first, with the close support of the Thirty-Fourth, Seventy-First, and Fifty-FourthBatteries, but now the men were exhausted. Therefore, when the Austro-Hungarians counterattacked during the night of August 21, although they were finally driven off, they managed to stop any further progress being made by the Alpini. It was necessary to suspend the operations for at least a couple of days, even disregarding repeated orders to push forward. The attacks were resumed on the twenty-fourth, but the enemy resistance had definitively stiffened, and the men that had fought for five days without proper rest needed to be replaced with fresh forces. The Alpini were therefore withdrawn from the line in the night between August 25 and 26, replaced by infantry units.

Farther to the south, the offensive of the XXIV Army Corps was more successful, and Italian troops, with the Battaglioni *Monte Tonale* and *Monte Pasubio*, were able to advance and conquer the Bainsizza Plateau, one of the objectives of the offensive. The battle came to its end on the twenty-ninth with an undoubted success; however, once more, the Austro-Hungarians had managed, with great effort and by moving in the last reserves, to close the gap and prevent the coveted, decisive breakthrough.

THE AUSTRO-GERMAN OFFENSIVE: A BITTER SURPRISE AT CAPORETTO!

The Austro-Hungarian army had parried the blow once more, but the commander of the Isonzo Armee (the Army of the Isonzo), General Boroevic, was convinced that the next Italian offensive would also be the last: his army had no more reserves, and his men were worn out. He expressed his fears to the high command in Vienna, which in turn, having no spare divisions to send to the southern front, called on its ally, Germany, for reinforcements. The German Imperial high command had already turned down the Austro-Hungarians the previous year, having no intention of committing any of its troops to a front that it considered secondary, but this time the new commanders, General Hindenburg and General Ludendorff, understood that their ally was on the verge of collapsing, with the real risk of dragging Germany down with it. The two German generals decided therefore to help Austria-Hungary in mounting a great offensive that would dispose of the Italians definitively or, at least, keep them quiet for a long time. It would be superfluous to say that the offensive would be planned by German officers.

The preparation for the offensive was very detailed. Units were transferred to the southern front from many different places, using hundreds of trains. The Austro-Hungarians were able to take advantage of the great confusion that reigned on the Russian front, where the Russian army was paralyzed by the explosive political situation that had followed the fall of the Romanov dynasty, and move a few divisions to the Isonzo area. Furthermore, for the first time, the German divisions applied the new tactics—which had been developed on the western front—to the southern front. On the other hand, the Italian Supreme Command underestimated the warning signs, which were plentiful and rather precise, of the impending attack. After years passed, it seemed unlikely that the Austro-Hungarians still had the necessary resources to mount a major operation.

The offensive started in the night between October 23 and 24, in the area between the stronghold of Tolmino, to the south, and the Basin of Plezzo, to the north. In a few hours, it was able to realize the breakthrough that the Italian army had been seeking for years, and the Austro-German troops were able to converge on the town of Caporetto from the gap. The Italian divisions in many parts of the front resisted bravely, but because of the confusion of these hours when German units were penetrating their rear, some regiments

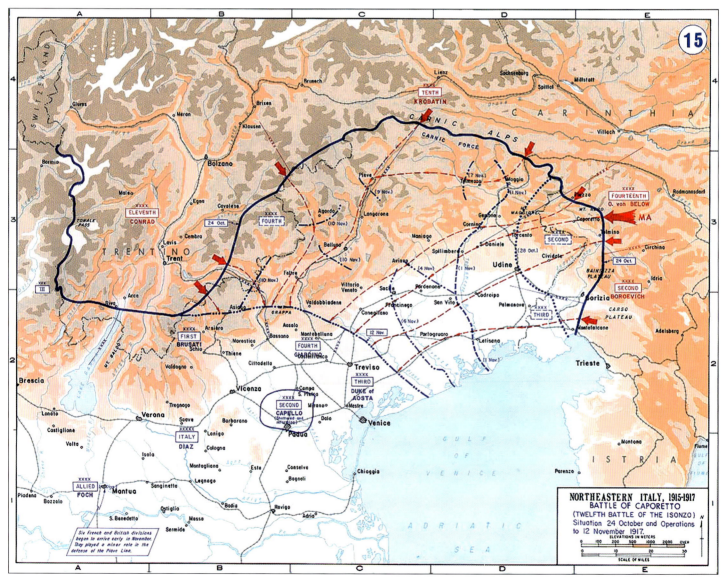

The Battle of Caporetto and the retreat of the Italian army toward the Piave River

Demolitions and road breaks made by the withdrawing Italian troops to slow down the advancing Austro-Germans. *Museo Nazionale Storico degli Alpini*

Equipment abandoned by the Italian troops in retreat. *Museo Nazionale Storico degli Alpini*

and divisions withdrew, fearing to be surrounded and cut off from their lines, due to a clear overestimation of the enemy forces and a poor knowledge of the Germans' tactics. On the afternoon of October 24, the whole front north of Tolmino was moving to the rear, and the Italian Supreme Command could do nothing other than to order, on October 26, a general retreat to the first strong natural position, the Tagliamento River, to gain time and put some space between its forces and those of the enemy. There, after a retreat of between 40 and 50 kilometers, it hoped to regroup its divisions and reorganize the line. The movement, which was rather chaotic indeed, was virtually completed on October 31, but, unfortunately for the Italians, this new line held firm for only a few hours. The Austro-Germans were so rapidly advancing, well motivated and, above all, enthusiastic because of the great success they were scoring, that they hoped they could even put an end to the war against Italy. On the opposite side, some of the Italian divisions had lost all semblance of the chain of command, the men were struggling just to reach safety, the logistic system was completely disrupted, and a great part of the artillery had been lost along the way. The Tagliamento line was broken during the night between November 2 and 3, the river was crossed at several points, and the Italian army resumed its retreat, directed toward the next great river, the Piave, about

50 to 70 kilometers farther west, where the movement was completed on November 8. There, thanks to the substantial shortening of the front and the tiredness of the Austro-Germans, who had been on the move for two weeks and had lost contact with their supply lines and heavy artillery, which could not follow at the same pace, the offensive was blocked.

It would be impossible to follow the fate of every Alpine unit in these chaotic events, which involved three Italian armies and an army corps, with dozens of Alpini battalions within their ranks. A "helicopter view" of the events involving them will be provided, with some specific references to relevant episodes that had Alpini as protagonists.

THE RETREAT FROM THE AREA OF THE ROMBON MASSIF

To the extreme north of the front of the offensive, on October 24, Austro-Hungarian troops assaulted the Italian positions on the Rombon massif, where they encountered the Battaglioni *Borgo S. Dalmazzo*, *Dronero*, and *Saluzzo*. The fighting was extremely hard, but the Alpini resisted an entire enemy regiment

An Austro-Hungarian supply column in march toward the frontline is crossing a deep gorge whose bridge has been destroyed by the withdrawing Italians. *Fondazione Museo Storico del Trentino Archivio Fotografico*

for the whole day. In the evening, the order was given to retreat to a rear position due to the gap created in the valley below, where a gas attack had exterminated an infantry battalion and from where the Germans had been pouring in since that morning. A few units of Alpini had tried to slow down the advancing enemy, but a company of the Battaglione *Ceva* had been nearly annihilated in the attempt. Meanwhile, the other two companies and the Battaglione *Mondovì* were positioned across the Isonzo River a few kilometers behind. Although they were able to maintain their positions intact, at half past 3:00 p.m., they had been ordered to retreat to the west to avoid being cut off from the Italian lines. The retreat from the Rombon massif was carried out rather chaotically due to the confusion of the commands and the horrible weather conditions. Two companies of the *Borgo S. Dalmazzo* did not receive the orders and remained isolated, being later overwhelmed by the advancing enemy, while the other units marched west in a blizzard that severely reduced visibility. In the morning of October 25, two companies of the Battaglione *Dronero* that moved as rearguard of the column were hit by artillery fire and were forced to stop and take cover, losing contact with their fellow Alpini. They put up a resistance on their improvised position, but in the morning of the twenty-sixth, the survivors, completely surrounded, surrendered. Those who remained

from the three battalions reached their destination, Sella Prevala, a pass that allowed access to the Raccolana Valley, and fell on the back of the XII Army Corps deployed in the Zona Carnia. Here, they met the forces sent there by the same XII Army Corps: the Battaglione *Val Fella* with the Fifty-Fifth Battery of mountain artillery and some infantry units. The pass and the surrounding mountains were attacked by overwhelming forces on the afternoon of the twenty-sixth and in the morning of the following day; the forces were barely repelled. However, that evening, the order came to retreat to the new line along the Tagliamento River since the whole position was at risk of being cut off by Austro-Hungarian troops coming from the north. The march west started on October 28, but in the morning of the following day, most of the units found themselves completely surrounded by enemy troops and, being completely worn out by the long days of march and fighting without supplies, had no other choice than to surrender. The Battaglione *Val Fella* alone managed to pass and reached the town of Tolmezzo, on the Tagliamento River, where it fought during the following days. When the general retreat to the Piave River started, the survivors of the battalion moved west, attached to the Gruppo *Alliney* (see below), on November 5, but on the sixth, they were surrounded and forced to surrender.

THE FIGHTING BETWEEN THE MONTE NERO RIDGE AND THE STRONGHOLD OF TOLMINO

The offensive opened in this area with a mine that blew up the Italian positions on Monte Rosso, garrisoned by infantrymen of the *Etna* Brigade, but the assailants did not manage to advance farther. To support the infantry units, the Battaglione *Belluno* was moved in. The situation on that stretch of the front seemed to be under the control of the Italian troops, but in the afternoon of October 24, the order by the divisional command to leave the position and retreat west arrived, and rather surprisingly, since a German column in the valley below had infiltrated the rear of the Italian line and was reaching the town of Caporetto. This hasty order created a lot of confusion among the troops, and, worst of all, did not reach all the subordinate units. Therefore, limiting our remarks to the actions of the Alpini, while the Battaglione *Belluno* made the movement, the *Monte Albergian*, deployed to the south on Mount Pleca, did not. And on the twenty-fifth, completely surrounded and attacked from every direction,

A postcard exhorting the Italian soldiers to resume the fight against the enemy and regain the Italian soil lost to the Austro-Germans, for the sake of those who have their family in the invaded areas

it was annihilated. Opposite the Tolmino stronghold, in the same afternoon, the Battaglione *Val d'Adige*, which was in the rear as a reserve, received the probably untimely order to advance and defend the positions on Mount Jeza, while the rest of the front was retreating in disorder. During the march, the battalions lost one-third of its men and, having reached its positions, discovered that the infantry units on its right and left flanks had already retreated west. The Alpini resisted the Jeza stubbornly the whole night, and in the morning, when they were finally ordered to move west, only a few men managed to break contact. However, the survivors were captured a few days later near the town of Codroipo, not far from the Tagliamento River, which they were trying to reach. The Battaglioni *Morbegno*, *Monte Berico*, and *Vicenza* were luckier, as they had been deployed to the extreme south of the front of attack. Confronted with an Austro-Hungarian mountain regiment, they fought bravely until they received the order to retreat. The battalions managed to march west and maintain their combat capabilities during the phases of the long retreat to the Piave River.

On the morning of the twenty-fifth, some units of Alpini and infantry were hastily deployed to defend Mount Stol and try to slow down the enemy advance until the retreating Italian units managed to form a continuous line of resistance. The Battaglioni *Monte Argentera* and *Monviso*, which had not yet been involved in the battle, joined what remained of the *Belluno* and *Mondovì*. These had already been weakened by the previous day's fighting as well as by some infantry units of the *Genova* Brigade that had managed, with great effort, to break contact with the Austro-Germans. Attacked by two mountain regiments, without artillery support, and with only a few machine guns, they lost the top of Mount Stol after a night of hard fighting, although they inflicted heavy casualties on the enemy. A handful of Alpini managed to retreat to the west and, after days of marching, reach the Piave River and were sent to reorganize to fight another day.

THE RETREAT OF THE XII ARMY CORPS FROM THE ZONA CARNIA

The XII Army Corps had not been directly touched by the Austro-German offensive, but as mentioned above, several roughly parallel valleys could lead the enemy forces from the Plezzo Basin to the rear of the divisions deployed there. Therefore, on October 24, the *Comando Zona Carnia* formed a special unit grouping the Alpine Battaglioni *Pinerolo*, *Monte Canin* and *Monte Mercatour*, the Fifty-Second Battery of mountain artillery and some infantry and *bersaglieri* units, named "Gruppo *Alliney*" (Alliney group), after the name of the commanding officer. The duty of the group was to seal the Resia Valley that runs straight to the Tagliamento. Over the following days, the men fought bravely, contesting every inch of terrain against the advancing Austro-Hungarian mountain troops and, beginning on October 28, when the order for a general retreat to the Tagliamento River was issued, acted as rearguard protecting the orderly movement of their fellow soldiers. On October 30, the Gruppo *Alliney* received the Battaglione *Val Ellero*, which had escaped from the Sella Prevala trap, and later, on November 5, the Battaglione *Gemona* as well. Following the general retreat from the Tagliamento to the Piave River, the group started to move west on November 5, when many avenues of retreat were already closed. From the sixth to the ninth, the units retreated, fighting to keep the line of withdrawal open but, little by little, lost cohesion and the remnants of the battalions were surrounded and overwhelmed by the enemy one by one. To the south, the Battaglioni *Valle Stura*, *Val Leogra*, and *Bicocca*, after several days of continuous retreat, were ordered to protect the accesses to the plain from the north and sacrificed themselves completely in their duties between November 3 and 5. The destiny of the Battaglioni *Monte Clapier* and *Valle Arroscia* was no different; after days of marching, they were deployed on some heights north of the town of Maniago. Only a handful of Alpini escaped being surrounded and were able to reach the Piave line. To the extreme west side of the Zona Carnia, another tactical group was formed from the Battaglioni *Tolmezzo*, *Monte Nero*, and *Assietta*, with mixed infantry units and a *bersaglieri* regiment. With the Alpini as rearguard, they retreated south toward the high valley of the Piave River, but during the march, the *Tolmezzo* remained isolated and its survivors were captured. The Battaglione *Susa* left its positions and, fighting its way toward the southwest, was able to reach the plain and the Italian lines in relatively good order.

THE FOURTH ARMY DELAYS THE RETREAT

The Fourth Army, deployed on the eastern side of the Trentino Salient, was issued the order to retreat from the northern part of its lines on the morning of October 27, at the same time as the troops of the XII Army Corps. But instead of complying, the command decided to hold its positions, considering the positions to be compatible with their defense needs within the Tagliamento River line. Therefore, when the general retreat toward the Piave River started, many units of the army, at serious risk of being cut off from the new southern line, had to move with haste and disorder, abandoning most of its heavy equipment. The Fourth Army included twenty-two battalions of Alpini at the time: the *Compagnia volontari Alpini Feltre*, the *Compagnia volontari Alpini Cadore*, and thirteen mountain artillery batteries. The Supreme Command, considering these troops to be invaluable as part of the new defenses that were being prepared on Monte Grappa—one of the key positions of the new line of defense—ordered that some battalions be transported south by truck and redeployed immediately. The Battaglione *Fenestrelle*, stationed near the Tre Cime di Lavaredo, acted instead as rearguard and fought its way south for days. During its march, it collected the remnants of the Battaglioni *Monte Nero* and *Assietta*, retreating from Zona Carnia. Together, they reached the town of Longarone, on the high course of the Piave River, on November 9. In the afternoon, a German unit, led by Lieutenant Erwin Rommel, an avant-garde of its advancing troops, managed to cross the river and close the way south, cutting the retreat of several thousands of Italian soldiers. What remained of the three battalions tried to pass through the mountains, but only a few hundred men reached the Italian lines. At Longarone, a few dozen German soldiers managed to capture more than 10,000 prisoners in total.

The retreat from the Marmolada massif and the Lagorai occurred in better order since the advancing Austro-Germans were far away and the Austro-Hungarian troops that faced the Italians in this area were not strong enough to be of real concern. The movement toward the Monte Grappa area was covered by a tactical group as rearguard, formed from the Battaglioni *Monte Pavione*, *Val Brenta*, *Monte Rosa*, and *Cividale*, part of the Battaglioni *Val Tagliamento* and *Monte Arvenis*, as well as some infantry units. The group would hold the enemy back effectively until November 13, gaining precious time for the units that were deploying on Monte Grappa.

To the south, the Supreme Command decided that it would be useful to help complete the retreat of the Fourth Army by maintaining a bridgehead east of the Piave River, at the town of Vidor, using the town's own bridge. Amongst the troops hastily deployed there were also the Battaglioni *Val Varaita*, *Val Pellice*, *Monte Granero*, and the *Compagnia volontari Alpini Feltre*. The defenses were rudimentary and improvised, with little barbed wire; furthermore, the time needed to improve them was very scarce. The Austro-Germans attacked the bridgehead on November 10, but the Italian troops held firmly, repelling the assailants, for probably the first time since Caporetto. However, the situation at Vidor was so precarious that the Supreme Command feared the enemy would take the bridge intact, it therefore gave the order to abandon the town and blow up the bridge, even though Italian units were still on the other side. Unfortunately, as had already happened in other circumstances, the order did not reach all the defenders: the *Compagnia volontari Feltre* remained barricaded in a building and, once the Alpini realized that they were surrounded and without ammunition, tried a sortie, charging with their bayonets; all were either killed or captured.

The events related to the retreat from the Isonzo to the Piave also involved the Third Army, deployed to the extreme south of the Isonzo front. The army had no Alpine troops assigned; therefore, events related to it are beyond the scope of this work. It is enough to know that this major unit managed to retreat in good order and formed the backbone of the defense of the lower part of the Piave line.

On the Piave line, the Italian army found the strength to face the enemy and stop its advance. The Austro-Germans had run out of momentum, their supply lines were stretched beyond their limits, and their artillery as well as their heavy equipment were far behind the advancing columns. They had reached that point out of enthusiasm, hoping to give a definitive blow to Italy, but when resistance stiffened, they could not find the strength to overwhelm it. The defeat had been severe: there were more than 40,000 casualties and 260,000 prisoners, and over 1,300 pieces of artillery and tons of supplies had been lost or destroyed before they could be taken by the enemy. But Italy was still standing.

THE DEFENSIVE BATTLE ON THE ASIAGO PLATEAU AND ON MONTE GRAPPA

After the hasty retreat from the Isonzo Valley, the *Regio Esercito* was now deployed along a new line that, starting from the west side of what had been the Trentino salient, comprised the southern Trentino, the old positions on the Pasubio massif, the Asiago Plateau, and the Monte Grappa massif. It then bent southeast, following the course of the Piave River. On this line, much shorter than the previous one and anchored on strong, natural obstacles, the army found the strength to put up an effective resistance against the advancing Austro-Germans.

The Asiago Plateau was manned by the right wing of the First Army, which had moved its XX Army Corps back slightly to follow the retreat of the Fourth Army, which was now deployed on the Monte Grappa and the other peaks of the massif. Along the Piave River, the Third Army, still in good order, mounted an effective defense. What remained of the Second Army, the most affected by the enemy offensive, was in the rear under complete reorganization. This phase of the defensive battle, also called the First Battle of the Piave River or *Battaglia d'Arresto* (blocking battle), saw the participation of many Alpine battalions and mountain artillery batteries.

THE STRUGGLE ON THE GRAPPA MASSIF

The Austro-Hungarians coming down from the lower Trentino tried to break through the Asiago Plateau. Meanwhile, to the east, the Austro-German forces that had pursued the retreating Italian troops were trying to conquer the pillar of the entire new line of defense, the Grappa massif. The massif is situated in the Veneto Prealps, between the valleys of the Brenta River and the Piave River, and is formed by a series of ridges that run in a roughly east–west direction; the highest peak is Monte Grappa itself, 1,775 meters (5,823 feet) above MSL. In the southern portion of the massif, the terrain becomes more regular, resembling a high plateau that descends gently to the plain. As seen, the massif was garrisoned by Italian troops of the Fourth Army, withdrawn from the Cadore area, some of them relatively fresh and not directly involved in the disaster of Caporetto. However, although great efforts had been made in the attempt to adequately fortify the area, not much was in place in terms of trenches, strongholds, or even barbed wire. The deployment of the Italian troops was completed on November 13, and the line was subdivided into four sectors, hinged on four mounts: from west to east, Monte Asolone, Monte Grappa, Monte Spinoncia, and Monte Tomba. The

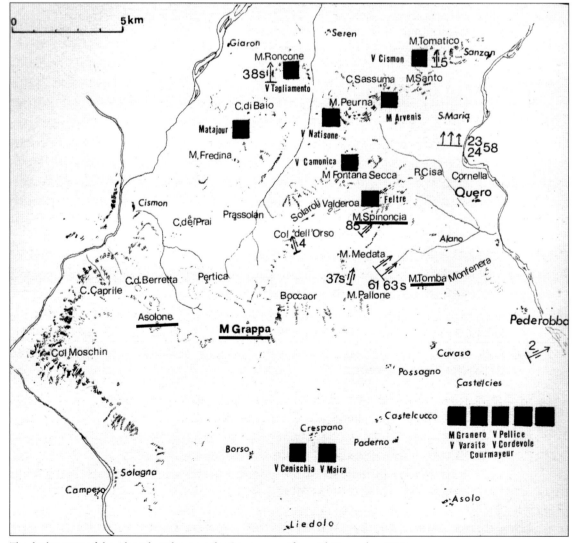

The deployment of the Alpini battalions on the Grappa massif in mid-November 1917

Alpine artillerymen in a stronghold on Monte Grappa. *Museo Nazionale Storico degli Alpini*

Italian soldiers in a trench on Monte Grappa

The defense of Monte Valderoa as imagined by the *Domenica del Corriere*

Monte Asolone sector was manned by the Battaglione *Monte Matajur* and a *bersaglieri* battalion and supported in the rear by three infantry battalions. In the Monte Grappa sector, the Battaglioni *Val Tagliamento* and *Val Natisone* were stationed on the first line, with a *bersaglieri* battalion and two infantry battalions at their rear. In the Monte Spinoncia sector, battalions were deployed that were almost entirely Alpine, the *Monte Arvenis* and *Val Cismon* in the front line and the *Val Camonica* and *Feltre* in the rear, reinforced with infantry units and supported by four batteries of mountain artillery. The Battaglioni *Val Cenischia* and *Val Maira* were kept as a reserve. The Monte Tomba sector was entrusted to the infantry, with four batteries of mountain artillery as close support, but the Battaglioni *Monte Granero*, *Val Pellice*, *Val Varaita*, *Courmayeur*, and *Val Cordevole* were kept in reserve.

The enemy, three Austro-Hungarian divisions and a German division strong, attacked on November 14, exerting their maximum efforts on the flanks, along the valleys of the Brenta River and the Piave River, with diversionary attacks against the first ridge of peaks that blocked their advance. The Alpini held their positions the whole day, suffering heavy losses. But, during the night, the Battaglioni *Val Cismon* and *Monte Arvenis* received the order to withdraw because, at some points, enemy units had penetrated the first line and they risked being surrounded. The following day, the *Monte Matajur* and the *bersaglieri* were heavily attacked and forced to retreat. The *Val Tagliamento* and the *Val Natisone*, which had so far resisted bravely, remained isolated and managed to disengage at a heavy toll due to these movements to their left and right flanks. On November 16 and 17, the attacks continued in the Piave Valley with a certain degree of success, forcing a general retreat of the right wing of the Italian line to the slopes of Monte Tomba, while they were contained along the Brenta Valley. On the sixteenth, the situation was rather critical, and the newly arrived battalion, the *Monte Rosa*, was hastily sent to Monte Pertica, the last height before Monte Grappa, which was manned at that time by only an infantry battalion with two batteries of mountain artillery. The following day, in the late afternoon, after two hours of artillery preparation, four Austro-Hungarian battalions moved to attack Monte Pertica. There, the Alpini of the *Monte Rosa* resisted for days, counterattacking each time they lost a trench until, on November 22, the few survivors were forced to retreat. However, the stiff resistance had worn out the enemy, who could not advance further, as well. In the Monte Tomba sector, the attacks were resumed on the nineteenth by German forces that continued their action until the twenty-fifth. Monte Tomba remained in Italian hands, but the nearby Monte Monfenera was lost, jeopardizing the line. Counterattacks were launched by the Battaglione *Val Pellice*, and by the *Val Pellice* again with the *Val Varaita* on the following day, but they could not reconquer the top of the mountain. However, the week of fighting had exhausted the Germans, who were forced to suspend the offensive, as well. After the enemy's progress on the right and on the left of the Italian line, the Spinoncia sector now formed a sort of wedge in the new Austro-German line. On November 21, after the usual heavy bombardment, enemy troops moved to attack, forcing the Italian troops, the Battaglioni *Val Camonica* and *Monte Arvenis*, to leave the more advanced positions. However, the second line, manned also by the Battaglioni *Feltre* and *Val Maira*, resisted. On the twenty-fifth, some stretches of the front gave in, but a brave counterattack by some companies of the Battaglioni *Val Cenischia* and *Val Cismon*, closely supported by the Fourth Battery of mountain artillery, managed to close the gap.

In the Asolone sector to the west, on November 22 and 23, Austro-Hungarian troops assaulted Col della Berretta but were beaten back by infantry units and the Battaglione *Val Brenta*. On November 26, new attacks made the Italian line waver, and it seemed that the enemy would set foot on Monte Asolone, but the decimated companies of the *Val Brenta* used their last ounce of energy for a desperate counterattack that stopped its advance. After these operations that had dented but not broken the Italian line, the Austro-Germans were forced to suspend the attacks and reorganize their ranks.

During the pause, both contenders moved reinforcements to the Grappa area. The Italian command managed to gather a few more Alpine units, although not at full strength, while the Austro-Germans were able to rotate all their first-line divisions in order to resume the offensive with fresh troops. On December 11, in the Asolone sector, the Austro-Hungarians assaulted Col della Berretta and the nearby Col Caprile again, after an artillery barrage that lasted five hours, aiming to circumvent the Monte Asolone itself from the west. Col della Berretta was finally lost, while on the Col Caprile, the *Monte Matajur* resisted until it was annihilated. The loss of these two positions was not acceptable to the Italian command; therefore, several counterattacks were mounted on the twelfth that were led by the Battaglioni *Monte Clapier*, *Val Natisone*, *Val Tagliamento*, and *Monte Rosa*. The only result was causing the

attacking units severe casualties—up to two-thirds of their men. On December 13, the Battaglioni *Tolmezzo*, *Pinerolo*, and *Susa* hastily replaced their exhausted fellow Alpini, who had been momentarily withdrawn from the front line. At dawn on the fourteenth, they were targeted by heavy bombardment that included the use of gas shells and then attacked by enemy infantry. In a few hours, they were almost completely wiped out. Over the following two days, it was again the Italians' turn to counterattack, with the infantry Brigade *Modena* supported by the Battaglioni *Courmayeur*, *Pallanza*, *Moncenisio*, and *Val Cordevole*, in an action that did not reach any significant result. Finally, on December 18, the Austro-Hungarians made their last attempt to break the Italian line, and after a short but terrific artillery barrage, the enemy infantry assaulted the decimated Italian units on the Asolone. *Val Natisone* and *Val Tagliamento*, in the front line again, resisted until they were destroyed; the *Monte Rosa* sacrificed its last Alpini in a desperate and useless counterattack. The *Courmayeur* suffered heavy casualties while some remnants of the *Pallanza* managed to escape. Monte Asolone seemed to have been lost, but a final counterattack led by the Battaglioni *Val Pellice* and *Val Varaita*, although repelled, managed to stop the advance of the Austro-Hungarians, who were likely as worn out as the Italians. On the nineteenth and twentieth, the Italians tried hard to retake Monte Asolone and Col Caprile, with no success; however, the enemy offensive on this stretch of the front had been definitively stopped, once again within a few kilometers of the coveted Veneto plain.

On December 11, the offensive was resumed in the Spinoncia sector as well, and the Austro-Germans were able to set foot on Monte Spinoncia itself, jeopardizing the whole sector. The gap was momentarily closed by the Battaglioni *Val Maira*, *Monte Pavione*, and *Cividale*, but the situation was very precarious, and a counterattack was deemed necessary to retake the mountain and restore the line. The counterattack launched on the twelfth was a complete failure and caused severe casualties to the three battalions. The positions north of the Spinoncia were now in serious danger, although the Alpini that manned them held out on their positions. On December 13, German units managed to crush the Battaglione *Val Cenischia* with a series of attacks, and only 120 men could retreat to the new Italian lines. The same fate was expected for the Battaglioni *Val Maira* and *Monte Pavione*, which were reduced to 400 Alpini by the end of the same day. On Monte Valderoa, to the northwest of Monte Spinoncia, the Battaglione *Feltre*, along with the remnants of the *Val Censchia* and units of the *Val Camonica*, resisted bravely, but the top of the mountain was lost on the fourteenth. That day, Monte Valderoa was conquered and lost several times, but the Germans were in control of it by the end of the day. The Battaglione *Val Cismon*, deployed on a new line behind Monte Valderoa, was attacked on December 17 by the Germans, after three hours of artillery preparation. The Alpini held their ground the whole day and also counterattacked successfully. This was the last combat of the Alpini during the *Battaglia d'Arresto*, because all the battalions, reduced to a few hundred men each, were withdrawn from the first line and sent to the rear to rest and replenish their ranks. However, on December 21, the Austro-Germans definitively suspended the offensive, having spent their last reserves without achieving that definitive success that they had sought.

THE DEFENSE OF THE ASIAGO PLATEAU

As mentioned, when the First and the Fourth Army started their retreat, the Austro-Hungarian troops that faced them in Trentino moved forward, following them and engaging them in some sporadic rearguard fighting. General Conrad von Hötzendorf, now in command of the troops stationed in Trentino, hoped to be able to break through the Italian positions on the plateau and reach the Veneto plain, to the rear of the Piave River line, with a sort of reedition of his spring offensive of 1916. However, beginning on November 13, the Italian retreat was completed, and resistance stiffened on the new line, which followed roughly the same positions as had already been desperately defended during that same offensive in this sector. In fact, it ran through Monte Tondarecar, Monte Castelgomberto, and Monte Fior, in the Melette area, and was defended by the infantrymen of the *Regina* Brigade with the support of many Alpini battalions.

As early as November 14, a company of the Battaglione *Monte Pasubio* thwarted the Austro-Hungarians' attempt to take the top of Monte Fior, still weakly garrisoned, by surprise. With an audacious counterattack, it even managed to expel the enemy from some important positions that had been conquered a few hours before. From then on, they were named "*Il Torrione*" (the keep), which would be one of the cornerstones of the Italian line in the area; to garrison the *Torrione*, the Battaglione *Monte Stelvio* was sent in. Monte Tondarecar was assaulted on the fifteenth and sixteenth, but the Italian troops, among them the Battaglioni *Sette Comuni* and *Cuneo*, did not back off; on the contrary, they were able to counterattack and improve their positions. A few days' pause followed, used by both parts to prepare for the next unavoidable phase of the offensive.

On the morning of November 21, under the supervision of the new emperor, Karl I,[2] the Austro-Hungarians resumed the offensive with a terrific artillery barrage, followed by an infantry assault on the twenty-second. The enemy concentrated its efforts on the left side of the Italian line, which had Monte Meletta Davanti as pillar, defended by two infantry battalions and the Alpini of the *Monte Cervino*. The Italians withstood the attack for two days, even counterattacking from time to time, reinforced during the course of the battle by the Battaglione *Bassano* until, on November 24, the offensive, which had produced no results, was called off. A new effort with fresh troops was mounted on December 3, anticipating a double attack against Monte Fior: *Torrione* to the west, and the area between Monte Tondarecar and the nearby Monte Badenecche to the east. This time, the Austro-Hungarians succeeded and broke through the Italian lines, threatening the rear of the units deployed on Monte Fior and Monte Castelgomberto. A desperate counterattack with the remains of the Battaglione *Monte Berico*, no more than 200 Alpini, against the eastern jaw of the attack was a failure, as was a similar action carried out by the Battaglione *Val Dora* against the western jaw; thus, the line collapsed. The Battaglione *Monte Cervino* was annihilated while trying to fall back from the advanced position of the *Torrione* to Monte Fior after a useless attempt to open a way out with a desperate bayonet charge. The *Monte Pasubio*, deployed to the south, was instead surrounded at its positions, and crushed. The *Monte Saccarello* and the companies of the *Val Dora* that were not yet engaged, retained as reserve so far, were sent in to try to close the gap but were in turn surrounded by enemy forces that poured in from various directions, and they were wiped out. The situation was a bit better on Monte Badenecche, where the enemy had been stopped for the moment. However, a counterattack launched by the *Bassano*, which had been sent to the first line again with a company of the *Vicenza*, failed. Monte Badenecche, in danger

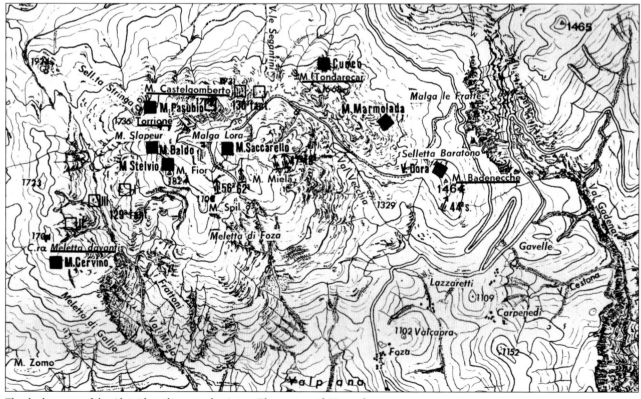

The deployment of the Alpini battalions on the Asiago Plateau in mid-November 1917

of being surrounded, was cleared. The Battaglione *Sette Comuni* did not withdraw in time and was surrounded; only a few Alpini managed to escape death or captivity. By the end of the day, Monte Tondarecar and Monte Fior were in enemy hands, and a few Alpini of the Battaglioni *Cuneo* and *Monte Marmolada*, who resisted bravely on Monte Castelgomberto, were completely surrounded and without support. During the night, some new units were sent to the plateau, among them the newly replenished Battaglioni *Monte Stelvio* and *Monte Baldo*, which were sent to the south of Monte Badenecche to reinforce the positions that were still manned by what remained of the Battaglioni *Vicenza*, *Bassano*, *Sette Comuni*, and *Monte Berico*. The hope was that these fresh units would manage to stop the advancing Austro-Hungarian troops and even counterattack to regain the lost positions. However, on December 5, the enemy was still on the attack; the Battaglioni *Cuneo* and *Monte Marmolada*, now reduced to a few hundred men, capitulated, and other positions that had so far resisted were wiped out.

On the other hand, these few hours of fighting in the area, although unsuccessful, allowed the Italian command to set up a new defensive line to the south. It was anchored on a new ridge of mountains, the last one before the plain: Sasso Rosso, Col d'Echele, and Col del Rosso. Every infantryman, *bersaglieri*, and alpino that was still available was deployed to these precarious positions, with full awareness that this would be a last stand before possible disaster. Here, the Battaglioni *Monte Stelvio* and *Monte Baldo*, and the few survivors of the *Vicenza*, *Bassano*, *Sette Comuni*, and *Monte Berico*, converged, and the momentum of the Austro-Hungarian attack, within a few kilometers of victory, died away. The enemy had spent all its reserves, and the heavy artillery had once more not kept pace with the infantry: access to the Veneto plain was still closed. A last effort was made between December 23 to 25, during what became known as the Christmas Battle; however, now the Italian lines were better prepared and garrisoned by fresh troops, the Battaglioni *Monte Stelvio* and *Val d'Adige* among them, and the offensive was a complete failure.

The Italian troops had proven impressively ready to fight and had shown a surprisingly high morale after days of retreat. They had managed to resist some of the best troops of the German army, at improvised positions, without shelter, and often even without eating or sleeping. After being on the brink of defeat, the Italian army had passed through the crisis and laid the foundations of the victory obtained in the following year.

A column of Alpini marching toward Monte Castelgomberto. *Fondazione Museo Storico del Trentino Archivio Fotografico*

The silhouette of the Melette and of Monte Grappa seen from the Austro-Hungarian positions on Monte Ortigara. *Fondazione Museo Storico del Trentino Archivio Fotografico*

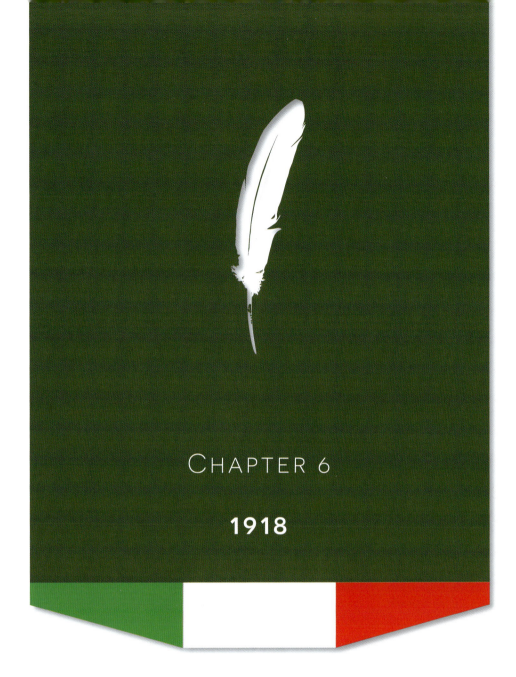

CHAPTER 6

1918

The year 1918 is commonly known for the Second Battle of the Piave River, or Battle of the Solstice, and overall for the Battle of Vittorio Veneto, the battle that gave Italy its victory over Austria-Hungary. Although the first six months of the year were relatively quiet, with both parties busy consolidating their positions, some important battles did indeed take place that involved the Alpini as well.

As a result of the defeat at Caporetto and the deep retreat to the Piave River, the supreme commander General Cadorna was removed from his office and replaced by General Armando Diaz,[1] who began a major reorganization of the army immediately after the appointment from both the material and the moral point of view, forging the military instrument that would gain victory for the Italians. On the other side of the front, the Imperial-Royal army was encountering ever-growing difficulties in its logistic system, and the cohesion among its several ethnicities was rapidly declining. However, in those months it found the energy to attempt a final effort.

Concerning the Alpini in particular, sadly, several battalions were disbanded due to the terrific losses they had suffered during autumn and winter 1917–18. In fact, in November 1917, seventeen battalions were disbanded: *Ceva, Val d'Arroscia, Val Ellero, Monte Mercantour, Val Stura, Monte Argentera, Monviso, Bicocca, Val Chisone, Monte Albergian, Monte Assietta, Val Leogra, Belluno, Gemona, Val Fella, Monte Canin,* and *Monte Nero*. In December,

General Armando Diaz, who replaced General Luigi Cadorna as supreme commander of the Italian army in November 1917

The reorganization of the army, after suffering the loss of both men and equipment, required much money. This poster invites the citizens to subscribe to the *Prestito Nazionale* (the national loan) to give the soldiers, here represented by an alpino, the resources necessary to cut the fingers of the greedy enemy.

A Decauville narrow-gauge train, used extensively during the war to transport equipment and supplies, since they were very easy to put in place and maintain. *Museo Nazionale Storico degli Alpini*

the battalions *Val Dora*, *Monte Marmolada*, and *Monte Saccarello*, of which remained, however, the 107th Company, followed suit. After the blocking battle, *Val Pellice*, *Val Piave*, *Val Varaita*, *Courmayeur*, *Val Tagliamento*, *Val Natisone*, and *Monte Matajur* were disbanded as well. At the end of this reorganization, fifty-eight battalions remained and were fully replenished; the *Monte Saccarello* would be re-formed in August.

In the spring of 1918, after similar experiences with infantry and *bersaglieri* units over the previous year, three special Alpine assault units were formed, called *Fiamme Verdi* (green flames) because of their collar insignia and whose members were called *arditi* (bold, daring): the III Reparto d'Assalto, who fought on the Adamello massif and then on the Grappa massif; the XXIX Reparto d'Assalto, who were active in the Vallagarina; and the LII Reparto d'Assalto, who were stationed on the Asiago Plateau.

The mountain artillery disbanded several batteries as well, but the most important measure was the suppression of the previously mentioned specialty of mule pack artillery that was finally absorbed into the mountain artillery, fulfilling a process that was already on course. The 70 mm gun was definitively abandoned in favor of the 65/17 gun, which was now produced in enough quantity to satisfy the needs of the specialty, and the allocation of mules was readjusted, resulting in a strengthened mountain artillery component.

THE ALPINI STRIKE BACK!

A few weeks after the Christmas Battle, it was the *Regio Esercito*'s turn to mount an offensive on the Asiago Plateau; it was certainly not a major, far-reaching offensive, which was not yet within the capabilities of the Italian army, but a limited action in that specific stretch of the front, with the scope of providing more depth and space of maneuver to a line that had been in great danger in December. The plan was to retake the ridge of relatively low mountains immediately to the north of the Italian positions from the Austro-Hungarians: Monte Valbella, Col del Rosso, and Col d'Echele, which had been lost during the last of the fighting in December. The action was known by the name "*Battaglia dei Tre Monti*" (battle of the Three Mounts), and the units assigned to it were the XX and XXII Army Corps. The latter had within its subordinate units the Fifty-Second Division, formed entirely from Alpine battalions and mountain artillery batteries, which were entrusted with the extreme right of the front of attack, including the Col d'Echele and a series of lower heights immediately east of it. The above-mentioned division had already included several Alpine battalions in the past, especially during the Second Ortigara Battle, but its organization chart became stable from this moment on. Thus, this can officially be considered the first real Alpine troops division. It would be formed by the following units until the end of the war:

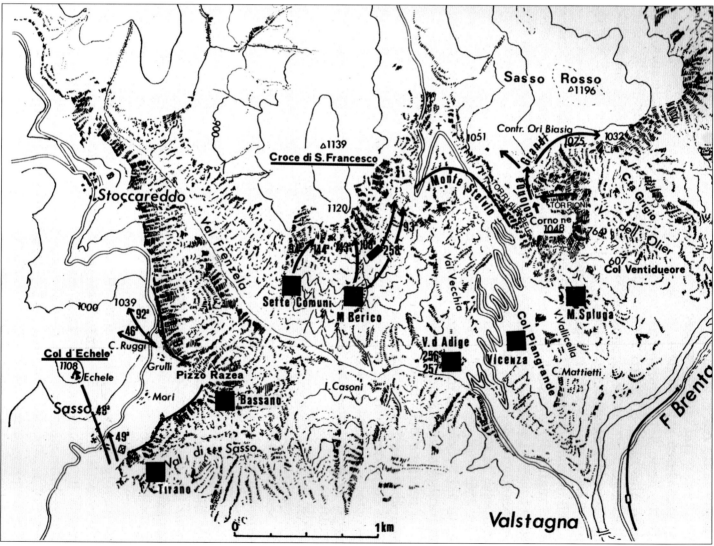

The operations during the Battaglia dei Tre Monti, in January 1918

I Raggruppamento Alpini, consisting of:
1° Gruppo Alpini, with the Battaglioni *Morbegno, Tirano, Monte Stelvio,* and the XXX Gruppo of mountain artillery
9° Gruppo Alpini, with the Battaglioni *Verona, Bassano, Monte Baldo, Sette Comuni,* and the LIII Gruppo of mountain artillery

II Raggruppamento Alpini, consisting of:
5° Gruppo Alpini, with the Battaglioni *Vestone, Valtellina, Monte Spluga,* and the LVII Gruppo of mountain artillery
10° Gruppo Alpini, with the Battaglioni *Vicenza, Val d'Adige, Monte Berico,* and the XXXII Gruppo of mountain artillery
10° Raggruppamento of mountain artillery

The offensive started on January 27, 1918, with a heavy and accurate artillery preparation that lasted many hours, concentrating, however, on a stretch of the front different from the one chosen for the main infantry attack, to deceive the enemy. During the following night, the Battaglioni *Sette Comuni* and *Monte Berico* tried a surprise assault against the enemy positions on Monte Croce S. Francesco; they climbed an 80-meter slope with ropes and managed to capture the height, which they were not however able to maintain, faced with a violent artillery reaction that forced them to retreat to their own line. On the twenty-eighth, after a new artillery bombardment, the Alpini launched the main attack against their target of Col d'Echele. At the beginning progress was limited, because the reaction of the Austro-Hungarians was very effective and the barbed wire lines were in many points still intact, but later during the day the Battaglioni *Tirano* and *Monte Baldo* were able to penetrate the enemy defenses, take the mountain and capture numerous prisoners. Another action was mounted to conquer the Monte Cornone, a height little more than 1,000 meters (3,280 feet) above MSL, a sort of wedge in the Italian line, carried on by a small party of expert climbers chosen among the Alpini of the Battaglione *Monte Stelvio.* On the afternoon of January 28, they climbed the mountain and took the enemy garrison by surprise, managing to extend the conquest to some surrounding heights as well, supported by units of the Battaglione *Val d'Adige.* Meanwhile, infantry units conquered the other mountains that were the target of this small-scale offensive. On the twenty-ninth, the Austro-Hungarians tried to counterattack, but they were pushed back everywhere. The return of the *Regio Esercito* to the offensive had been an undoubted success.

To the extreme west of the front as well, on the Adamello massif, the Alpini mounted a new offensive to conquer a ridge of peaks that was still in enemy hands. This offensive, known as the *Battaglia Bianca* (the White Battle), with reference to the terrain covered in snow and ice, was entrusted to the Battaglioni *Monte Mandrone, Monte Cavento, Edolo, Monte Granero, Pallanza, Monte Rosa, Val Brenta,* and *Tolmezzo,* which had formed one special assault platoon each and were supported by the IV, XXXI, XLV, XLVII, XI, and XII Gruppi of mountain artillery, plus the Eleventh and Forty-Seventh Batteries, an impressive number of pieces of artillery in comparison with

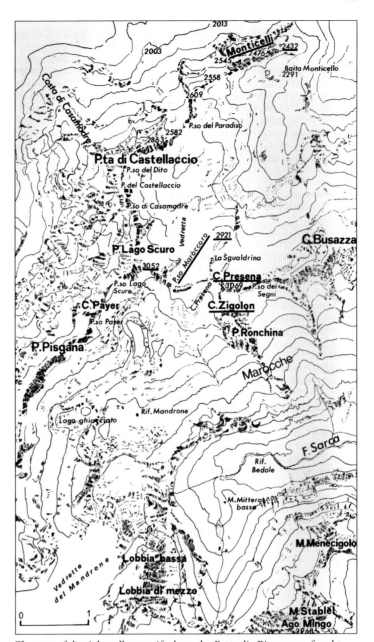

The area of the Adamello massif where the Battaglia Bianca was fought

the actions carried out in the previous years. The first aim of the offensive was the conquest of the ridge whose main peaks were, from north to south, Hill 2,921, 2,921 meters (9,583) above MSL; Monte Zigolon, 3,048 meters (10,000 feet) above MSL; Cima Presena, 3,069 meters (10,065 feet) above MSL; Hill 3,052, 3,052 meters (10,013 feet) above MSL, which stood a bit isolated to the west; and the Maroccaro Pass. Once this action was completed successfully, the attackers would move north against the Monticelli Ridge, which had already been attacked several times without success in the past three years. As it is easy to imagine, the action had all the characteristics of a real enterprise, both because of the extremely difficult terrain and climate and because the mountains were heavily manned with numerous machine guns in caves that covered all the accesses, and so were able to protect each other with crossfire.

The attack was launched in the morning of May 24, with artillery preparation and air bombardment as well. Then, at 11:30 a.m., the assault platoons of the Battaglioni *Edolo* and *Monte Mandrone* moved against Hill 3,052 while those of the Battaglione *Monte Cavento* assaulted Monte Zigolon and those of the Battaglioni *Val Baltea* and *Pallanza* assaulted Cima Presena. The first two actions succeeded quickly because the

Injured Alpini are transferred to the valley below by cableway. *Museo Nazionale Storico degli Alpini*

Alpini of the Battaglione *Monte Mandrone* ascend the slopes of a peak in the Adamello. Massif *Museo Nazionale Storico degli Alpini*

A unit of Alpini skiers. *Museo Nazionale Storico degli Alpini*

The top of Monte Zigolon shelled by Italian mountain artillery. *Museo Nazionale Storico degli Alpini*

La guerra sui ghiacciai. Gli alpini con la loro bandiera vittoriosa raggiungono Cima del Zigolon.

The conquest of Monte Zigolon by the Alpini of the Battaglione *Monte Cavento* celebrated on the *Domenica del Corriere* of June 9, 1918

Alpini managed to climb the steep slopes of the mountains and reach the top, where they overwhelmed the defenders; the latter, instead, proved more problematic since Cima Presena was effectively protected by the fire coming from Hill 2,921, and all attempts to climb it failed. It was not until the evening, when the Battaglione *Monte Cavento* moved in to join the attack, that Cima Presena was taken. The following day, the battaglioni *Monte Cavento* and *Monte Mandrone* assaulted Hill 2,921, while the Battaglione *Edolo* and the special assault platoons of the *Val d'Intelvi* and *Monte Granero* moved against the Monticelli, with the difficult task to eliminate, one by one, the numerous strongholds that the Austro-Hungarians had dug there since 1915. Hill 2,921 fell on May 25, while the Monticelli resisted stubbornly until the twenty-seventh, when almost the whole ridge was conquered, apart from the very last peak, located at 2,432 meters (7,979 feet) above MSL, which remained in enemy hands. The White Battle had come to its end and, all in all, it had been another important success for the *Regio Esercito* and for the Alpini in particular, who had proven their extreme ability in the difficult conditions of mountain warfare once more.

THE LAST AUSTRO-HUNGARIAN COUNTERMOVES

In June 1918, the Austro-Hungarian High Command thought it was time to try to retake the initiative on the southern front and planned a new offensive along the stretch of the front that went from the Asiago Plateau to the course of the Piave River, following a scheme that was not very original indeed. In fact, the Imperial-Royal army could count on substantial reinforcements coming from the eastern front, which was now pacified after the conclusion of the peace at Brest-Litovsk in March with the new Soviet Russia, which had succeeded in dethroning the czar and putting an end to a very unpopular war. Similarly, a great number of German divisions were moving to the western front.

The great offensive, known as the "Second Battle of the Piave River" or the "Battle of the Solstice," represented a double effort led by the Austro-Hungarian army, the first from the southern Trentino toward the plain in the direction of Vicenza, a sort of replay of the spring offensive and the First Battle of the Piave River; and the second, along the Piave River itself. It started on June 15 and did not see Alpine units directly involved, since the Fifty-Second Division was in reserve. Although many batteries of mountain artillery were involved on the Asiago Plateau, on the Grappa massif and even along the Piave River, a full description of the offensive would be beyond the scope of this book. It is enough to say that it seemed clear from the very beginning that the Italian lines would not be broken. The attacks on the Asiago Plateau and on the Grappa massif did not achieve any result, and from the late afternoon of the fifteenth, the Italians counterattacked effectively. The Austro-Hungarians obtained some degree of success along the Piave River during the first three days, without giving any impression that they would be able break through. But on the nineteenth, the *Regio Esercito* counterattacked, restoring the situation. The fighting continued until June 23 but was only a waste of men and material.

THE *LAWINE EXPEDITION*

The abovementioned offensive along the Piave River was to be preceded by an action launched in the northern area of the Adamello massif and across the Tonale Pass, called the *Lawine Expedition* (Avalanche Expedition). The main idea was to break through the pass and penetrate Lombardy,

taking the Italians by surprise, with the city of Milan as the final, and indeed farthest-reaching, target. At worst, this offensive would cause the transfer of Italian troops to this area, removing them from the Piave line. On June 12, the day of the attack, the whole area was covered by heavy fog and rain was pouring down; therefore, the artillery bombardment was suspended several times due to the extremely poor visibility. Notwithstanding this bad start, on the thirteenth, the Austro-Hungarian infantry moved to attack the pass and the heights to the north of it, Cima Cady; and to the south, the much-contended Monticelli. The attacks on the mountains obtained some small success since some positions on Cima Cady fell, as did some of the strongholds of the Monticelli, which had recently been lost to the Italians. In the valley below, on the contrary, the Battaglione *Monte Rosa* did not yield an inch, threatening the loss of the assailants's morale. By the end of the morning, the offensive could be considered to be a failure, and the Alpini counterattacked everywhere to retake the few positions lost. On the Cima Cady, units of the Battaglioni *Monte Clapier* and *Valcamonica* threw the Austro-Hungarians back to their lines while the Alpini of the *Monte Rosa* reconquered all of the lost strongholds on the Monticelli except for one.

Emperor Karl I inspects his soldiers not far from the Tonale Pass just before the *Lawine Expedition*. *Museo Nazionale Storico degli Alpini*

IN ACTION AGAIN ON THE ADAMELLO MASSIF

Other small-scale actions were led by both parties on the Adamello massif while the Battle of the Solstice raged on the plain.

On June 15, the Austro-Hungarians carried out a surprise assault on the Corno di Cavento, lost to the Italians the previous year. The peak was manned by a unit of the Battaglione *Val Baltea*, which was overwhelmed by an assault party that emerged suddenly near the stronghold from a tunnel excavated across the glacier that divided the Italian line from the Austro-Hungarian line. The action had been very skillful and called for an immediate response from the Alpini, which was planned for July 18. Two companies of the *Val Baltea* itself, with the assault platoons of the Battaglione *Val Baltea*, *Monte Mandrone*, and *Val d'Intelvi*, moved from the Cavento Pass, and at noon, the top of the Corno di Cavento had been reconquered. The action had been supported once more by the fire of the 149 mm gun Ippopotamo, which fired effectively from Cresta della Croce. This remarkable success convinced the local Italian command to plan a small-scale offensive to snatch the last peaks of the massif from the enemy, giving the Alpini the opportunity to descend to the valleys below. A series of attacks had to be launched contemporaneously on August 6, a date that was then postponed to August 13 due to the abundant snowfall.

As mentioned, the Italians had already conquered the ridge of the Lobbia Alta, Lobbia Bassa, and the Crozzon di Lares in 1916 and had advanced to the Crozzon di Fargorida. The Austro-Hungarians still kept Monte Stablel, 1,849 meters (6,037 feet) above MSL, and Monte Menecingolo, 2,686 meters (8,812 feet) above MSL, east of the Lobbie and north of the Crozzon di Fargorida. The attack was entrusted to the assault platoons of the Battaglioni *Monte Mandrone*, *Val d'Intelvi*, *Edolo*, and *Val Baltea*. On the appointed day, the Alpini moved against their objectives, but this time the reaction of the enemy was very effective, and the assailants were forced back after a promising beginning.

To the north, a similar assault was planned against the Marocche, the last Austro-Hungarian stronghold on the ridge of Cima Presena-Zigolon, which had been conquered by the Italians two months earlier. Units of the Battaglioni *Monte Tonale* and *Val d'Intelvi* moved south from the Zigolon and, notwithstanding the difficulties of the terrain and the active enemy reaction, managed to overwhelm the defenders during the day and the following night.

A sentry on the Corno di Cavento wearing a heavy fur coat. *Museo Nazionale Storico degli Alpini*

Across the Tonale Pass, the Italian command was strongly decided to get rid of the last enemy strongholds on the Monticelli once and for all and, at the same time, to extend their hold on the north side of the pass from Cima Cady to Monte Eastern Tonale. This latter peak was attacked with a pincer movement by the Battaglione *Monte Clapier,* moving from the south and by the *Pinerolo,* advancing from the north, with the close support of the IV and XXXI Gruppo of mountain artillery. The action did not make much progress, due to strong enemy reaction, and was soon suspended to avoid casualties not necessary in an action that was considered not to be decisive for the outcome of the war. This caused the failure of the attack on the Monticelli, which was on the south side of the Tonale Pass, where, on the other hand, the Battaglione *Tonale* had not advanced much along the ridge. Better results had been obtained by the *Monte Rosa,* climbing up from the pass. But without the support of the other units, it was forced to retreat.

After a series of successes on the Adamello massif, the Alpini had registered a setback this time.

THE BATTLE OF VITTORIO VENETO: THE *REGIO ESERCITO* FORCES THE PIAVE RIVER

After the battles fought in late spring and summer, the operational capacity of the Austro-Hungarian army started to decline dramatically, and the crisis that gripped the empire extended to its armed forces. The long-lasting naval blockade imposed by the entente was irremediably affecting the possibility of supplying its factories with raw materials and, consequently, of producing the goods necessary to continue the war. For the units on the forefront, the Battle of the Solstice had been a sort of turning point: the last hope of victory having faded, the willingness to go on fighting was lacking more and more. In many areas of the empire, the population, deprived of everything, was revolting against the state, and the soldiers, who were aware of the situation, desired to go back home. In other words, the empire was rapidly disintegrating. In Germany, the situation was no better: the offensives launched in the spring by the Imperial army had been successful in the beginning, but had again not been a decisive resolution; the German population was exhausted, as well.

On the Italian front, the *Regio Esercito* did not plan any actions in summer or autumn although the allies of the entente and the Italian government itself made great pressure for an offensive. In fact, Supreme Command General Diaz was not willing to take any risks and preferred to go on with his work of reorganizing and strengthening the army, avoiding new, bloody battles of attrition against an enemy that was still deployed on strongly manned positions, convinced as he was that a failure would undermine the newly restored Italian morale and, contrary to his intent, boost the low morale of the Austro-Hungarians. On the other hand, it was common opinion that the war would continue well into the year 1919; therefore, the final clash could wait until the following spring now that time favored the entente.

However, at the beginning of autumn, the military situation evolved more rapidly than expected, with the victorious conclusion of the campaign in Macedonia, where the Bulgarian army mutinied, forcing the Bulgarian government to bid for an armistice, and with the positive progress of the offensive on the western front, where the Germans were repeatedly retreating. The Italian supreme command saw the opportunity to engage the enemy in a decisive battle in this moment and executed the plans that had been prepared during the summer, which included the forcing of the Piave River to be followed by an offensive on the Grappa massif. The execution of the plans was fixed for October 18, but due to the bad weather conditions that had also swelled the flow of the Piave River, the date was postponed, and it was also decided to attack the Grappa first and then force the river.

The area where the Italian army launched its final offensive on October 24, 1918

Italian assault units advancing on the Grappa massif

In September, a new Alpini division was formed for the oncoming offensive, the Eightieth, which grouped twelve battalions and many groups of mountain artillery. The organization chart was the following:

VIII Raggruppamento Alpini, consisting of
6° Gruppo Alpini, with the Battaglioni *Aosta*, *Monte Levanna*, *Val Toce*, and the III Gruppo of mountain artillery
13° Gruppo Alpini, with the Battaglioni *Pieve di Cadore*, *Val Cismon*, *Monte Antelao*, and the XXV Gruppo of mountain artillery
IX Raggruppamento Alpini, consisting of:
17° Gruppo Alpini, with the Battaglioni *Exilles*, *Monte Suello*, *Monte Pelmo*, and the XV Gruppo of mountain artillery
20° Gruppo Alpini, with the Battaglioni *Cividale*, *Monte Saccarello*, *Monte Cervino*, and the XLVIII Gruppo of mountain artillery
1° Raggruppamento of mountain artillery

The division was assigned to the XXX Army Corps, entrusted with a stretch of the Grappa front and the mission to attack Monte Valderoa and the Solaroli Ridge, but at first it was put to the reserve.

The battle started on October 24 with the assault of the infantry brigades *Aosta* and *Lombardia*, which were successful on the Valderoa but not in managing to set foot on the Solaroli, which was still strongly defended. The Alpini were called in on the following day, when the Battaglioni *Val Cismon*, *Monte*

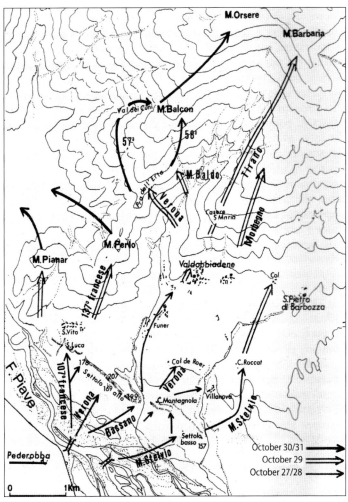

The progresses of the Alpini of the Fifty-Second Division over the Piave River

Pontoon bridges built by Italian engineers over the Piave River, crossed by Italian units. *Museo Nazionale Storico degli Alpini*

The Battaglione *Monte Antelao* reaches the town of Predazzo, in the Fiemme Valley, eastern Trentino, and is welcomed by the population, which displays the Italian flag. *Museo Nazionale Storico degli Alpini*

Antelao, and *Monte Saccarello* supported the infantrymen against the Solaroli Ridge, but with scarce results. The artillery had not been able to break the barbed wire lines, and the attackers were easily targeted by the enemy machine guns. Instead, the *Monte Levanna*, along with a company of the *Aosta*, was sent to Monte Valderoa, where the Austro-Hungarians were not resigned to defeat and were counterattacking with every ounce of their energy. The battalion was almost annihilated during the fighting, as had happened to the *Monte Rosa* between the twenty-fifth and the twenty-sixth, when the Austro-Hungarians managed to retake the Valderoa, ousting the few survivors from the battalion. An immediate counterattack was mounted with the Battaglione *Pieve di Cadore*, units of the *Val Toce,* and the remnants of the *Monte Rosa* but failed due to heavy artillery fire that hindered the movements of the Alpini. Another counterattack organized the following day, again by the Battaglioni *Pieve di Cadore* and *Val Toce*, was unsuccessful as well. Meanwhile, on October 26, the attacks by the *Monte Saccarello*, *Cividale*, and *Val Toce* continued against the Solaroli and were again driven off with heavy casualties by the defenders, who were determined to maintain their positions no matter what happened in other parts of the front.

Meanwhile, during the night between October 26 and 27, the offensive along the Piave River started as well, with the battalions of the Fifty-Second Alpine Division entrusted with the forcing of the river in the area of the town of Pederobba, on the middle course of the river, in cooperation with a French division. The river was crossed between 1:00 a.m. and 6:00 a.m. by a French regiment and the Battaglioni *Bassano* and *Verona*, but then the pontoon bridge suffered a direct artillery hit and blew up with a great number of Alpini on it. Attempts to repair it were unsuccessful because the area was under heavy fire; thus, the units on the eastern bank remained cut off from supplies and reinforcements throughout the day of October 27. However, although targeted by artillery and machine guns, French infantrymen and Alpini managed to dig in, even seizing some enemy strongholds, and resisted every counterattack launched that day. During the night the pontoon bridge was repaired, allowing another French regiment and the Battaglione *Monte Stelvio* to cross the river, but the following morning it was again hit by accurate Austro-Hungarian artillery fire. However, now enough troops were on the other side; thus, the *Verona* and the *Monte Stelvio* were able to mount an attack and, with a brief fight, overwhelm the enemy stronghold that had prevented all progress so far. From that moment on, the troops moved forward steadily, while the resistance put up by the Austro-Hungarians weakened more and more. During the night of October 30, the enemy troops that still resisted on the Grappa massif were forced to retreat northward to avoid being outflanked and surrounded by the advancing Italians, who were pursued by the Alpini of the Eightieth Division.

Over the following few days, the front moved everywhere, and Italian columns pushed forward, often overcoming the columns of Austro-Hungarians that retreated hastily northward and eastward, having abandoned their weapons and equipment. On November 3, the light cavalrymen of the Alessandria Regiment entered the town of Trento, followed by the Alpini, who, however, continued their march some 30 kilometers more.

Negotiations for an armistice were already in progress at Villa Giusti, in Padua, since the first of November, but only on the third did the parties sign the document, with the ceasefire fixed for 3:00 p.m. on November 4.

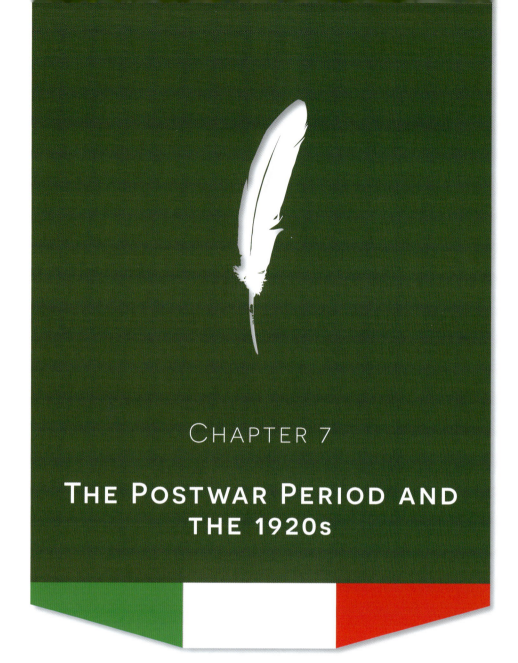

CHAPTER 7

THE POSTWAR PERIOD AND THE 1920s

THE DEMOBILIZATION AND ORGANIZATIONAL EVOLUTION

At the end of the First World War, the Italian army had over three million men under arms, ranging from the class of 1874 to the class of 1900. Among the mobilized units, there were sixty-one Alpine troops battalions and sixty-three battalions of mountain artillery. The demobilization started almost immediately, the older classes first, but gradually, both to ensure that the newly conquered areas were adequately manned as well as to reinsert these men slowly and methodically into civilian life. By January 1919 the classes between 1874 and 1879 were dismissed, followed during the year by the classes up to 1896, while the younger men had to wait until the beginning of 1920. Meanwhile, many units were progressively disbanded, thus returning to the prewar situation of twenty-six Alpine battalions grouped in eight regiments, and nine groups of mountain artillery battalions grouped in three regiments. During the following years, the Alpini were involved in the several reorganizations that affected the *Regio Esercito* over relatively few years, aimed at finding the correct balance between a large army and little money.

The first peacetime organization plan was enacted in 1919[1] by the ministry of war General Alberico Abricci, who established, among other provisions, that the Alpini regiments be grouped in four brigades. It was replaced very soon by the organization introduced in 1920[2] by the new minister Ivanoe Bonomi, the first civilian to be appointed to that office. The plan included three Alpine divisions, consisting of three regiments and one mountain artillery regiment each, anticipating to a certain extent what would be accomplished about a decade later. In 1923,[3] General Diaz being the minister of war, a further reorganization abolished the divisions, replacing them with the *Raggruppamenti* Alpini, a situation that was reminiscent of the war years. Finally, in 1926,[4] an organizational structure was enacted that was destined to remain valid until the mid-1930s, ascribed to Benito Mussolini himself, at the time minister of war as well as prime minister, although planned by his undersecretary, Ugo Cavallero, a personality we will encounter again during the Second World War at the apex of the *Regio Esercito*. This reform, renowned because the *Regio Esercito* abandoned the four-regiment division in favor of the three-regiment division, with respect to its impact on the Alpini, was organized to be a total of three brigades, consisting of three regiments each, with a total of twenty-seven battalions, and three mountain artillery regiments, consisting of three artillery battalions each, with a total of twenty-seven batteries.

Beginning with its enactment, the organization chart was as follows:

I Brigata alpina, formed by

1° Reggimento Alpini, with Headquarters in Mondovì, consisting of the Battaglioni *Ceva*, *Pieve di Teco*, and *Mondovì*

2° Reggimento Alpini, with Headquarters in Cuneo, consisting of the Battaglioni *Borgo San Dalmazzo*, *Dromero*, and *Saluzzo*

3° Reggimento Alpini, with Headquarters in Turin, consisting of the Battaglioni *Pinerolo*, *Fenestrelle*, *Exilles*, and *Susa*

4° Reggimento Alpini, with Headquarters in Ivrea, consisting of the Battaglioni *Ivrea*, *Aosta*, and *Intra*

1° Reggimento of mountain artillery, with Headquarters

Mountain artillerymen of the 1° Reggimento in 1919. *Museo Nazionale Storico degli Alpini*

in Turin, on the Gruppi *Susa*, *Aosta*, *Pinerolo*, and *Mondovì*

II Brigata Alpina, formed by

5° Reggimento Alpini, with Headquarters in Milan, consisting of the Battaglioni *Morbegno* and *Tirano*

6° Reggimento Alpini, with Headquarters in Brixen, consisting of the Battaglioni *Edolo*, *Vestone*, *Verona*, and *Trento*

7° Reggimento Alpini, with Headquarters in Belluno, consisting of the Battaglioni *Feltre*, *Pieve di Cadore*, and *Belluno*

2° Reggimento of mountain artillery, with Headquarters in Bergamo, consisting of the Gruppi *Vicenza*, *Belluno*, and *Bergamo*

III Brigata alpine, formed by:

8° Reggimento Alpini, with Headquarters in Tolmezzo, consisting of the Battaglioni *Tolmezzo*, *Verona*, and *Cividale*

9° Reggimento Alpini, with Headquarters in Gorizia, consisting of the Battaglioni *Vicenza* and *Bassano*

3° Reggimento of mountain artillery, consisting of the Gruppi *Conegliano* and *Udine*

Aside from the organization of the Alpine specialty within the *Regio Esercito*, the peacetime battalions lost most of the special units that had been attached to them earlier to increase their firepower. The special assault platoons, called *arditi,* were abolished in 1919, as was the platoon armed with the Stokes trench mortars, the flamethrower platoon, and the platoon armed with the 37 mm trench gun; the machine gun companies assigned to each battalion were also eliminated, replaced by a single platoon. Thus, the resulting battalion was now formed by three rifle companies, each consisting of three rifle platoons and a machine gun platoon with two weapons.

The mountain artillery from 1920, on the other hand, replaced its 65/17 gun with the Austro-Hungarian 7.5 cm Gebirgskanone M15 Skoda howitzer, obtained as war booty and war reparation. It was renamed the "73/13" howitzer by the Italians, and was much better suited for mountain warfare and was able to fire from defiladed positions, unlike the 65/17; it would remain the standard piece of Italian mountain artillery until the end of the 1950s.

DEPLOYMENT DURING THE 1920S

The end of the Great War did not bring with it the long-sought peace throughout the world; quite to the contrary, in the early 1920s there were several areas that experienced tension, inducing many governments, the Italian government among them, to deploy troops that found themselves in combat situations from time to time.

MOUNTAIN ARTILLERY IN SIBERIA

The war had not yet even ended when, in July 1918, a section of mountain artillery consisting of two pieces left Naples with a unit of *Reali Carabinieri* and a unit of about fifty infantrymen headed to Siberia, where the clash between the revolutionary army, supported by Germany, and the czarist army, supported by the entente, was raging. Once they had landed in Tientsin, in China, these personnel were joined by about a thousand Italian-speaking Austro-Hungarian prisoners of war in order to form an infantry battalion. The unit was then transferred by railroad to the town of Krasnoyarsk, in central Siberia,

View of the town of Krasnoyarsk at the time of the Italian deployment in the area. *Museo Nazionale Storico degli Alpini*

where it arrived on November 24, by which time the war in Europe had ended a couple of weeks before. Between May and June 1919, the battalion was engaged in a series of operations aimed at the conquest of the town of Narva, on the Mana River, a tributary of the Yenisej River, and on the ejection of the Red Army from the area. By June 15, the Italian unit, with the mountain artillery section often at the forefront, had engaged in several combat actions and had performed its duty very well. The artillerymen went back to Krasnoyarsk, where they arrived on June 20, and in August the entire Italian contingent was sent back to Tientsin to be repatriated. The last soldiers arrived in Naples at the beginning of April 1920.

THE ATTEMPT TO RECONQUER LIBYA

When the Great War ended, one of the first concerns of the Italian government was to send a large expeditionary corps to Libya to reaffirm Italian rule. During the European conflict, the Italian presence in the colony had been reduced to a few towns along the seacoast due to the lack of interest of the supreme command in this decentralized front, which had been left almost devoid of troops, and due to the aid provided to the Arab insurgents by Turkey and Germany. However, between January and March 1919, three divisions were sent to Libya that had no mountain troops within their ranks. But they were supported by five mountain artillery battalions, consisting of three batteries each, which had proved themselves very useful in that operational theater during the recent Italo-Turkish war. In Libya, they also found the six mountain artillery batteries—two of which were now manned by Libyan artillerymen—that had remained deployed in Libya since 1914. The expeditionary force was formed from:

Thirty-Eighth Division, with XIV, XXXVII and XLIV Gruppo of mountain artillery
Eighty-First Division, with XLIII Gruppo, the Libyan indigenous batteries, and two of the Italian batteries already deployed in Libya
First Assault Division, with IX and XXIX Gruppo[5]

However, these forces did not see any combat since negotiations started immediately with the Libyan notables that led, in May 1919, to the conclusion of a peace agreement that was followed in June by the enactment of a specific Libyan statute, establishing a local parliament for both Tripolitania and Cyrenaica and a sort of Italian citizenship for the Libyans. Although both acts turned out to be rather ephemeral, and the revolt would soon resume, the three divisions were sent back to Italy, while six mountain artillery batteries remained in Libya.

ALPINI IN ALBANIA

Much more challenging was the duty performed by Alpini and mountain artillerymen in Albania between 1919 and 1920. The port of Valona, in the south of the country, had been garrisoned by Italian troops since 1914, and the following year, a whole army corps had landed on the other side of the Adriatic

Sea to occupy the southern part of Albania and prevent its conquest by the Austro-Hungarians. In 1918, the Italian occupation was extended to the whole country. The Italian government had unilaterally proclaimed its protectorate over the recently independent Albania;[6] thus, it tried to obtain the confirmation of the Italian trusteeship during the peace conference and, furthermore, the annexation of the port of Valona. These maneuvers were a source of great insult in the eyes of the Albanians, who—facing the risk of losing their independence and having their national territory curtailed—revolted against the Italians.

In 1919, only two infantry divisions remained in Albania, supported by seventeen batteries of mountain artillery; but in August, six Alpini battalions were sent there, grouped in two *Gruppi* Alpini: the 2° Gruppo, with the Battaglioni *Dronero*, *Saluzzo*, *Intra*, and the 2227th Machine Gun Company; the 14° Gruppo, with the Battaglioni *Borgo San Dalmazzo*, *Fenestrelle*, *Feltre*, and the 1740th Machine Gun Company. All these units, however, were understaffed and periodically saw personnel reduced by the dismissal of the older classes, a situation that continued steadily throughout the assignment. Furthermore, they could not even count on the arrival of young replacements from Italy because public opinion in Italy was strongly against this adventure. Some units even mutinied when they feared that they would be sent to Albania, and the government was not

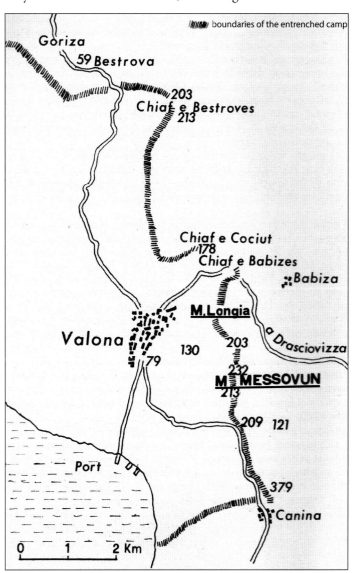

The stronghold of Valona in 1919

strong enough to impose its will. In such a situation, although it became more and more difficult every day to oppose the bands of armed Albanian men, the Italian soldiers did not falter. The garrisons stationed in the interior were withdrawn progressively in order to concentrate the forces in a few places along the coast. Then, in 1920, the Italian contingent was concentrated in Valona, and part of it was definitively repatriated. What remained was the Thirty-Sixth Infantry Division with the 2° Gruppo Alpini as reinforcement. Unfortunately, the whole Gruppo, which was formed by three battalions on paper, could really count only on no more than 600 Alpini. By now, the Albanians felt that victory was at hand and attacked Valona in force from June on. At the beginning of June, an attack was partially successful because some advanced strongholds were abandoned; however, on June 11, the assault against the main line of defense of Valona was bloodily repelled. The Alpini manned Mount Longia and Mount Messovun, more hills than real mountains, being about 200 meters (656 feet) above MSL; these positions were attacked with particular fury by the Albanians because they were very close to the center of the town, and their fall would entail the rapid fall of the whole line. The Alpini of the Battaglioni *Intra* and *Dronero*, supported by the guns of the XXI and L Gruppo, fought doggedly and were even able to counterattack. The assailants took a couple of weeks of pause to reorganize, counting on the negotiations that were ongoing between Italy and Albania; furthermore, they were perfectly aware that time worked in their favor and against the Italians.

On June 24, however, they resumed the offensive, with fresh forces that had grown to 15,000 men, against an entrenched camp that now numbered no more than 1,500 soldiers. Once again, the maximum effort was directed against the line between Mount Longia and Mount Messovun, where the Albanians managed to overwhelm a small party of Alpini of the Battaglione *Dronero* that manned the saddle between the two hills and advanced a few hundred meters toward the suburbs of Valona. There, they were pinned down by the accurate fire of the mountain artillery deployed in the strongholds and of the guns of the cruiser *S. Marco* docked in the port. This gained enough time for the Alpini of the *Dronero* and *Saluzzo*, with the assault troops of the *IX Reparto d'assalto* (IX assault unit), to mount a counterattack that restored the situation, causing the assailants hundreds of casualties. This was the last action of this undeclared war because, at the beginning of August, Italy and Albania reached an agreement, and the Italian troops were withdrawn from Valona but maintained a garrison on the island of Sazan, which was strategically placed between the Strait of Otranto and the entrance to the Bay of Valona.

THE DISPUTE OVER THE TOWN OF FIUME

Over the fifteen months between 1919 and 1921, an event took place in the town of Fiume, which is today's Rijeka in

The famous poet and writer Gabriele D'Annunzio eats a ration from a mess tin with some soldiers, a few Alpini among them, at Fiume.

Croatia. Although, according to the Treaty of London, the town should have been assigned to Italy like most parts of Dalmatia, the new Kingdom of Serbs, Croats, and Slovenes—the future Yugoslavia—disputed this assignment and reclaimed the port as part of its national territory. After months of inconclusive international negotiations that rendered the town ungovernable, on September 12, 1919, some hundreds of volunteers, led by the renowned Italian poet and writer Gabriele D'Annunzio, marched on the town and occupied it. The reaction of the Italian government was to establish a military blockade around it. This unusual situation dragged on several months until, in November 1920, Italy signed the Treaty of Rapallo with neighboring Yugoslavia, so it was established that Fiume would become a free state; then, it decided to remove D'Annunzio's volunteers from the town by force. On both sides of the barricades, there were units formed by Alpini: two companies of the Battaglione *Morbegno* had joined the volunteers since November 1919, while the Thirty-Fourth Division, charged with the assault, had assigned the Battaglioni *Aosta*, *Vestone* and *Edolo*, and, a few days before the action, the Battaglioni *Dronero*, *Saluzzo* and *Fenestrelle* as well. The two sides clashed on December 24, 1920 and again on the twenty-sixth, having observed a truce during Christmas, and the *Edolo* suffered some casualties. However, faced with this firm attitude of the Italian government, D'Annunzio negotiated an honorable surrender and left Fiume with his volunteers at the beginning of January 1921. A garrison of Alpini remained in the town until 1924, when Italy and Yugoslavia agreed with the Treaty of Rome to divide the territory of the Free State between them: Italy kept the town itself, inhabited predominantly by Italians, with a strip of territory that connected it to Italian territory, while Yugoslavia was granted the hinterland, where the Slavic population represented the great majority.

A Brief Appearance in Turkey

In spring 1919, an Italian expeditionary corps landed in Anatolia, in Turkey, that according to the Treaty of London was supposed to come under the control of Italy. The troops landed in Antalya and extended the occupation to some other ports, like Bodrum and Kusadasi, but the Italian units were not able to set foot in Smyrna, today's Izmir, which was already occupied by Greek troops. There were no *Alpini* in the expeditionary corps, but there were five batteries of mountain artillery—the 102nd, 105th, 108th, 187th, and 190th—because the intention was to seize some mountain areas of the interior. In fact, the batteries never left the coast and were repatriated during 1920, when Italy, faced with strong Turkish resistance led by Mustafa Kemal, lost interest in the expedition. The last units left Turkey in 1922, and the whole area returned under the rule of the new Turkish republican government led by Ataturk.

The Battaglione *Monte Baldo* in Upper Silesia

In 1919, the Battaglione *Monte Baldo*, which had been disbanded a few months before, was re-formed to be sent at the beginning of 1920 to Upper Silesia, attached to the Italian contingent that was charged with the public order of the region, along with French and British units. Upper Silesia was disputed between Germany and Poland, and its population was called to decide which country to join by a plebiscite. The battalion, as well as the rest of the Italian troops, remained in the area until the plebiscite took place, and Upper Silesia was delivered to German troops in 1922. Once repatriated, the battalion was disbanded again.

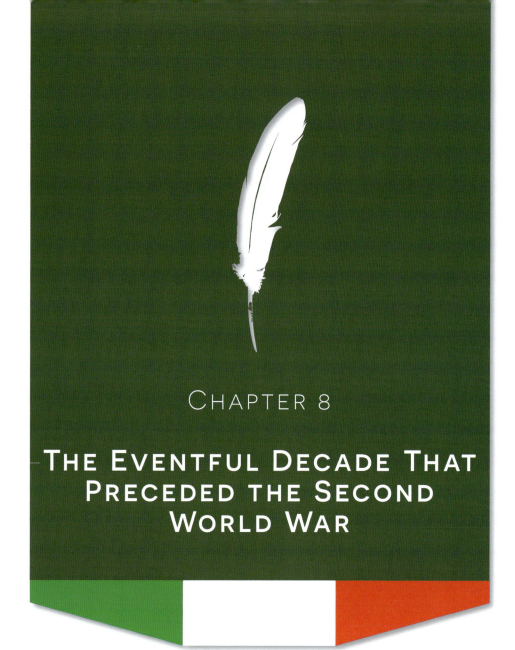

CHAPTER 8

THE EVENTFUL DECADE THAT PRECEDED THE SECOND WORLD WAR

THE REORGANIZATION DURING THE 1930S

During the 1930s, several innovations were introduced to the mountain troops specialty, both from the organizational and from the equipment points of view. The first important provision of the decade was in 1933, which saw the increase of the number of brigades from three to four and, consequently, the creation of a fourth mountain artillery regiment. However, the total number of battalions and batteries did not increase, insofar as the existing ones were simply redistributed. A few months later, the mountain artillery changed its denomination, being called *artiglieria alpina* (Alpine artillery) from then on, to stress further that it would be assigned to operate in strict contact with, and only with, the Alpini units.

A new organization chart was enacted in 1934[1] by the undersecretary of war and army chief of staff, General Federico Baistrocchi. The chart did introduce important changes as

far as the Alpini were concerned; the most relevant provision was the elimination of the brigades, replaced by four *Comandi Superiori Alpini* (Alpine superior commands), with the same duties and prerogatives as the brigades. These commands were named "*Taurinense*," "*Tridentino*," "*Julio*," and "*Cuneense*," in reference to the prevalent area of recruitment of the men.

In April 1935, a new battalion was formed, named "*L'Aquila*," which was recruited in Abruzzo, a mountain area across the Appennines, in central Italy. The new battalion was assigned to the 9° Reggimento Alpini and entailed the creation of a new Alpine artillery group, named "*Udine*," assigned to the 3° Reggimento artiglieria alpina.

In October 1935, finally, the *Comandi Superiori Alpini* were transformed into proper divisions, whose names they maintained, and the specialty was freed from the duty it had been created for—the defense of the Alpine borders—to be entrusted with the new task of penetrating impervious enemy territories, in line with a rhetoric that called for the whole army to be exclusively devoted to attack.[2] To carry out this new

Alpini of the Sixty-Third Company of the Battaglione *Bassano* during an excursion on Monte Scherbina, today Vrh nad Škrbino, in Slovenia, in 1933. *Museo Nazionale Storico degli Alpini*

Alpini of the 6° Reggimento lined up at Vipiteno in 1936. *Museo Nazionale Storico degli Alpini*

Machine gunners practicing with a FIAT mod. 14 machine gun and gas mask in the mid-1930s. *Andrea Tallillo*

assignment, a *compagnia genio* (engineer company), consisting of four platoons, was attached to each division; these companies were initially formed directly by the engineer regiments of the army with personnel detached from their ranks, instead of adhering to the recruitment rules of the Alpini; it was established, however, that men with particular physical prowess should be chosen for these Alpine engineer companies. Beginning in 1938, the Alpine engineers were recruited according to the same criteria as the other Alpini, and special courses were activated for officers and NCOs at the school of military Alpinism, created in 1934 in Aosta.

Very soon, however, this organization chart was again revised due to the outbreak of the war against the Empire of Ethiopia in 1935. On December 31, 1935, in the town of Brunico, in northeast Italy, the new Fifth *Pusteria* Division was formed, with the precise intent to send it to East Africa; the division consisted of two new Alpine regiments and a new Alpine artillery regiment, although the total number of battalions and batteries did not change, because there was a redistribution of the existing ones. Thus, the new division was formed with the 7° Reggimento Alpini, consisting of the Battaglioni *Feltre*, *Pieve di Teco*, *Exilles*, and 11° Reggimento Alpini, consisting of the Battaglioni *Trento*, *Intra*, *Saluzzo*, the 5° Reggimento artiglieria alpina, consisting of the Gruppi *Belluno* and *Lanzo*, and the 5ᵃ Compagnia genio. For the needs of the war, two replacement battalions were also created: the VII, attached to the 7° Reggimento, and the XI, attached to the 11° Reggimento. The Battaglioni *Pieve di Cadore* and *Belluno*, formerly of the 7° Reggimento, were assigned to a newly created 12° Reggimento.

In 1936, two new battalions that were not attached to any regiment were created, but planned to remain independent: the Battaglione *Duca degli Abruzzi*, formed at the school of Aosta, and the Battaglione *Uork Amba*, formed in Ethiopia from the VII replacement battalion of the *Pusteria* Division (see infra).

Once the division was repatriated from East Africa, the whole organization was revised again, with the disbanding of the 12° Reggimento and the reassignment of its battalions to the other regiments, and, a little later, with the creation of the new Battaglione *Bolzano*, assigned to the 11° Reggimento.

In 1939, two new provisions assigned the Alpine divisions a sequence number in August and upgraded the engineer companies to battalions, consisting of a company of sappers and a signals company, in September.

At the end of these changes, shortly before the outbreak of the Second World War, the organization chart of the Alpini involved five divisions with ten regiments and twenty-nine battalions assigned to them, plus two autonomous battalions, five engineers battalions, five Alpine artillery regiments with ten Alpine artillery battalions, distributed as follows:

1ᵃ Divisione alpina *Taurinense*, with Headquarters at Torino, consisting of:
3° Reggimento Alpini, with the Battaglioni *Pinerolo*, *Fenestrelle*, *Exilles* and *Susa*
4° Reggimento Alpini, with the Battaglioni *Ivrea*, *Aosta* and *Intra*

1° Reggimento artiglieria alpina, with the Gruppi *Susa* and *Aosta*
I Battaglione genio.

2ᵃ Divisione alpina *Tridentina*, with Headquarters at Merano, consisting of:
5° Reggimento Alpini, with the Battaglioni *Morbegno*, *Tirano*, and *Edolo*
6° Reggimento Alpini, with the Battaglioni *Vestone* and *Verona*
2° Reggimento artiglieria alpina, with the Gruppi *Bergamo* and *Vicenza*
II Battaglione genio.

3ᵃ Divisione alpina *Julia*, with Headquarters at Udine, consisting of:
8° Reggimento Alpini, with the Battaglioni *Tolmezzo*, *Gemona*, and *Cividale*
9° Reggimento Alpini, with the Battaglioni *Vicenza* and *L'Aquila*
3° Reggimento artiglieria alpina, with the Gruppi *Conegliano*, and *Udine*
III Battaglione genio.

4ᵃ Divisione alpina *Cuneense*, with Headquarters at Cuneo, consisting of:
1° Reggimento Alpini, with the Battaglioni *Ceva*, *Pieve di Teco*, and *Mondovì*
2° Reggimento Alpini, with the Battaglioni *Borgo San Dalmazzo*, *Dronero*, and *Saluzzo*
4° Reggimento artiglieria alpina, with the Gruppi *Pinerolo*, and *Mondovì*
IV Battaglione genio

5ᵃ Divisione alpina *Pusteria*, with Headquarters at Brunico, consisting of:
7° Reggimento Alpini, with the Battaglioni *Feltre*, *Pieve di Cadore*, and *Belluno*
11° Reggimento Alpini, with the Battaglioni *Bassano*, *Trento*, and *Bolzano*
5° Reggimento artiglieria alpina, with the Gruppi *Lanzo* and *Belluno*
V Battaglione genio.

With regard to the equipment, a new caliber 6.5 mm light machine gun was adopted in 1930: the Breda mod. 30, one of which was distributed to each rifle squad within the platoons. A few years later, the FIAT mod. 14 heavy machine gun of the Great War was replaced by the modern FIAT mod. 35 and Breda mod. 37, both caliber 8 mm, two of which were assigned to each company. The small 45 mm Brixia mortar, tested during the war against Ethiopia, was adopted, and a squad of three mortars was assigned to each company. At the same time, the very effective CEMSA mod. 35 81 mm mortar was adopted, and each battalion had a platoon of four weapons. Finally, not much before the outbreak of the war, the Carcano mod. 91 rifle was replaced by the mod. 91/38 carbine, directly derived from it, with the same 6.5 mm caliber but much easier to handle.

Alpini carrying out shooting training with the Breda mod. 30 light machine gun at the school of Aosta in the 1930s

In September 1934, the Twenty-First Battery of the Gruppo *Vicenza* of Alpine artillery carried out some tests with the newly designed 75/18 mod. 34 howitzer in northern Italy. The official report advised against the adoption of the piece of artillery. *Museo Storico Italiano della Guerra*

Top and above: additonal images showing the tests carried out on the 75/18 mod. 34 howitzer in 1934. *Museo Storico Italiano della Guerra*

An alpino training with the CEMSA 81 mm mortar. *Storia Militare*

In 1934, the Alpine artillery was submitted a new 75 mm howitzer, produced by the Ansaldo firm and developed specifically to be carried by a pack mule or towed in the mountains. However, experiences were disappointing, particularly because the components of the new weapons were heavier in comparison with the previous 75/13 howitzer, creating an additional burden for the mules, while the ballistic characteristics did not improve notably.[3] Therefore, the gun used by Alpine artillery that remained in use throughout the war was the previously mentioned former Austro-Hungarian 75/13 howitzer.

THE ALPINI IN EAST AFRICA

In the mid-1930s, the tormented decade that preceded the Second World War, Italy was involved in a war against the only African state not already colonized by another European state, the empire of Ethiopia.

After the defeat at Adua in March 1896, which ended the first Italo-Ethiopian War, and the signing of the Treaty of Addis Ababa the following October, the relationship between Italy and Ethiopia had been rather quiet, as both nations were busy consolidating their possessions in the area. However, Italy had not completely abandoned its designs on Ethiopia, or at least certain parts of it. With the rise to power of fascism, Italian diplomacy from the late 1920s onward started to undertake diplomatic efforts with France and, overall, with Great Britain, to isolate Ethiopia and enhance Italian presence in the country, both political and economic. On the other hand, the ambiguous contacts with those Ethiopian governors, the Ras, who ruled the regions of the empire bordering the Italian colony of Eritrea, began anew with the aim to weaken the central Imperial

A postcard celebrating the Gruppo *Susa* of Alpine artillery, attached to the *Sabauda* infantry division during the Ethiopian campaign. *Roberto Rossini*

Alpine artillery marching on the Eritrean front. *Vito Zita*

After the conquest of the Amba Aradam, Alpini are watching the Italian flag hoisted on top of it. *Museo Nazionale Storico degli Alpini*

A gruppo of Alpine artillery is training in Ethiopia, in 1936. *Museo Nazionale Storico degli Alpini*

A stronghold armed with Alpine artillery howitzers in East Africa. *Museo Storico Italiano della Guerra*

Alpini of the Divisione *Pusteria* with an old FIAT mod. 1914 on the Amba Aradam. *Museo Nazionale Storico degli Alpini*

government. The emperor of Ethiopia, the Negus Haile Selassie, was perfectly aware of the Italian maneuvers; therefore, his annoyance and his distrust toward the Italians grew day by day. Indeed, the war awaited only a *casus belli*, which happened in December 1934 near the water wells of Ual Ual, along the unclear border between southern Ethiopia and the Italian colony of Somalia, with a gunfight between two groups of irregular armed men in service with the opposite countries. International diplomacy started to work tirelessly to avoid open war, submitting to the parties several plans to settle the dispute, however, the Italian government was inclined toward war for propaganda and prestige reasons, while the empire of Ethiopia, which had also been a member of the League of Nations since 1923, felt strong enough not to make any concessions to a counterparty that it considered to be, rightly or not, an aggressor. At the end of the day, the months that had elapsed in useless negotiations only served to make the two parties prepare for the armed clash that started in the night between October 2 and 3, 1935, when Italian troops crossed the border between Eritrea and Ethiopia. It would be beyond the scope of this book to follow the whole unfolding of this war; thus, it will focus on the battles in which Alpini units were involved.

Remembering very well what had happened forty years before at Adua, this time Italy set up an expeditionary corps strong enough to avoid any surprises: in a few months, thirteen divisions arrived in Eritrea and Somalia, of which seven were of the *Regio Esercito* and six of the *Black Shirts*, complete with artillery and state-of-the-art equipment. Insofar as the Alpini are concerned, the first unit to arrive in Eritrea was the *Susa* Alpine artillery battalion, mobilized in the spring of 1935 and sent to Massaua the following June, then attached to the

Sixteenth Artillery Regiment of the *Sabauda* Infantry Division. At the beginning of October, the Battaglione *Saluzzo*, consisting of four companies, arrived as well, and was assigned to a special unit formed with a battalion from the *Granatieri di Sardegna* Division and another formed by the *Guardia di Finanza* (customs police); however, the *Saluzzo* did not take part in any combat until it joined the *Pusteria* Alpine division, once it landed in Massaua during January 1936. The unit had been requested specifically by the commander of the Italian troops in East Africa, Marshal Pietro Badoglio, to launch an offensive against the Ethiopian troops in the high mountains of the region of Tigray. The division was 13,000 men strong and had almost 4,000 mules; once it had arrived and regrouped in Massaua, it had to move hundreds of kilometers to the interior to reach its assigned area. The men moved partly on trucks but partly also on foot, marching up to 50 kilometers per day, while the mules covered the distance entirely on foot, arriving at their destination already exhausted. Once there, the units had only a few days to rest and reorganize before the offensive, called the Battle of Endertà, or Battle of Amba Aradam, was launched. The aim of the action was to annihilate the army of Ras Mulugheta, which numbered 80,000 men, with numerous machine guns and some artillery pieces that manned the Amba Aradam, which was located to the south of the Ethiopian town of Mekelle. Amba Aradam was a large plateau 2,700 meters (8,858 feet) above MSL and prevented any attempt to move south. The Italian plan included a pincer movement with two columns attacking to the east and to the west of the Amba Aradam moving south, with the aim to surround it and isolate it. The I Army Corps was assigned the eastern arm of the pincer, with the *Pusteria* and *Sabauda* divisions, and the Black Shirts

3 *Gennaio* Division as reserve. The *Pusteria* was deployed to the right of the line, with the Battaglioni *Feltre*, *Pieve di Teco*, and *Exilles* supported by the guns of the Gruppo *Belluno*, close to the slopes of the Amba Aradam, while the Battaglioni *Intra* and *Saluzzo*, with the *Trento* as reserve, supported by the Gruppo *Lanzo*, acted as "marching wing" of the encircling movement, with the infantrymen of the *Sabauda* covering their left flank. The attack was launched on the morning of February 15, 1936, after several hours of artillery shelling and aerial bombing, using a certain number of gas shells, and the Battaglioni *Intra* and *Saluzzo* immediately ran into the stiff resistance put up by the Ethiopians, although the Alpine artillery was advancing with the first line and firing at close range on the enemy strongholds. Soon it became necessary to move in the reserve, the Battaglione *Trento*. However, in the morning of February 16, the eastern arm met the western arm of the pincer, thus completing the surrounding of the Amba. Meanwhile, in the afternoon of the fifteenth, the Battaglioni *Feltre*, *Pieve di Teco*, and *Exilles* had moved to make a direct attack against the eastern slopes of Amba Aradam, where they met

The development of the Italo-Ethiopian War between 1935 and 1936

Legend
- Border
- ★ Capital
- Railroad
- Street
- ✕ Battle
- → Badoglio
- → Graziani

heavy fog and heavy enemy fire that rendered the movement extremely slow. In any case, in the morning of the sixteenth, the top of the Amba was reached since the Ethiopians, once aware of being surrounded, broke contact and ran away in disorder, pursued by Italian airplanes that completed the defeat. After a few days of rest, the I Army Corps resumed its march and on February 28 occupied the Amba Alagi massif.

During the same period, the two replacement battalions, VII and XI, were, quite surprisingly,[4] assigned to the Eritrean indigenous army corps and took part in the fighting known as Second Battle of Tembien, grouped in a task force with a battalion of the *Granatieri di Sardegna* division and a Black Shirt battalion. The aim of the offensive was to defeat another of the Ethiopian armies, the one led by Ras Seyoum Mangasha and Ras Kassa Haile Darge, and for that purpose, a classic plan with a pincer maneuver was developed. The plan was for the Eritrean army corps to move south and meet with the III Army Corps, which was moving north, behind the town of Abyi Addi, about 50 kilometers west of Mekelle, thus encircling the enemy. The Eritrean army corps needed to pass through the Worsege Pass, dominated to its right by the major peaks of Uork Amba, which had to be taken to ensure the transit of the columns through the pass below. The plan was that about thirty volunteers from the VII replacement battalion would climb the steep slopes of the amba and conquer the southern peak, while at the same time a handful of Black Shirts of the CXIV Legion would do the same and take the northern peak. A unit of Alpini of the VII replacement battalion was to attack the saddle between the two peaks. The action was launched in the night of the February 27. The first to reach their target were the Black Shirts, who managed to conquer the northern peak by surprise before the Alpini were able to assume an advantageous position for their assault; therefore, once they were able to move forward, the defenders were on alert and started to fire on the assailants. The attack against the saddle failed, while the southern peak was taken despite the resistance of the Ethiopians. For this action the VII replacement battalion was awarded the Bronze Medal and, as a further reward, became a regular battalion, assuming the evocative name "*Uork Amba.*" Curiously, it would be the only Alpini battalion to remain in East Africa after the *Pusteria* Division's return to Italy, and it would fight in East Africa during the Second World War.

After the battles fought in the Tigray,[5] the Italian forces were able to move south, with the I Army Corps in the lead and the *Pusteria* Division as spearhead. Between the Italian divisions and the capital city of Ethiopia, Addis Ababa, lay the sole enemy army, led by the emperor himself. The army counted within its ranks the only unit organized, trained, and armed in the European fashion, the Imperial Guard, 6,000 men strong. The place chosen by the emperor for the final clash was at Maychew, near the border between Tigray and Shewa, some 650 kilometers north of Addis Ababa. The first to reach the area were the Alpini of the Battaglioni *Feltre* and *Exilles* and the batteries of the Gruppo *Belluno*, with the *askari* of the XXV Eritrean battalion, on March 17. They immediately took possession of the Western Mecan Pass and the Eastern Mecan Pass, ensuring access to the valley below, and dug in, waiting for reinforcements. Between March 19 and 20, the other battalions and batteries of the *Pusteria* arrived, followed

immediately by the whole Eritrean army corps and, on the twenty-fifth, by the *Sabauda* Division. The Imperial army reached the area on March 21 but, rather surprisingly, did not immediately attack the relatively few Italian forces that were still deploying. On the contrary, the emperor lingered a few more days, giving the Italian troops the needed time to improve their defensive preparations for the battle. It was the opinion of the Italian command that the Ethiopians would not be able to occupy defensive positions and wait for the Italian attack, due to their dislike for that kind of operations and to their poor logistics; their only option would be an impetuous frontal attack hoping to break the Italian line and overwhelm them.

The *Pusteria* deployed its battalions on the front line, with the *Intra* defending the Western Mecan Pass, the *Feltre* occupying the heights between the latter and the Eastern Mecan Pass and the *Pieve di Teco* on the western slopes of the Eastern Mecan Pass. The right flank of the *Intra* was guarded by the Battaglioni *Trento* and *Saluzzo*, while the Battaglione *Exilles* was deployed to the left of the line, 1 kilometer behind the Eastern Mecan Pass, connected with the *askaris* of the Second Eritrean Division. Regarding artillery support, the mechanically towed heavy guns of the army corps were a long way behind, waiting for the engineers to build a road; therefore, the only available artillery was the mule pack divisional artillery. The support of

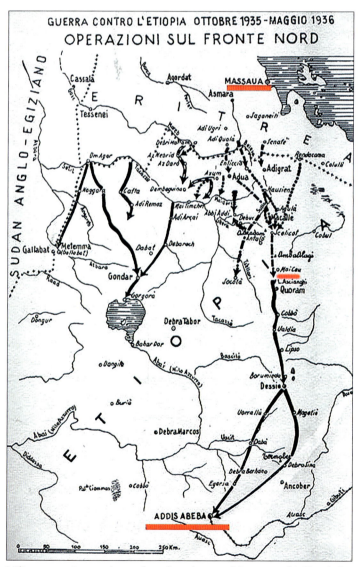

Military operations on the northern front, between Massawa and Addis Ababa, the area of Mai Ceu, where the emperor of Ethiopia fought his last battle

the front-line units was furnished by the howitzers of the Gruppi *Belluno* and *Susa*, along with the guns of the First Artillery Battalion of the Sixteenth Artillery Regiment of the *Sabauda* Division. Behind the Battaglioni *Trento* and *Saluzzo*, the 75/13 howitzers of the Gruppo *Lanzo* and those of the Second Artillery Battalion of the *Sabauda* were deployed, while the Eritrean divisions had their own mule pack artillery as support. The Alpine artillery pieces were deployed very close to the first line, in direct support of the Alpini strongholds, in order to be able to shell the areas were the assailants grouped for the attacks and support the counterattacks with direct fire. The guns of the *Sabauda* occupied more defiladed positions, with the mission to hit the no-man's land just in front of the Italian trenches. Due to the lack of mules, who had suffered greatly from the fatigue caused by marching uninterruptedly since they had landed in Massaua, the artillerymen had to carry a shell each in their backpacks themselves in order to ensure a load of at least 1,500 shells per battery.

The Ethiopians launched their attack at 5:30 a.m. on March 31, 1936, and in the initial phase, they concentrated particularly on the strongholds of the Battaglione *Intra*, aimed at conquering the Western Mecan Pass, with a diversion against the positions of the Battaglione *Trento*. Three attack waves were repelled by the Alpini, well supported by the artillery, although with a high casualty toll. Around 10:30 a.m., the enemy actions shifted direction and concentrated on the Eastern Mecan Pass, aimed at outflanking the positions of the Battaglione *Pieve di Teco*, but the reaction of the *Exilles* and of the *askaris* frustrated this maneuver as well. In a desperate attempt to find a weak point in the Italian line, the Ethiopians launched an assault against the Eritreans, but they did not achieve any positive result. The last attack of this morning of hard fighting was directed against the juncture point between the Battaglioni *Intra* and *Trento*, who, with great difficulty, managed to contain it. At 11:30, the Ethiopian offensive faltered, a sign that the assailants were tired and their morale was low; therefore, a first counterattack was mounted with the *askaris*, who moved forward from their positions. However, the action had been premature, since the Eritreans were beaten back by the enemy machine guns and were forced to retreat, pursued by the Ethiopian hordes. After a few hours of rest and reorganization and faced with the strength of thc Italian line, at 4:00 p.m., the emperor ordered a general attack by all the forces at his disposal, directed against the whole front, but the Italians fended off his warriors again. In the evening, the fighting subsided, and the emperor's army started to retreat slowly, leaving behind some rearguard forces to cover the movement

and hold back the pursuers. On April 3, the remains of the last Ethiopian army were retreating toward the town of Korem, but the divisions of the I Army Corps and of the Eritrean army corps were at their heels and managed to cut their retreat: the capital city of Addis Ababa lay 600 kilometers to the south and there was nothing that could stay in the way of the advancing Italian forces. A swift, truck-mounted column was organized to reach Addis Ababa, with the Battaglione *Trento* representing the Alpini. Notwithstanding the bad state of the Ethiopian roads, Addis Ababa was reached on May 5, the day that marks the official end of the Italo-Ethiopian war.

The other battalions of the *Pusteria* Division moved south to Dessie, where they arrived after days of marching that cost the loss of the last mules of the division, and the Alpini were able to enjoy a few days of rest and to repair their personal equipment. Later, however, they were used to work on building roads until they were sent to the capital to carry out garrison activity and protection of the labor squads. In March 1937, the order to repatriate arrived; therefore, the units started to move to Massaua and, once there, embark for Italy, where they arrived during the month of April. Only the Battaglione *Uork Amba* remained in East Africa. The campaign had cost the loss of twenty officers and 200 Alpini.

THE NONPARTICIPATION OF ALPINI UNITS IN THE SPANISH CIVIL WAR

Between 1936 and 1939, Italy was intensely involved in the Spanish Civil War, supporting the Nationalist side against the Republican side. Since the beginning of the confrontation, the common ideology between Fascist Italy and Nationalist Spain seemed obvious; thus, the Italian government did not think long before deciding to send an expeditionary corps, represented to the public as a volunteer army, to the Iberian Peninsula.

At the beginning of 1937, a division called *Penne Nere* (black feathers) appears within the ranks of the Italian expeditionary corps. Although the name might suggest that it was an Alpini unit, it was a Black Shirt division.

It was not until March 1939 that two battalions, *Vestone* and *Edolo*, arrived in Cadiz with two batteries of 75/13 howitzers. They were renamed "I Battaglione *Alpini*" and "II Battaglione *Alpini*" to maintain the pretense of non-regular army units, but they did not take part in any action since a few days later, Madrid fell, and the war ended with the victory of the Nationalist side.

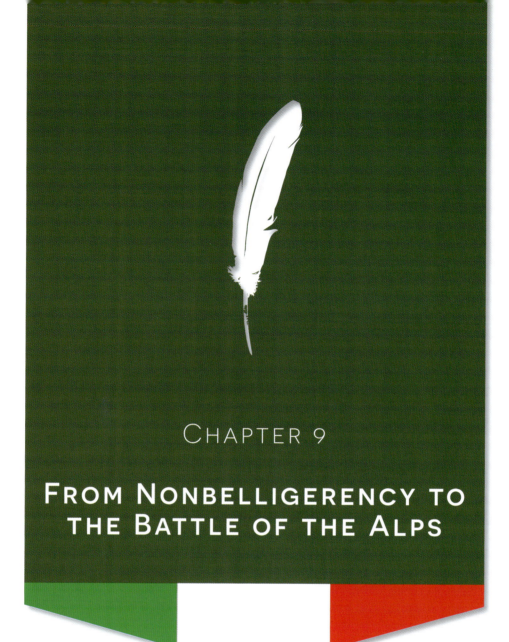

Chapter 9

From Nonbelligerency to the Battle of the Alps

Italy's Ambiguous Behavior at the Outbreak of the Second World War

On September 1, 1939, Germany invaded Poland and set in motion the domino effect that led to the outbreak of the second terrific world war in less than twenty-five years. Nazi Germany had risen as a European power in the second half of the 1930s, overwhelming the fragile, diplomatic texture that maintained peace in Europe. From the remilitarization of the Rhineland in 1936, violating the Treaty of Versailles, which banished all weapons from that region, to the annexation of Austria, the well-known *Anschluss*, carried out in March 1938[1] and from the occupation of the Czech *Sudetenland*,[2] obtained as a result of the Munich Agreement in September 1938, to that of Bohemia and Moravia, in March 1939,[3] Germany had seen all of its claims satisfied, always indulged by Great Britain and France, who were too concerned with avoiding the war to be aware that this weak attitude was actually paving the way to war. Throughout the decade, Fascist Italy had been attracted to the German orbit little by little until, in May 1939, it had signed the Pact of Steel with its powerful neighbor, an alliance that was meant to ensure mutual military assistance not only in case one of the parties were to be attacked by third parties but also in case one of the parties were to be the aggressor. However, when the moment came to fulfill the obligations contained in the treaty, Italy was completely unprepared for the events, and Mussolini himself realized that the Italian armed forces were in no condition to fight a war. Thus, Italy did not declare war on France and Great Britain, as it should have done. But to appease Germany and its dictator Adolf Hitler slightly, on September 1, 1939, the council of ministers declared *nonbelligerency*, a curious formula concerted with the ally meaning that, although there was no war declared, Italy would do its best to favor Germany, thus forcing its enemies to maintain a high degree of alert toward Italy, indirectly subtracting resources from the war.

Since the month of August, the Italian armed forces were fully mobilized and deployed along the eastern and western borders, albeit with a solely defensive attitude. The five Alpine divisions, as well as the rest of the army, were completed to reach wartime manning levels, and twenty-eight new battalions and nine new artillery battalions were formed, named after Italian valleys. During the war, they would often be grouped into what were called *Gruppi Valle*, functioning as regiments. To garrison Mont Blanc, rising 4,808 meters (15,774 feet) above MSL, a special unit was created at the school of military Alpinism of Aosta, the *Reparto autonomo Monte Bianco* (Independent Mont Blanc Unit), 250 men strong. Later, in May 1940, another special unit was formed at the school of Aosta, the *Reparto Alpini Alpieri*, particularly trained for warfare in the highest peaks. In East Africa, the staff of the Battaglione *Uork Amba* was brought up to strength and assigned to the *Granatieri di Savoia* Division. In many cases, the deployment of the Alpini along the Eastern Alps entailed changes in the organizational chart of the divisions and the creation of new units, called *Raggruppamenti*, of various composition.

Uniform and equipment of the alpino shortly before World War II. He wears the model 1937 jacket, which was replaced by a new model in 1940; the model 1935 trousers with the old-style puttee, used by the Italian infantry throughout the war; and the model 1929 boots, for mountain troops. On his shoulders, he has the backpack with the tactical bag attached to it and the blanket under it. The personal equipment is completed with the model 1933 helmet, the snowshoes, and the ice ax. *Museo Nazionale Storico degli Alpini*

A platoon of Alpini is marching through a village in Piedmont in late spring 1940. *Museo Nazionale Storico degli Alpini*

An alpino taking care of the mule that has been entrusted to him. *Storia Militare*

The Alpine front against France was under the responsibility of the Gruppo *Armate Ovest* (Western Army Group), under the nominal command of the Prince of Piedmont, Umberto, son of the king, consisting of the First and Fourth Army, twenty-three divisions in total, 300,000 men strong; the line was subdivided into seven sectors. Each, except for one, had Alpine units assigned to it. From north to south:

Sector *Baltea-Orco-Stura*
Divisione *Tridentina*, consisting of
5° Reggimento, with the Battaglioni *Morbegno*, *Tirano,* and *Edolo*
6° Reggimento, with the Battaglioni *Vestone* and *Verona*
2° Reggimento of Alpine artillery, with the Gruppi *Bergamo* and *Vicenza*
II Battaglione genio
Battaglione *Duca degli Abruzzi*
Reparto autonomo Monte Bianco
Reparto Alpini Alpieri
Divisione *Taurinense*, consisting of
4° Reggimento, with the Battaglioni *Aosta*, *Val Baltea,* and *Val d'Orco*
4° Gruppo *Valle,* with the Battaglioni *Ivrea*, *Val Piave,* and *Val Cordevole*
1° Reggimento of Alpine artillery, with the Gruppo *Aosta* and two batteries of the Gruppo *Val d'Adige*
I Battaglione genio
Raggruppamento *Levanna*, consisting of the Battaglioni *Intra*, *Val Brenta*, *Val Cismon*, the Gruppo *Val d'Orco* of Alpine artillery, and one battery of the Gruppo *Val d'Adige*
The two Divisions and the Raggruppamento formed a *Corpo d'Armata Alpino* (Alpine Army Corps)

Sector *Moncenisio-Bardonecchia*
The Battaglioni *Susa* and *Val Cenischia* with three batteries of Alpine artillery detached from the Gruppi *Susa*, *Val Chisone*, and *Valle Isonzo* were attached to the *Cagliari* Infantry Division
The 3° Gruppo *Valle,* with the Battaglioni *Exilles*, *Val Dora* and *Val Fassa*, and three batteries detached from the Gruppi *Susa*, *Val Chisone,* and *Val d'Adige* was attached to the *Superga* Infantry Division

Sector *Monginevro*, without Alpine units assigned

Sector *Germanasca-Pellice*
3° Reggimento, with the Battaglioni *Pinerolo*, *Fenestrelle*, *Val Pellice* and *Val Chisone*, two batteries of Alpine artillery detached from the Gruppo *Susa*, and two more from the Gruppo *Val Chisone*

Sector *Po-Stura-Maira*
II Raggruppamento Alpini, consisting of
5° Gruppo *Valle,* with the Battaglioni *Val Chiese*, *Val Camonica*, *Valtellina* and *Val d'Intelvi*, and the Gruppi *Val Po* and *Val Camonica* of Alpine artillery
Battaglione *Val Maira*, attached to the *Forlì* Infantry Division
Battaglione *Val Stura*, attached to the *Acqui* Infantry Division

Sector *Alta Roja-Gessi*
I Raggruppamento Alpini, consisting of
6° Gruppo *Valle,* with the Battaglioni *Val Ellero*, *Val Arroscia*, *Val Tanaro*, *Val d'Adige* and *Val Venosta*, and the Gruppi *Val Tanaro* and *Val Piave* of Alpine artillery

Sector *Media e Bassa Roja*
Battaglione *Ceva*, attached to the *Ravenna* Infantry Division

Western Alps, 1940. His Majesty the Prince Umberto, commander of the Gruppo *Armate Ovest*, reviews a unit of Alpini. *Museo Nazionale Storico degli Alpini*

The *Pusteria* and *Cuneense* Division were kept in the reserve, although they were called into action as soon as war was declared.

Other Alpine units were deployed along the eastern border with Yugoslavia, with a defensive purpose:

Raggruppamento Alpini *Alto Isonzo*, consisting of
1° Gruppo *Valle*, with the Battaglioni *Val Tagliamento*, *Val Natisone*, and *Val Fella*

2° Gruppo *Valle*, with the Battaglioni *Val Leogra* and *Val Pescara*
Gruppi *Val Tagliamento* and *Valle Isonzo*, less the battery detached to the *Superga* Division listed above

The *Julia* Alpine Division, on the other hand, had been deployed in Albania since April 1939, when that small state had been occupied.

Alpini of the 2° Gruppo *Valle* patrolling the eastern Italian valleys in 1940. *Museo Nazionale Storico degli Alpini*

ITALY DECLARES WAR

The nonbelligerency period lasted until June 1940 as the Italian dictator Benito Mussolini became more and more restless and was willing to join Germany in its victorious ride on the one hand, while at the same time aware of the poor state of the Italian armed forces on the other hand. His goal was to enter the war at the very moment when Italian action would definitively decide the outcome, so as to be counted among the winners with the minimum possible effort. Confronted with the overwhelming advance of the Wehrmacht to the west, the surrender of Belgium and the Netherlands in a few days, the reboarding of the British expeditionary corps at Dunkirk and the expected fall of Paris, Mussolini considered that the right moment had arrived and that to wait further would mean to arrive too late. The declaration of war was delivered to the French and British ambassadors on June 10, 1940, but, paradoxically, the guidelines issued to the army considered a strictly defensive behavior, quite strange for an aggressor, while the navy and the air force were issued vague orders to attack wherever possible. Those who, like the Germans, awaited some surprise action planned thoroughly during the long months of inactivity, remained very disappointed since the Italian armed forces for the first few days did not fire a single bullet, leaving the initiative to the French.

In June, although many divisions had been moved to the northern front, the French *Armée des Alpes* still counted 85,000 men, well protected behind the *Maginot des Alpes* (Maginot of the Alps), a deep defensive line provided with concrete strongholds and positions dug into solid rock, with numerous machine guns and artillery. The soldiers still showed good morale, not being involved in the disastrous fighting against the Germans, and were eager to fight. Unlike the Italian Supreme

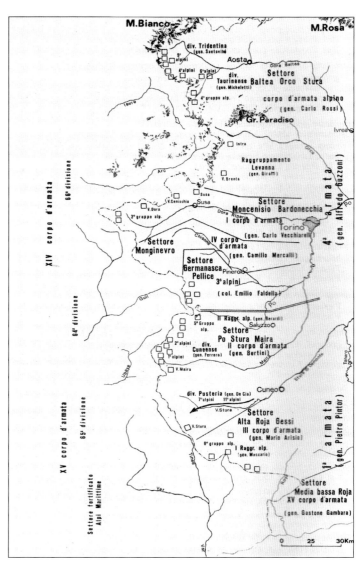

The deployment of the Alpini units in the Western Alps on June 21, 1940

Alpine artillery on the Western Alps in a propaganda postcard, which reads "Struggle at 3,000 meters"

Command, the French commander of the small *Armée* decided to adopt an aggressive behavior, launching a series of coups de main in order to take some dominant positions and further improve the situation. On June 13, a small unit tried, without success, to conquer the Galisia Pass, between the Val d'Orco and the Val d'Isére, defended by a platoon of the Battaglione *Intra*, while another unit managed to capture a patrol of the *Ivrea* in Valgrisenche. Faced with this French activity, the Italian army carried out some limited actions in response.

Furthermore, on June 14, a force of the French navy approached the Italian coast unseen and shelled Savona and Genoa without any Italian reaction. From a strictly military point of view, the action did not produce any relevant result, with its very limited damage caused to the infrastructure of the ports. But politically, it came as a shock, from the lack of opposition of the coastal artillery and of the nearby Italian navy. Benito Mussolini was in a rage and ordered some retaliatory attacks, to be launched immediately, that would precede a general offensive along the whole Alpine front. They were planned for June 18 then postponed to June 26, due to the great difficulty in changing the deployment of the troops and in changing the artillery from defensive to offensive in four days. However, on June 17, France delivered the request of an armistice to Germany; therefore, the whole preparation was interrupted, while the Italian dictator went to Munich to confer with Adolf Hitler. Unexpectedly, when he was back, Mussolini ordered that preparations be resumed and to begin the offensive on the twenty-first. The objections of the general staff were, as

usual, rather weak, and the troops were moved forward, including the two Alpine divisions *Cuneense* and *Pusteria*, thus far kept in reserve; however, due to the short time and the very bad weather conditions, most of the heavy artillery could not be moved in time and remained useless; during the offensive, the troops could count only on the divisional artillery, and particularly on the Alpine artillery, which was the only artillery that could move in the mountains without roads and under almost any weather conditions. The offensive, as expected, did not acheive relevant results, although it caused severe casualties, due more to frostbite than to French fire; however, the Italian infantrymen and Alpini did their best to make up for the inadequate preparation.

June 21, 1940, A column of Alpini crosses the Italo-French border. *Antonio Tallillo*

Unit of Alpini with some mules under a snowfall in the Western Alps. *Museo Nazionale Storico degli Alpini*

One of the main actions of these few days of war was carried out to the north of the front, in the *Baltea-Orco-Stura* Sector, with the French town of Bourg St. Maurice as a target, some 12 kilometers, as the crow flies, into the French territory, in Val d'Isère. It anticipated an attack along the road of the valley floor, carried out by the *Trieste* motorized division, with the direct support of the Battaglione *Val Baltea*, soon reinforced by the Battaglione *Val Cismon*, which moved along the mountains to the north of the road, and the Battaglione *Aosta*, which moved to the south. Flanking attacks were planned to the north, in the Mont Blanc massif, along peaks over 3,000 meters (9,842 feet) above MSL, carried out by the *Tridentina* Division, and to the south, entrusted to the 4° Gruppo *Valle*.

The main attack was blocked very soon near the Piccolo San Bernardo Pass by a French stronghold called *Fort de la Redoute Ruinée* (Forte di Traversette, in Italian), which could not be conquered, due to the lack of heavy artillery. The Battaglioni *Val Baltea*, *Val Cismon*, and *Aosta* barely managed to advance in the snow and reached the mountains that overlook the Val d'Isère, even pushing patrols to the surroundings of Bourg St. Maurice itself. In these positions, the Alpini received the order to cease fire on June 24 since the armistice between France and Italy had been signed.

To the north, the Battaglioni *Duca degli Abruzzi*, *Edolo*, and *Tirano* pushed forward in forbidding environmental and weather conditions, opposed by artillery fire that could not be counteracted, while the Alpini *Alpieri* protected the right flank of the columns. From June 21 to June 24, the Alpini were able to advance between 3 and 5 kilometers until they reached the French defensive line, where they were pinned down by enemy fire until the end of the hostilities.

To the south, the Battaglioni *Val Cordevole*, *Ivrea*, and *Val Piave*, with the guns of the Gruppo *Val d'Adige*, were able to cross the border during the few days of war, overwhelming some minor strongholds and reaching the eastern side of the Val d'Isère. However, they were not in any condition to attack the strong defenses on the western side of the valley, strongly manned with artillery and machine guns, when the ceasefire was ordered.

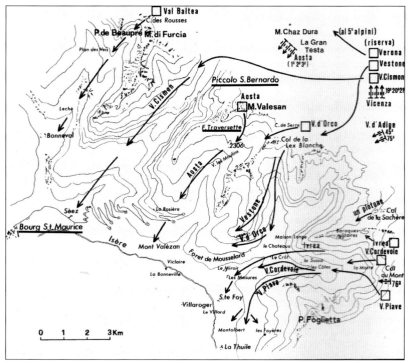

Western Alps, June 1940, the action of 4° Gruppo *Valle* of the Divisione *Taurinense* in French territory between the twenty-first and the twenty-fourth

Mule train of the Battaglione *Val Fassa*. *Museo Nazionale Storico degli Alpini*

Progress in the other sectors was even more meager, as difficult as that may be to believe, in spite of strenuous efforts made by the soldiers.

In the *Moncenisio-Bardonecchia* Sector, the target of the operations was the valley of the Arc River. The Battaglione *Susa*, with a Black Shirt battalion, managed to cross a glacier over 3,000 meters (9,850 feet) high, descend to the other side, march through a side valley, and set foot on June 24 in the Arc valley, near the town of Lanslebourg, achieving complete surprise. In fact, the French were so sure that no danger could come from that area that the Italian column, once sighted, was mistaken for a French one. The Battaglioni *Val Cenischia* and *Val Dora* aimed instead at the town of Modane, some 5 kilometers from their line, as the crow flies, through the mountains, while the infantrymen of the *Cagliari* Division advanced in the valley below. Progress was very slow and constantly under artillery fire that took a heavy toll, but on June 24, the units had just come into contact with the French advanced defenses, very far from their target.

In the *Germanasca-Pellice* Sector, the French defenses were very close to the border, protecting the area around the village of Abriés; even in this case, the Italian heavy artillery was useless, due to the bad weather and the poor visibility. Every effort to conquer or bypass the strongholds failed, and when the armistice was signed, the Alpini of the 3° Reggimento had advanced only a few hundred meters.

More to the south, in the *Po-Stura-Maira* Sector, the *Cunenese* and *Pusteria* Divisions were hastily deployed, recalled from the rear, and had to march three days in adverse weather conditions just to reach the front line. The *Cuneense* was able to move on June 22, with the valley of the Ubaye River as target, a valley that runs roughly parallel to the Italian-French border in northern Provence. The Alpini had to advance crossing 2,000-meter-high (more than 6,000 feet) peaks, where even the mules were not able to move; thus, most of the material was transported on the backs of the soldiers. As along most of the front, the advance was stopped by the first line of the *Maginot des Alpes*, against which the Alpini had little more than their rifles, and some units were so worn out that they needed to be recalled. The *Pusteria*, originally stationed between Liguria and Piedmont, only managed to reach the line on June 23, and all movement forward was hindered by high snow, blizzards, and persistent fog; thus, the Alpini were able to advance less than a couple of kilometers before the armistice.

The hostilities ceased officially at 1:30 a.m. on June 25; the four-day offensive had obtained very scarce results at a toll of a total of 642 dead; 2,631 injured; 2,151 men with frostbite, even though it was late June; and 616 missing in action.

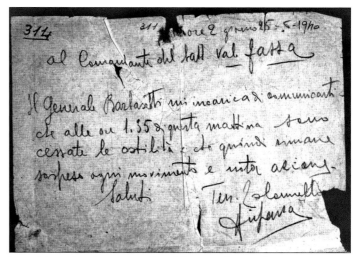

Note delivered to the commander of the Battaglione *Val Fassa* announcing the end of the hostilities with France and ordering a halt to operations of the battalion. *Museo Nazionale Storico degli Alpini*

Alpini marching on a mountain path in the summer of 1940. *Museo Nazionale Storico degli Alpini*

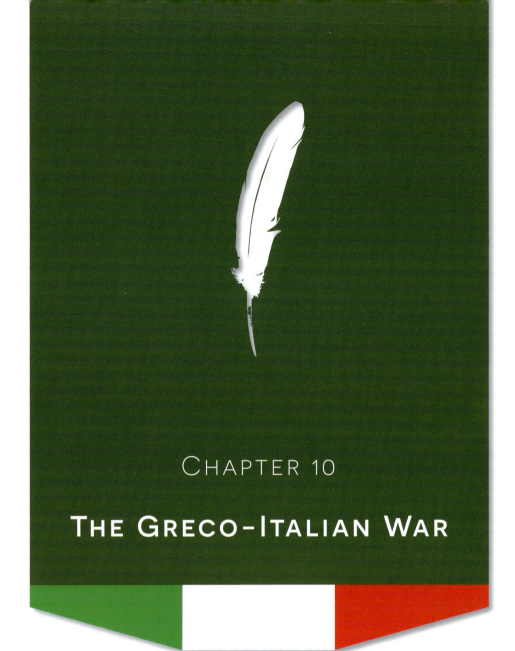

CHAPTER 10

THE GRECO-ITALIAN WAR

A HASTY DEMOBILIZATION

After the armistice with France had been signed, the Alpine divisions were withdrawn from the front and were given a period of rest and reorganization, while the *Valle* battalions remained on the Western Alps a few more months, guarding the armistice line. The Alpini of the 1° and 2° Gruppo *Valle,* instead, remained deployed on the eastern border with Yugoslavia. The special units created for the campaign in the Alps were disbanded.

During the summer months, however, the winds of war continued to blow, this time against Greece and Yugoslavia, countries that had for a long time had a rather bad relationship with Italy.[1] Both projects were set aside in late summer due to the insistence of Germany, which was already secretly planning its campaign against Russia and needed the Balkans area to be as quiet as possible; thus, it was decided to demobilize the army. The plans were that between October 15 and November 15, about 600,000 men of the classes between 1910 and 1916 would be sent back home, a welcome return, given the harvest and other farm needs, since Italy remained basically an agricultural economy. Concerning the Alpini in particular, all the *Valle* battalions and Alpine artillery battalions were disbanded, while many divisional units remained with very few personnel. This provision did not affect the units deployed in Africa nor those already stationed in Albania—the *Julia* Division among them—that were nevertheless withdrawn from their advanced positions and sent to the barracks for the wintertime.

Things changed dramatically on October 7, when the Wehrmacht entered Romania and occupied the country, with the consent of the Romanian government, which feared an aggression by the USSR, as it was said at the time. The truth was that Romania had the only important source of oil within German reach, the oil field of Ploesti, which was essential for the war effort, and the country was a good base for the invasion of the southern part of the USSR. From the Italian point of view, and above all that of the Duce, this German move completely changed the balance of power in the Balkans, an area that he had always considered strictly within Italian influence, shifting it dangerously toward Germany. Furthermore, Mussolini was notified by a simple message from his fellow dictator once the occupation had been rapidly completed, leaving him literally furious. He decided on the spot that an appropriate retaliation would be the invasion of Greece without any communication to his German ally. The decision was shared on October 12 with the undersecretary of war, General Ubaldo Soddu, with the general chief of staff, Marshal Pietro Badoglio, the following day, while the army deputy chief of staff, General Mario Roatta became aware of it only on October 14, during a meeting in the office of Benito Mussolini. The navy and air force chiefs of staff were notified in that same afternoon, while the army chief of staff, General Rodolfo

Graziani, was not even in Italy, but in Libya as commander of the Italian troops there. The following day, during another meeting, Mussolini, Badoglio, Soddu, and Roatta were joined by the lieutenant general of the king in Albania, Francesco Jacomoni, and by the commander of the Italian troops in Albania, General Sebastiano Visconti Prasca, and on this occasion the dictator imposed that the date for the beginning of the offensive be October 26, later postponed to the twenty-eighth. The guidelines for the operations expected it to begin with the occupation of the northern Greek region of Epirus moving from southern Albania, a landing on the island of Corfu, and then a triumphal march on Athens. This complacency was justified by the politicians with the assurance that the political climate in Athens was such that, as soon as Italy would declare war, the Greek army would mutiny and a coup d'état would replace the current government with another that would immediately surrender: this course of events had also been enhanced by generously bribing Greek generals and politicians for months. The Italian military chose to take these assurances for granted and did not argue further.

The Italian troops in Albania, grouped under the *Comando Superiore Truppe Albania* (Troops in Albania High Command), were rather weak, limited to nine divisions consisting of two regiments each, totaling about 150,000 men. Along the Albanian-Greek border in Macedonia were deployed the *Parma* and *Venezia* infantry divisions, while in Epirus, the theater of the

Columns of Alpine artillery of the Divisione *Julia* in Albania in the summer of 1940. *Luigi Manes*

A propaganda postcard with a small unit of Alpini on a rock spur with a Breda mod. 30 light machine gun. *David Zambon*

main Italian offensive effort, were stationed the *Ferrara* and *Siena* infantry divisions, the *Centauro* armored division, and the *Julia* Alpine division. Along the coastline, the *Raggruppamento Litorale* (Coastline Group) would move with the Third Regiment of the *Granatieri di Sardegna* Division and two cavalry regiments. The *Arezzo* Infantry Division remained for the moment deployed to the north, along the Albanian-Yugoslavian border, to avoid surprises from that direction. On the other side, Greece was able to deploy up to fourteen infantry divisions, with three regiments each, and a cavalry division: a total of about 300,000 soldiers.

The Italian plan considered an active defensive attitude in Macedonia to pin down a substantial part of the Greek army, and a reckless push forward in Epirus, with two columns that were to advance: one along the coastline and another following the largest of the few roads of the interior, the Kilibaki-Giannina-Arta, both having the Gulf of Arta as their first target. The *Julia* Division had the extremely precarious task to advance in the wild and mountainous area of the Pindus massif to protect the left flank of the Italian penetration.

Once the offensive started and was met with increasing Greek opposition, it became clear that the assurances of the politicians had been unrealistic, and it would be necessary to fight a hard war. From that moment, reinforcements were sent in from Italy in a hurry, with little room for planning.

As far as the Alpini were involved, during the month of November, the Gruppi of Alpine artillery *Val Tanaro*, *Val Po*, *Val Chisone*, and *Val d'Orco*, which, fortunately, had not yet been disbanded, were sent to Albania. The newly re-formed Battaglioni *Val Tagliamento*, *Val Fella*, and *Val Natisone* as well as the Gruppo *Val Tagliamento* of Alpine artillery, grouped in the 1° Gruppo Alpini *Valle* and the Battaglioni *Val Leogra* and *Val Pescara*, grouped in the 2° Gruppo Alpini *Valle*, which also included the Gruppo *Valle Isonzo* of Alpine artillery, arrived in Albania the following January. These latter units were formed, for the most part, with unexperienced recruits because the government decided it would be too unpopular to call the men who had been recently discharged and sent to Albania back to arms. They had little to no training since the situation of the Italian troops there worsened day by day. Meanwhile, the Alpine divisions were replenished and sent to the front one by one to join the *Julia*, starting with the *Tridentina* in early November, then the *Pusteria* between the end of the month and the beginning of December, and finally the *Cuneense* in mid-December.

In January 1941, the Battaglioni *Intra* and *Susa* followed, detached from the *Taurinense* Division, *Val Chiese* and *Val Cismon*, as well as the aforementioned Gruppo *Valle Isonzo* of Alpine artillery. Furthermore, the School of Aosta formed two special ski units, the Battaglioni *Monte Cervino* and *Monte Rosa*, sent to Albania in January and March, respectively.

At the beginning of 1941, the Battaglioni *Val Pellice*, *Val Cenischia*, and *Val Toce* were also re-formed, along with the Gruppo *Val d'Adige* of Alpine artillery, which were grouped in the 3° Gruppo Alpini *Valle*, and the Battaglioni *Val Chisone* and *Val d'Orco*, which were grouped in the 4° Gruppo Alpini *Valle*. These units would remain stationed in Italy for the time being.

THE *JULIA* DIVISION ON THE PINDUS MASSIF

The Pindus is a Greek mountain range about 180 kilometers long with a course roughly from northwest to southeast, and divides Epirus from Thessaly, with peaks above 2,000 meters (6,561 feet) above MSL, with very few natural resources and, at the time, poor routes and little population. The *Comando Superiore Truppe Albania* was eager to take control of it, with the aim of isolating the Epirus itself. The plan was to reach the Metsovo Pass, about 70 kilometers, as the crow flies, from the Albanian-Greek border, take control of it, and defend the position to prevent any movement of Greek troops to either withdraw from Epirus or send reinforcements to the region. To obtain this result, the *Julia* Division had to advance as rapidly as possible to surprise the Greek defenses and swoop down on the pass in full force, without even occupying any intermediate position during the march. Hence, the units left behind all the equipment that was considered not strictly necessary and took with them supplies of food and ammunition for at least five days, during which time it was expected the Alpini would be isolated in enemy territory. Since the territory was devoid of roads, trucks were not taken into consideration, and everything needed to be packed on the mules or, more often than not, on the men's backs.

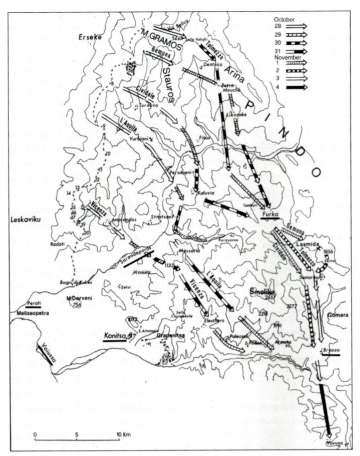

The march of the Divisione *Julia* on the Pindus massif

The beginning of the Greco-Italian War, with the advance of the Regio Esercito into Greek territory

The division was divided into two task forces, corresponding to its two regiments. The 8° Reggimento was in turn divided into three columns, with the Battaglione *Tolmezzo* taking the extreme left, the Battaglione *Gemona* with two batteries of the Gruppo *Conegliano* in the center, and the Battaglione *Cividale* with the third battery of the *Conegliano* to the right. They were to proceed southeast toward the village of Furka and then directly south to Metsovo, where, once they had arrived, they were to deploy facing east. The 9° Reggimento marched to the right of the 8° Reggimento and was divided into two columns, with the Battaglione *L'Aquila* and a battery of the Gruppo *Udine* to the left and the Battaglione *Vicenza* with another

A unit of Alpini pushes on, shouldering the necessary supplies and equipment. *Antonio Tallillo*

A postcard dedicated to the 3° Reggimento artiglieria alpina of the *Julia*, which took part in the unfortunate offensive on the Pindus massif. *Roberto Rossini*

The valley of the Sarandaporos River, with a column of Alpini facing the first serious obstacle to its advance

After days of uninterrupted fighting, these tired Alpini rearrange the little remaining equipment before beginning their march anew. *Antonio Tallillo*

battery of the *Udine* to the right; their target was the village of Peristeri, about 10 kilometers west of the Metsovo Pass, where they were to deploy facing west. A battalion of Albanian volunteers, whose mission was to occupy the basin of Konitsa and protect the advancing forces against attacks coming from Epirus, acted to the extreme right of the division. The engineer battalion was subdivided into five units, each attached to one of the columns. Rather optimistically, the enemy presence had been evaluated as being about four battalions with two or three artillery battalions, although an entire division was already stationed east of the Pindus and would be able to move quickly.

On October 28, before dawn and in the pouring rain, the operations started, and the Alpini pushed forward on the few mule tracks on the Pindus that, moreover, had become a sea of mud because of the rain. The Greeks put up stiff resistance from the very beginning, which was overwhelmed thanks to the action of the artillery and mortars. Soon, however, the columns reached a major first obstacle, the Sarandaporos River, which ran roughly across the route of the Alpini and was swollen by the rain; on the opposite bank, the Greeks awaited the Italians with numerous machine guns. Between the evening of October 29 and the night of the thirtieth, the Alpini managed to force the river, wading the icy waters, with the cover of the artillery that tirelessly shelled the Greeks during the crossing and the subsequent fighting on the opposite bank. The following day, the columns pushed forward rapidly and the battalions of the 8° Reggimento reached the area of Furka, occupying the nearby pass; to the right, the 9° Reggimento took positions on the lower slopes of Mount Smolika, the highest peak of the Pindus massif. The action had been really impressive so far, taking into consideration the territory and the weather conditions; thus, the Greeks, worried that the Alpini would be really able to occupy the Metsovo Pass, sent substantial reinforcements

to the area: between November 1 and 3, the Greek command managed to deploy nine battalions against the five battalions of the *Julia*, and at some points, Greek forces started to occupy positions behind the Alpini, threatening to surround the whole division. The supplies of the Italian columns were getting lower and lower; furthermore, many mules had been lost due both to enemy fire and to the hardship of their service. Thus, more and more equipment had to be abandoned along the way. Above all, the Italian offensive in the Epirus had been a complete failure, and the advance of the infantry divisions toward Arta had progressed only a few kilometers: it was therefore clear that the *Julia* was now completely isolated behind the enemy lines, without a supply chain and engaged by more and more Greek forces supported by automatic weapons and artillery.

After a few days of advancing farther and farther into Greek territory, the division was forced to stop and try to gather its forces with a new purpose: to get back to the Italian lines before being annihilated. On November 4, the Battaglioni *Tolmezzo* and *Gemona*, with the Fourteenth and Fifteenth Battery of the Gruppo *Conegliano*, deployed near the village of Bryaza and were joined the following day by the Battaglione *Cividale* and the Thirteenth Battery, which had tried to push forward a little more, but were now retreating hastily. The right flank of the division was covered by the Battaglioni *L'Aquila* and *Vicenza*, which manned the eastern and western slopes of Mount Smolika, trying to keep the way to Konitsa open, which now seemed to be the only one open for withdrawal to the Italian lines. On November 6, the Greeks attacked Bryaza from the south and the north, and the fighting went on the whole day, with the Alpini clinging desperately to their improvised positions and the howitzers doing their best to supply their supporting fire everywhere it was necessary. In the evening, the Greek momentum subsided a bit; thus, the *Tolmezzo* counterattacked, managing to escape being surrounded and open an escape route. The next day, the decimated units were marching toward Konitsa, always under the covering fire of the Alpine artillery batteries that retreated and redeployed in turn to ensure their continuous action. On November 9, the Gruppo *Conegliano* was marching, escorted by two *Alpine* companies, when it was attacked by overwhelming Greek forces. The men fought for over six hours, the guns shooting at point blank range against the advancing enemies until they ran out of ammunition, and then the artillerymen fought like infantry along with their fellow Alpini. In the dark, the survivors managed to escape, launching a desperate bayonet charge, even taking with them four of the howitzers. On November 10, what remained of the *Julia* Alpine division, which had lost 20 percent of its men and the greatest part of its equipment, reached Konitsa, where it met the infantrymen of the *Bari* Division. The most worn-out men were sent back to the rear, but part of the 8° Reggimento and the Gruppo *Udine* remained on the front line, attached to the *Bari* Division, fighting to defend the eastern access to the town. On November 15, the situation was again very critical, therefore the 9° Reggimento was redeployed on the forefront, after only four days of rest, while the entire Italian line backed off some kilometers in order to shorten the line that needed to be manned. This was only the beginning of a series of maneuvered retreats, called by the supreme command's daily bulletin a "strategic withdrawal" that would characterize the next few weeks, until January. The Battaglioni and Gruppi of the *Julia* were deployed near the confluence of the Sarandaporos River with the Vojussa River, in the area of the town of Perati. On November 18, the division was reinforced with the Battaglione *Val Tagliamento*, which had just arrived in Albania without its mules and some of its equipment, and was immediately sent to the front line. Between November 20 and 21, confronted with repeated Greek attacks, which always employed fresh units, the newly formed Italian VIII Army Corps ordered a general retreat; thus, the Alpini broke contact with the enemy and moved northwest along the Vojussa River. However, it was not yet time for the *Julia* to rest, and the division would fight for months without interruption.

THE REORGANIZATION OF THE ITALIAN TROOPS

On November 7, the Italian offensive had already been halted by bad weather and by the Greeks; furthermore, an enemy counteroffensive was in the air. General Visconti Prasca himself realized it and that very day sent two alarming messages to the ministry of war. The following day, the undersecretary, General Soddu, made some major decisions, such as the division of the

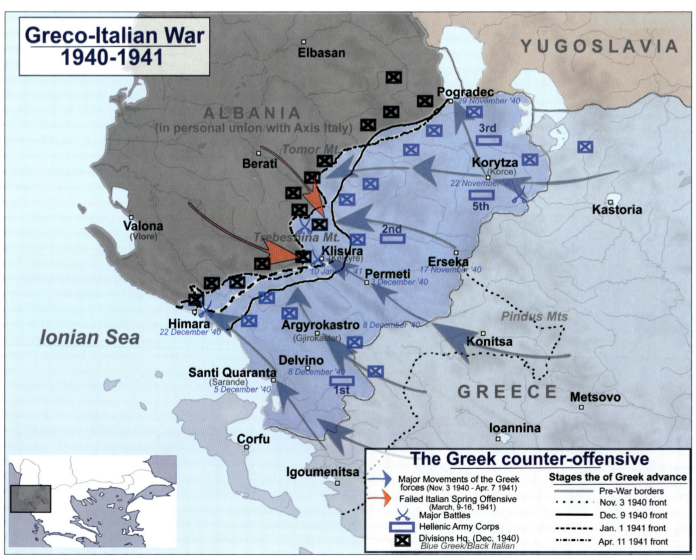

The second phase of the Greco-Italian War: the Greek counteroffensive

A unit of Alpini transported on a column of air force trucks, as the number plates show, confirmation of the extreme confusion that reigned in Albania during the Italo-Greek war. *David Zambon*

An alpino is boarding the plane that will hastily transfer him and his fellow soldiers to Albania with only their individual equipment. *Antonio Tallillo*

long frontline in two sectors under the responsibility of two newly created armies, which were in turn grouped in an army group under his personal command:

- Ninth Army, with responsibility for the Macedonian sector, from the Yugoslavian border up to the Pindus massif, under the command of General Mario Vercellino, consisting of the III Army Corps, with the *Venezia* and *Arezzo* Divisions, the latter coming hastily from northern Albania, and the XXVI Army Corps, with the *Piemonte* and *Parma* Divisions

- Eleventh Army, with responsibility for the Epirus sector, from the Pindus massif to the sea, under the command of General Carlo Geloso, consisting of the VIII Army Corps, with the *Bari* and *Julia* Divisions, and the XXV Army Corps, with the *Ferrara*, *Siena*, and *Centauro* Divisions

This settled, the dramatically difficult part of his job began: to transport the necessary reinforcements from Italy to Albania, which started with the most complete chaos.

First of all, it was necessary to bring the recently depleted divisions up to strength, which in and of itself took several weeks.

Second, it was necessary to organize their passage from Italy to Albania, dealing above all with the problem of the scarce capacity of the Albanian ports: in fact, the only two destinations were Durres to the north of the country and Vlore, to the south, and they were far from satisfactory.

Third, the reinforcements and the equipment needed to be dispatched to the frontline from the ports, but the road system of Albania was quite primitive. The roads that allowed truck traffic were very few, and most of the units could be reached only via mule tracks.

As a result, the entire system was affected by a series of bottlenecks, with men and supplies languishing for days in the Italian ports waiting to be embarked; they then waited hours and sometimes days in the Albanian ports before disembarking and, finally, needed even more days to reach their destinations.[2] More often than not, men moved toward the front line on foot, while their equipment and supply remained far behind, waiting for unloading and transporting, and arrived without suitable clothing and heavy weapons to be thrown immediately into the furnace of fighting.

THE *TRIDENTINA* DIVISION DISEMBARKS IN ALBANIA

The first Alpine division to arrive in Albania was the *Tridentina*, hastily brought up to strength and sent to reinforce the XXIV Army Corps in Macedonia; the move took several days, from November 10 to 19, but some units managed to join the division only at the end of the month. The first battalions to arrive were the *Morbegno* and the *Edolo*, which were delivered directly by air to the Tirana airfield between November 10 and 12, while the rest of the division as well as the heavy equipment were ferried from Apulia. The two battalions were not able to wait for their fellow Alpini and their mules but were immediately transported by truck to the area of the Albanian town of Korça, near the border with Greece, and between the thirteenth and the fifteenth, they took positions between the *Parma* and *Piemonte* divisions, to reinforce their thin line. Since the divisional artillery was still far behind, the battalions had the Gruppo *Val d'Orco*, which had arrived a few days earlier, temporarily

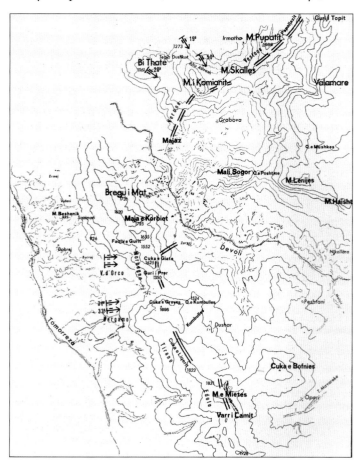

The deployment of the battalions of the Divisione *Tridentina* along the Devoll River

A mule carrying one of the loads of a 75 mm mountain howitzer struggling in the mud in the winter of 1940–41. *Luigi Manes*

A unit of Alpini climbs the slopes of an Albanian mountain whitened by snow. *Museo Nazionale Storico degli Alpini*

assigned. On November 16, the battalions were joined by the Battaglione *Tirano*; thus, the 5° Reggimento became fully operational. On the nineteenth, the 6° Reggimento arrived as well, transported on trucks and without its mules, and was deployed to the left of its fellow 5° Reggimento, replacing the now weary infantrymen of the *Parma* Division, which was temporarily withdrawn from the front. However, the Italian troops deployed in the area were still not adequate to defend the whole line;[3] therefore, the headquarters of the army, in accordance with the army group, ordered a deep retreat to shorten the line and to gain some time and space to put between its troops and the advancing Greeks. The withdrawal took place between November 21 and 22 and was preceded by some local attacks launched by the Battaglioni *Vestone* and *Verona*, supported by the howitzers of the Gruppo *Vicenza*, newly deployed and fresh, to relieve the enemy pressure a bit and hide the Italians' real intentions. The retreat was conducted in good order, although most of the divisional mule train was yet not available, so the Alpini transported a lot of equipment on their backs, and the units were redeployed in the upper valley of the Devoll River, with the 6° Reggimento on the left bank of the river, in contact with the *Arezzo* Division on the right flank of the III Army Corps; and the 5° Reggimento on the right bank,[4] linked with a battle group formed by the few combat-ready troops of the *Parma* and *Piemonte* divisions. Unfortunately, pressure from the Greeks increased again after a few days, and from November 25 on, the Alpini, who had not been able to dig adequate defenses and shelters, were subjected to hard fighting in extremely difficult environmental and weather conditions. Fortunately, the Gruppo *Bergamo* of Alpine artillery arrived a few days later and was assigned to the 5° Reggimento, and its fire support was a great relief; furthermore, at the beginning of December, the division was joined by its II Battaglione genio. It had the necessary equipment to improve its defensive positions and, since it had arrived with the complete mule train, its supply chain. On the new defensive line, the Alpini fought furiously, and although they were slowly forced to move back, they fought the Greeks for every meter of ground. In a few days, the units paid a heavy toll of casualties, the battalions were reduced to the strength of companies and the companies to platoons; the remnants of the Battaglione *Edolo* and of the Gruppo *Val d'Orco* had to be retired from the frontline in mid-December to be completely replenished. But the situation **was slowly getting better, and** reinforcements were on their way.

THE *CUNEENSE* DIVISION MOVES IN

THE 1° REGGIMENTO ON THE DEVOLL RIVER

While the *Julia* and the *Tridentina* divisions were desperately fighting to avoid the collapse of the front, the *Cuneense* Division started to disembark in Albania. On December 15, the entire 1° Reggimento Alpini arrived in Durres, miraculously with its full equipment and all its mules, and was immediately sent to reinforce the XXVI Army Corps. Unfortunately, the needs of the frontline prevented this unit from being deployed organically: the Battaglione *Mondovì* was hastily transferred to its destination by truck, where it arrived on December 17, while the Battaglioni *Ceva* and *Pieve di Teco* followed on foot and arrived between the twentieth and the twenty-first. The *Ceva* was assigned to

Alpini disembark at the port of Durres. The capacity of the Albanian ports was far from satisfactory for the needs of the front; furthermore, the poor condition of roads in the county made it even more difficult to deliver supplies to the units on the line. *David Zambon*

the *Parma* Infantry Division, by now a mere ghost of a division, while the other two battalions were attached to the 5° Reggimento of the *Tridentina*, which deployed them to replace its exhausted *Tirano* and *Morbegno*. However, the influx of fresh units gave new strength to the defenders, who even managed to mount some local counterattacks to improve the difficult situation a bit. On December 29, the Greeks launched the last great offensive in the sector that was defended by the XXVI Army Corps; thus, the *Tridentina* was forced to recall the Battaglioni *Tirano* and *Morbegno* to the frontline after only a few days of rest, but the Alpini managed to bear the impact without further retreats. On these positions, the Italians would be able to resist for the next few months, waiting to retake the initiative in the spring. On December 31, the Battaglione *Val Leogra*, which had arrived in Albania on the twentieth with the 2° Gruppo Alpini *Valle,* joined the *Tridentina* as well and was assigned to the 6° Reggimento and sent to replace the weary *Vestone.*

At the end of 1940, the Italian deployment in the upper valley of the Devoll River saw, on the right bank of the river, the 1° Reggimento of the *Cuneense* with its Battaglioni *Pieve di Teco* and *Ceva*, returned from its assignment to the *Parma* Division on the frontline; and the Battaglione *Mondovì* as reserve, supported by the howitzers of one surviving battery of the Gruppo *Val d'Orco*; and the 5° Reggimento of the *Tridentina*, with the Battaglioni *Tirano* and *Edolo* on the frontline and the Battaglione *Morbegno* as reserve, supported by the Gruppo *Bergamo*. The Gruppo *Mondovì* was arriving as well. On the left bank, the 6° Reggimento was deployed with the Battaglioni *Verona* and *Val Leogra* on the frontline and the Battaglione *Vestone*, just withdrawn, as reserve, supported by the guns of the Gruppo *Vicenza.*

THE 2° REGGIMENTO IN THE SUSHIÇA VALLEY

The 2° Reggimento of the *Cuneense* was not as lucky as the 1° Reggimento, since it had been airlifted to Albania and arrived woefully short of its equipment. On December 20, while some of its units were disembarking from the planes, the rest of the regiment was still at the port of Bari or on its way to Durres by ship, as was the IV Battaglione genio. The mule train, on the other hand, was still stationed at the headquarters in Cuneo. The Alpini, with just what they had on them, were immediately sent south toward Vlore, assigned to what was known as the *Divisione alpina speciale* (special Alpine division), entrusted with the defense of the valley of the Sushiça River. The river flows roughly parallel to the coast, in a south–north direction, until it joins the Vojussa River a little north of Vlore, which is roughly 40 kilometers away. Apart from the 2° Reggimento, the *Divisione alpina speciale* was formed by a cavalry regiment fighting on foot and two machine gun companies. The Battaglioni *Saluzzo* and *Dronero*, along with the Gruppo *Pinerolo* of Alpine artillery, arrived in the valley between December 20 and 21, transporting all the necessary equipment on the backs of their Alpini, and replaced the remnants of the *Siena* Infantry Division—who had been fighting for two months without rest—on the frontline. The Battaglione *Saluzzo* occupied the eastern bank of the river; the *Dronero*, the western one; with the *Pinerolo* ensuring its supporting fire. The command of the *Divisione alpina speciale* had planned a local counterattack with these fresh forces, but the Greeks anticipated it and moved against the Alpini during the night of December 26. The fighting went on for two days, but the Italian line was now firm enough, and when the Battaglione *Borgo San Dalmazzo* finally arrived in the area as further reinforcement

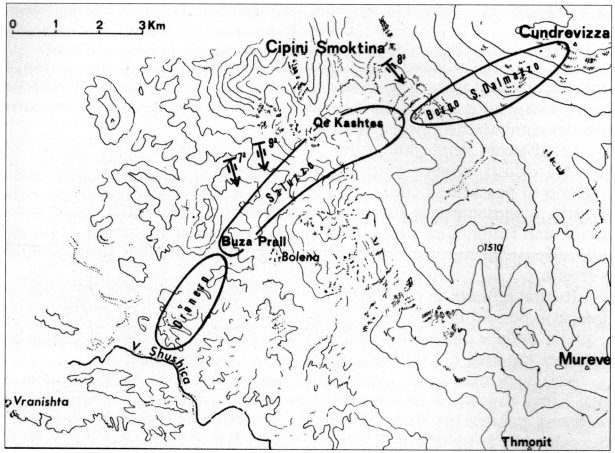

The positions defended by the 2° Reggimento of the Divisione *Cuneense* in the Sushiça River Valley

Alpini get off the planes that have airlifted them to Albania. This system for transferring troops was one of the symptoms of the chaotic situation throughout the whole campaign. *Luigi Manes/Antonio Tallillo*

on the twenty-eighth, the Greeks gave up. A few days later, the newly arrived *Cuneo* Infantry Division further thickened the Italian forces, and the three Alpine battalions redeployed on the left bank of the Sushiça River, leaving the right bank to the 7° Reggimento of the *Cuneo*. After two months, the defensive line was now strong and manned enough to be considered solid and able to ensure the possession of Vlore, whose loss would have endangered the Italian presence in Albania. By now, the supply line between Vlore and the southern front was short and was provided with roads suitable for trucks, while the Greeks were far from their depots and their supply lines were very stretched.

THE ARRIVAL OF THE 1° GRUPPO *VALLE* AND THE *PUSTERIA* DIVISION

Around mid-November, the Battaglioni *Val Fella*, *Val Tagliamento*, and *Val Natisone* of the 1° Gruppo Alpini *Valle* started to arrive in Albania, without mule trains, as was common in these weeks, and without the artillery of the Gruppo *Val Tagliamento*, which would arrive only a month later. The units were dispatched to the east, to deploy at the back of the *Julia* Division, which, as seen, had been retreating along the Vojussa River, and to defend the accesses to the town of Klisura. However, once it had arrived, the Battaglione *Val Tagliamento* was assigned to the 8° Reggimento of the *Julia* and sent to the frontline in the area of Perati (see above), while the *Val Fella* was assigned to the 9° Reggimento. The division also received the Gruppi *Val Po* and *Val Tanaro*, less one battery, significantly increasing the artillery support for the subordinate units.

A postcard celebrating the 11° Reggimento of the Divisione *Pusteria*. *Roberto Rossini*

General Esposito, commander of the Divisione *Pusteria*, inspects the positions manned by his Alpini. *Museo Nazionale Storico degli Alpini*

Between the end of November and the beginning of December, the *Pusteria* Division started to disembark in Albania, in the same dramatic situation common to every Italian unit transferred in those chaotic weeks: without its mule train and heavy equipment. In principle, the division had been assigned to the VIII Army Corps and was meant to fill the gap in the line across the Osum River that was still completely open to Greek penetration toward the town of Berat, which was located some 50 kilometers behind the frontline, thus linking the left flank of the Eleventh Army to the right flank of the Ninth Army. As often happened, several units of the division were diverted to other stretches of the front that needed reinforcements. The Battaglione *Feltre* reached the assigned area at the end of November, deploying two companies near the village of Cerevoda and one company some 10 kilometers south of it. A few days later, it was joined by the Battaglione *Pieve di Cadore*, which took position to its left flank on the other bank of the river, and shortly afterward, by the Battaglioni *Trento* and *Bassano*, which took position along the western bank of the same river. With the artillery still trudging behind, they received the Gruppo *Udine*, detached from the *Julia* Division, as support, but it had been reduced to little more than a battery. The Battaglione *Belluno* was instead reassigned to the 1° Gruppo Alpini *Valle,* which, as mentioned above, had seen its battalions ceded to the *Julia* Division, less the *Val Natisone*, and sent to the Zagoria Valley (see below). The Battaglione *Bolzano* remained for a while as reserve of the VIII Army Corps, but was later assigned to the *Modena* Infantry Division, as well as the Gruppo *Val Tagliamento* of Alpine artillery, formerly of the 1° Gruppo Alpini *Valle* (see below).

THE DEFENSE OF THE OSUM RIVER VALLEY

With the new battalions, the VIII Army Corps planned to mount a small-scale operation across the Osum River to reconquer some positions and halt the enemy advances in the area, at least momentarily. There was to be an attack by the Battaglione *Pieve di Cadore* to the south, toward the bend where the Osum River starts to flow due northwest, with a flanking movement of the Battaglione *Feltre* and a contemporary attack of the Battaglione *Trento* that was to cross the river itself. The aim was to annihilate the Greek units taken between the *Pieve di Cadore* acting as a hammer and the *Trento* acting as an anvil. On December 8, the Alpini moved out of their positions, but soon they met significant enemy forces, which were in turn moving to attack the Italians: what followed was a series of very confused fights, with little artillery support. The fighting ended with a setback for the *Pusteria*. The Alpini were pushed back across the Osum River and its tribuary Cerevoda, and they lost their few positions that they still held on the opposite bank, but managed to maintain at least that line. In the following days, the Greeks mounted several attempts to force the rivers, attacking both the *Pusteria* and the *Julia*, positioned to the south, but were not able to make any progress, although the support of the Alpine artillery, which had now no more than a handful of howitzers, was inadequate.

A view of the valley of the Osum River

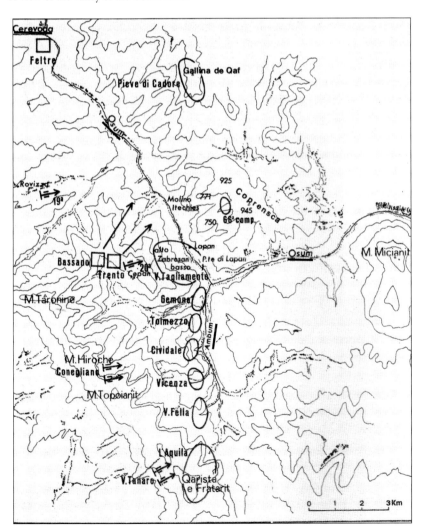

The Divisioni *Pusteria* and *Julia* deployed along the Osum River and its tributary, the Ambum River, in December 1940

What followed was a relatively calm period that saw the highly sought arrival of the two divisional Gruppi *Lanzo* and *Belluno* of Alpine artillery that enhanced the defensive capabilities of the *Pusteria* battalions. The division had also assigned a Black Shirt battalion and an infantry battalion that permitted the rotation of the units on the frontline and made it even possible to organize some coups de main to conquer better positions and improve the line. On December 23, the Greeks attacked the two divisions again; they did not obtain any significant result against the *Julia* and the 11° Reggimento of the *Pusteria* to the south of the bend of the Osum River but endangered the Italian lines to the north of the bend, where the 7° Reggimento had its units more scattered, and still lacked a firm link with the right flank of the Ninth Army. In a few days, the Battaglioni *Feltre* and *Pieve di Cadore* were reduced to a handful of men with few supplies and ammunition, while the Gruppo *Belluno* had been decimated by enemy machine guns and artillery; furthermore, the Alpini had lost their link with the Black Shirt battalion. The end of the year saw the worn-out 7° Reggimento, a regiment only on paper, gathering its surviving men on the slopes of Mount Tomor, the highest mountain of Albania, with its 2,417 (7,927 feet) above MSL, located between the Osum River and the Devoll River. Here it received the reinforcement of the Battaglione *Val Pescara*; thus, it was able to reconnect with the Black Shirts and to put up a resistance line.

OPERATIONS IN THE ZAGORIA VALLEY

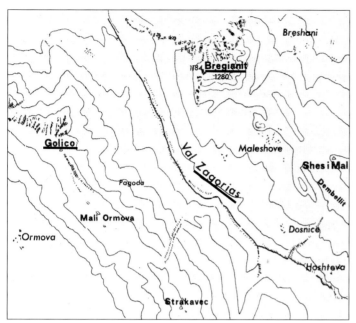

Map of the valley of the Zagoria River, closed to the north by Mount Bregianit and Mount Golico, ferociously fought against the Greeks by the Alpini of the 1° Gruppo *Valle*.

The Zagoria Valley, crossed by the river of the same name, is located in southern Albania, some 60 kilometers southeast of Vlore. The Zagoria River is a tributary of the Vojussa River in a stretch of this latter river's course where it bends due west before resuming its northwest course, drawing a sort of "S." The valley was a fragile point because the line of separation between the XXV Army Corps and the VIII Army Corps passed there and offered to the Greeks the possibility to break into the valley of the Vojussa River and threaten the town of Tepelenë, an important road junction for the southern front lying some

10 kilometers west along the valley. On November 24, the 1° Gruppo Alpini *Valle* arrived in the area with the only unit that remained, the Battaglione *Val Natisone*, with the support of only one battery of the Gruppo *Val Tanaro*, the twenty-seventh, and the two units were immediately engaged in hard fighting; on November 28, the battalion was joined by the Battaglione *Belluno*, detached from the *Pusteria* Division. During the whole month of December, the enemy did not cease to attack along the valley, forcing the Alpini to retreat slowly, but were never able to break through. Toward the end of the month, the remnants of the two battalions were gathered in the lower part of the valley, barely clinging to the last heights of the stretch of the front where the Zagoria River flows into the Vojussa River. The *Val Natisone* held the slopes of Mount Bregianit, on the left, whose top, however, it was not possible to occupy because it was constantly shelled by Greek artillery; the *Belluno* was entrenched on the Golik Mount, on the opposite bank of the Zagoria. The battery of the *Val Tanaro*, positioned on the northern bank of the Vojussa River, tirelessly supported its fellow Alpini. On these positions the two battalions resisted tenaciously during the following weeks.

THE BATTAGLIONE *BOLZANO* ON MALI I THATË

The Battaglione *Bolzano* detached from the *Pusteria* Division and was assigned as reserve to the VIII Army Corps, which planned to use the fresh Alpini for a small-scale action aimed at relieving at least for a while the Greek pressure to the south of Tepelenë. Notwithstanding the horrible weather conditions and the lack of adequate artillery support, the attack was initially successful, forcing the enemy to leave some of its positions. However, the battalion was not strong enough to face the ferocious counterattack launched by the Greeks and was forced

Unit of Alpini marching in the snowy Albanian mountains. *Museo Nazionale Storico degli Alpini*

to withdraw on December 4. The battalion was immediately dispatched southwest of Tepelenë to reinforce the infantrymen of the *Modena* Division, who were on the brink of collapsing. The Alpini deployed on Mali i Thatë, some 10 kilometers southwest of Tepelenë, where they resisted every attack until December 22. When the mountain was surrounded by enemy forces, the survivors opened their way to the Italian lines by launching a bayonet attack, but only a handful of about forty men were able to retreat. In the same area in mid-December, the Gruppo *Val Tagliamento* of Alpine artillery arrived, which made a great contribution to the defense of Tepelenë.

A CHANGE IN THE COMANDO SUPERIORE TRUPPE ALBANIA

On December 20, General Ugo Cavallero, freshly appointed general chief of staff, replacing the dismissed Marshal Badoglio, scapegoat of the embarrassing failure in Greece, landed at the airport of Tirana. He immediately met the army group commander, General Soddu, and the commanders of the two armies, General Vercellino and General Geloso, for an evaluation of the situation

Albania. The building shows clear signs of recent fighting. *Museo Nazionale Storico degli Alpini*

Columns of Alpini move toward the frontline along mountain paths and on footbridges built over a river. *Museo Storico Nazionale degli Alpini*

in Albania. During the following days, he inspected several points of the front, met the higher officers of the army corps, and gave some directions for the assignment of the new units that were arriving from Italy, trying to plan some local-scale actions to enhance morale and relieve the still strong Greek pressure. After just a few days, on the twenty-ninth, Cavallero himself assumed command of the army group, sending Soddu back to Italy.

Meanwhile, the situation in many stretches of the front was still rather precarious, but not as desperate as it had appeared only a few weeks before. Although sometimes a bit chaotically, now the reinforcements and supplies arrived from Italy regularly enough; thus, the line was now manned by a sufficient number of soldiers. An assessment made on December 28 ascertained that the Eleventh Army was now 130,000 strong, while the Ninth Army was 77,000 men strong; to these numbers were added about 8,000 Albanians and 25,000 civilian workers. The battalions and regiments were still intermixed in some places, but the necessary rotation and reorganization was now in motion, and the weariest divisions were retired from the front for a period of rest and replenishment. The capacity of the Albanian ports and road system had been enhanced, and furthermore, now the supply lines were much shorter than before. The sore point remained the scarce number of vehicles, about 8,500; and of mules, no more than 28,000. This sometimes made it difficult to deliver the supplies quickly to the frontline, but it was getting better. On the contrary, the Greek army was in the opposite situation, with divisions that started to feel the tiredness of weeks of fighting and having now inadequate supply lines that were stretched to their limits.

This situation, however, did not allow the Italians to regain the initiative, which remained firmly in Greek hands. There would be other enemy offensives and some defeats, but at least it was now ensured that the Italian presence in Albania was not in serious danger of being permanent anymore.

THE FALL OF THE TOWN OF KLISURA

The month of January opened with a new offensive effort by the Greek army, with the objective of conquering the important road junction of Klisura and, in case of success, pushing forward in the direction of Berat some 70 kilometers beyond, causing the break of the Italian frontline and, it was hoped, its collapse. The offensive hit the positions occupied by the 11° Reggimento of the *Pusteria* Division, still deployed along the Osum River, and the adjoining *Julia* Division, which manned a line that run along the Ambun River, a tributary of the Osum River, with its units facing east. The key position of the line was Mount Mal Topojan, defended by a very depleted Battaglione *Val Tagliamento*, which had on its left the Battaglioni *Val Fella*, *Cividale*, *Tolmezzo*, and *Gemona*, deployed along the previously mentioned Ambun River and on its right flank, the infantrymen of the 139th Regimento of the *Bari* Division, who defended a stretch of the front that bent to the southeast toward the town of Klisura. On January 8, at 7:30 a.m., the Greeks launched an attack against Mount Mal Topojan from the west and the south and, after fierce fighting, managed to conquer it, expelling the Alpini. This endangered the entire line defended by the *Julia*,

Alpini are digging trenches in the deep snow while another unit is passing by. *Museo Nazionale Storico degli Alpini*

The hard fighting of the winter 1940–41 has decimated the Alpini; a few fallen in combat rest in a small war cemetery. *Museo Nazionale Storico degli Alpini*

An alpino skier of the Battaglione *Monte Cervino* is reconnoitering the terrain in front of him. The *Monte Cervino* fought to the very last man on the Mal Trebeshine and on the Shendeli, in February 1941. *Antonio Tallillo*

which was forced to retreat some kilometers to the north: in the evening, about a thousand survivors of the *Julia* gathered on the slopes of Mali Taroninit. This movement, however, opened a gap to the left of the *Bari*, leaving the way to Klisura dangerously opened. Therefore, the newly arrived *Lupi di Toscana* Infantry Division was immediately dispatched there and entrusted with a counterattack to restore the line. Since the divisional artillery had not arrived yet, fire support was provided by the few howitzers of the Gruppi *Udine*, *Val Tanaro*, and *Lanzo*, as well as by the guns of one artillery battalion of the *Bari*. The counterattack was a complete disaster. The infantrymen, not acquainted with the territory and without adequate heavy fire support, were annihilated by the Greeks, who took Klisura in the night between January 9 and 10. The fighting went on, and the weary Alpini remained on the frontline between what remained of the *Bari* and the *Lupi di Toscana*. These forces resisted to the limits of their ability until, on January 25, the *Cacciatori delle Alpi* Infantry Division arrived and deployed in the area; only then, finally, were the remnants of the *Julia* retired from the line and sent to the rear to rest and replenish after three months of continuous fighting.

The fall of Klisura opened a dangerous gap between the left flank of the XXV Army Corps, pushed back to the west of the town, and the right flank of the VIII Army Corps, which had been pushed back some 15 kilometers toward the northwest. Between the two army corps was the Mali Trebeshine massif, which was hastily garrisoned with units gathered wherever possible but remained weakly manned. Fortunately for the Italian command, the Greeks were weary as well; thus, the offensive lost some of its momentum, and this circumstance gave General Cavallero the opportunity to reinforce the sector with fresh units and even to mount some small-scale actions to regain some of the lost positions, although not always successfully. An attempt to retake Klisura failed.

January saw a few changes in the assignment of the Alpine battalions, due to the arrival of some new units from Italy and to the need to garrison some important positions that were still weakly defended. The Battaglioni *Intra* and *Susa*, which had

been assigned at first to the depleted *Cuneense* Division, were soon detached and sent to the area of Mount Tomor, between the valleys of the Osum River and the Devoll River, under the command of the 2° Gruppo Alpini *Valle* and of the *Parma* Division first and later of the 1° Gruppo Alpini Valle, respectively. The *Pusteria* received the Battalione *Val Chiese* and the Gruppo *Valle Isonzo* of Alpine artillery as reinforcements. The Battaglione *Val Cismon* and the Battaglione sciatori (ski battalion), *Monte Cervino*, was assigned to the VIII Army Corps and immediately sent to Mali Trebeshine. Later, in March, the Battaglione sciatori *Monte Rosa* arrived as well and was attached to the *Tridentina* and, later, to the *Parma* Infantry Division.

THE STRUGGLE FOR THE TOWN OF TEPELENË

The last important offensive effort of the Greek army was planned, aimed at the conquest of the important Italian logistics center of Tepelenë, some 15 kilometers west of Klisura, and from there swoop on Vlore itself, which lay less than 50 kilometers to the northwest, as the crow flies. To achieve this result, the Greek command gathered its best forces in the Mali Trebeshine area, to the north of the Vojussa River, and in the lower Zagoria Valley, to the south of the river. On Mali Trebeshine, the Italians had been able to deploy some Black Shirt battalions and the Alpini of the Battaglioni *Monte Cervino*, *Val Cismon*, and *Bolzano*, already battered by the continuous fighting in the area since the fall of Klisura, with the support in the rear of a regiment of the *Sforzesca* Infantry Division. In the Zagoria Valley, the remnants of the Battaglioni *Val Natisone* and *Belluno* had still been clinging tenaciously

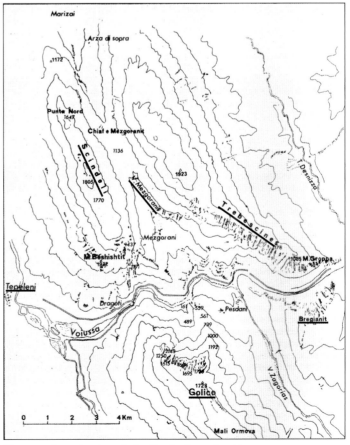

The area where the struggle for Tepelenë was fought

March 1941, a 75/13 howitzer of the Alpine artillery. *David Zambon*

to Mount Bregianit and Mount Golik, respectively, since December. Between Mali Trebeshine and the Zagoria Valley, in a fragile stretch of the front across the Vojussa River, the line was defended by the *Legnano* Infantry Division, some Black Shirt battalions, a few units of *bersaglieri*, and a handful of M13 medium tanks.

The Greek attack was launched on February 13, to the north of the Vojussa River, and managed to rapidly dislodge the haggard Italian force from Mali Trebeshine. However, it was stopped a little farther on by the line of resistance manned by the Italian reserves, which leaned now on Mount Shendeli and Mount Mezgoranit; the fighting went on during the whole day, but the Italians put up a stiff resistance and repelled the enemy. The following day, the Italians managed to organize a counterattack that forced the Greeks to stop their offensive temporarily and withdraw from some exposed positions, but then the Greeks took the initiative again with a series of attacks that, although they did not manage to break the line, put a strain on the Italian defenses. During this fighting, the *Monte Cervino* ski battalion was almost annihilated.

On February 15, the Greeks attacked as well to the south of the Vojussa River, toward the positions defended by the Alpini on the Bregianit and the Golik; in a few days the already depleted Battaglione *Val Natisone* was reduced to no more than fifty Alpini while the *Belluno* did not reach the force of a hundred men, however the enemy did not break through.

From February 20 to 26, the terrible weather conditions induced a pause to the operations that gave the Italian command the opportunity to reinforce the line and send in the *Julia* Division, which had been replenished and reorganized during the few weeks that it had spent in rear, and the Battaglione

Susa moved from its positions on Mount Tomor. The 8° Reggimento was sent to the south of the Vojussa River, on Mount Golik, with the Battaglioni *Tolmezzo* and *Cividale*, joined soon by the *Susa*, on the frontline and the Battaglione *Gemona* as reserve; the 9° Reggimento was sent to shore up the line on Mount Shendeli, with the Battaglione *L'Aquila* on the frontline and the *Vicenza* in the rear, supported by both Alpine artillery battalions, *Udine* and *Conegliano*. On the twenty-eighth, the area of the Golico was attacked by the Greeks, but the *Cividale* and the *Susa* held their line firmly and were able to mount some counterattacks that discouraged the enemy to continue its actions.

The offensive was resumed on March 7, with great vigor, by the Greeks, who saw the town of Tepelenë within reach since the Italian line, although not broken, had withdrawn slowly and now had very little space to maneuver: the next retreat would mean abandoning Tepelenë and deploying west of the town. During the day, the enemy managed to snatch a few positions away; some Italian units fought until they ceased to exist, like the Battaglione *Gemona*, which sacrificed itself—to the last man—on the Golik. Again, the Italian command thought it necessary to send the Battaglioni *Val Natisone*, *Val Tagliamento*, and *Val Fella* to the area as support. They had been withdrawn a few days before and were still largely incomplete, and even the engineers of the III Battalion fought with their fellow Alpini. During the following days, while the Greeks renewed the attacks with fresh units, the *Susa* was reduced to having only two surviving officers and had lost all its equipment, while the *Val Natisone* was completely lost, overwhelmed while trying to defend, along with a handful of Black Shirts, a stretch of the valley floor.

The casualties had been terrific for both contenders; the *Julia* Division, recently replenished, had lost almost 4.000 Alpini in fewer than fifteen days of fighting; this, however, was the swansong for the Greeks, who by now were as weary as the Italians, and they suspended the offensive. Furthermore, the Italian command had managed to mount a counteroffensive in the Trebeshine area that included an attack from the north toward the south along the eastern side of the Mali Trebeshine massif. It was to hit the right flank of the enemy penetration, reach the valley of the Vojussa River a little east of Klisura and retake the town, encircling all the Greek units between the advancing Italian columns and the Italian line. The action, entrusted mainly to the infantry divisions with a limited participation of Alpini units, started on March 9, and although it did not achieve the expected results, it at least forced the Greeks to stop their attacks and change their deployment to a defensive one.

THE EPILOGUE OF THE GRECO-ITALIAN WAR

The epilogue of the Greco-Italian War came a few weeks later, due to the evolution of the situation in the Balkans. At the beginning of March, Bulgaria had joined the Tripartite Pact, and German forces had entered the country, menacing the Greek-Bulgarian border. A few days later, the British government decided to send an expeditionary corps to mainland Greece. On March 25, Yugoslavia joined the Tripartite Pact as well, but a few days later, a coup d'état overthrew the government and repudiated the treaty. All of these events were leading toward a rapid German intervention in the area to secure the large rear front of its impending invasion of the USSR. Operation *Marita*, the offensive against Yugoslavia and Greece, started on April 6, when German forces invaded Macedonia and Thrace, easily overwhelming the meager forces that remained to guard that

area. On April 12, the advancing Germans threatened the rear of the Greek forces engaged against the Ninth Italian Army; hence, the Greek command was forced to order a general retreat from the Albanian front toward the south, while Italian forces advanced rapidly. The end of hostilities came on April 23.

The Greco-Italian War cost the Italian armed forces heavy losses, with few results. The *Regio Esercito* lost more than 100,000 men, including killed, wounded and missing soldiers, and a further 52,000, more or less, who were diseased. Among these casualties, 7,754 were Alpini of the *Julia* Division, the unit that suffered the heaviest toll and had its regiments awarded with the Gold Medal. The *Pusteria* had 2,534 casualties; the *Tridentina*, 1,511, with its 5° Reggimento awarded the Gold Medal as well; the *Cuneense*, 872.

A column of Alpine artillery and one of mechanically towed field artillery push forward. *Antonio Tallillo*

Alpini try to free a truck from a stream after an improvised wooden bridge has given way under it. *Antonio Tallillo*

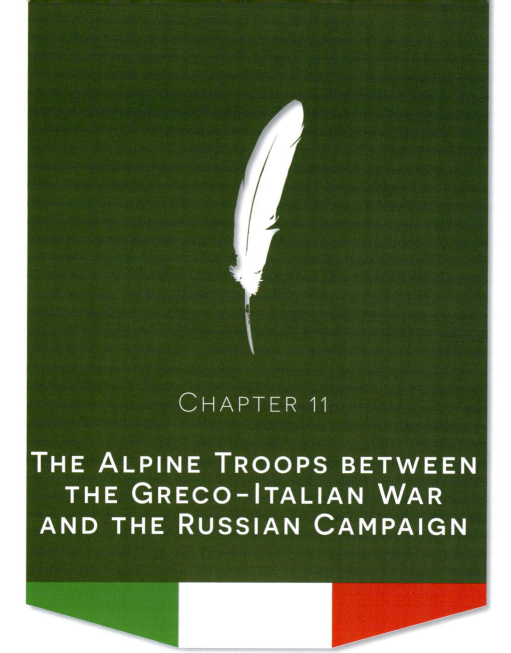

THE ALPINE TROOPS BETWEEN THE GRECO-ITALIAN WAR AND THE RUSSIAN CAMPAIGN

In the time frame between the end of the Greco-Italian War and the unfortunate expedition of the *Corpo d'Armata Alpino* (the Alpine Army Corps), in the USSR, some Alpine units were engaged in operations on several fronts.

THE SHORT WAR AGAINST YUGOSLAVIA

Axis occupation of Yugoslavia

Between April 8 and 18, the *Regio Esercito* campaigned, along with the German armed forces, against Yugoslavia: Italian columns moved from their bases in Friuli-Venezia Giulia and Istria, to the northeast of Italy, aiming at Ljubljana; from the town of Zara, an Italian enclave in Dalmatia, moving south along the coastline, to meet with the troops that moved north from Albania; and from Albania to the east, along the long Yugoslavian-Albanian border.

To the north, the Second Italian Army was deployed, commanded by General Vittorio Ambrosio, which had among its subordinate units the 3° Gruppo Alpini *Valle*, re-formed in January to be positioned in the area of Plezzo, in the upper valley of the Isonzo River. When war was declared, the unit started its march in a southeast direction, covering the flank of the mobile troops that moved toward Ljubljana. The city was captured on April 11, and a little later the Italians met with the German troops; thus, the Alpini were dispatched for some days to the southeast of the city. In Albania, the new northern front was entrusted to the *Firenze* Infantry Division and to the *Cuneense* Division, which had all of its subordinate battalions at its disposal again after many months. The division had been withdrawn from the southern front between March 15 and 20 and gathered in Berat for a period of rest and reorganization, when it had been replenished with new recruits in view of a new deployment against the Greeks. When it became clear that sooner or later something would happen with Yugoslavia, the division was sent to the north and deployed on a long stretch of the border, so far left unmanned. The 1° Reggimento covered a line along the Drin River, while the 2° Reggimento was positioned a little behind, guarding against possible Yugoslavian penetrations toward

Alpini of the Battaglione *Mondovì* march toward the Yugoslavian town of Debra, transporting the dead body of an officer fallen in combat.

Spring 1941, a unit of Alpini moves on trucks in Croatia. *Museo Nazionale Storico degli Alpini*

The campaign in the Balkans is over; Alpini and German soldiers' parade together. *David Zambon*

Tirana. The movement of the division started on April 3 and was, as usual, rather chaotic: some units were transported on trucks, while others had to march on foot in terrible weather; part of the equipment was left behind and reached its destination later. Furthermore, on April 8, when the division was still regrouping and reorganizing, the order arrived to advance into Yugoslavian territory, across the Drin River, and take the town of Dibra before the German mobile columns, which were already near Skopje, reached the area. On the following day, the 1° Reggimento moved forward and crossed the Drin, with the Battaglioni *Mondovì* and *Pieve di Teco* in the forefront and the *Ceva* taking the rear, and with the artillery support of the Gruppo *Mondovì*. On the tenth, the Italians came into contact with the Yugoslavian defenses, and entered Dibra on April 11 after some hours of hard fighting. The 2° Reggimento, too far behind, did not take part in the offensive.

Another Alpini unit, the Battaglione *Intra*, was transported on trucks to the border with Yugoslavia to be attached to the *Arezzo* Infantry Division and deployed hastily over a large area to the north of Lake Ohrid but was not involved in any fighting.

THE BATTAGLIONE UORK AMBA IN EAST AFRICA

While the battle for Tepelenë was raging in Greece, the British offensive was unfolding in Italian East Africa, and the decisive battle for the Italian presence in that part of Africa was being fought near the town of Keren. The operations in East Africa had started with the Italians' conquest of British Somaliland and with limited actions toward the towns of Kassala, in southern

A drawing on the front page of the *Domenica del Corriere* dedicated, in celebratory terms, to the Battle of Keren

Alpini of the Battaglione *Uork Amba* encamped near Addis Ababa. *Museo Nazionale Storico degli Alpini*

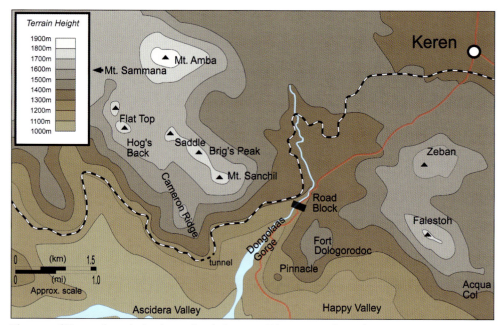

The area of Keren where the battle was fought between February 2 and March 27, 1941

Alpini of the Battaglione *Uork Amba* on the slopes of the mountain headquarters of the First Platoon, Third Company during a rare moment of rest, and the burial of a fellow alpino. Mid-February 1941. *Vito Zita*

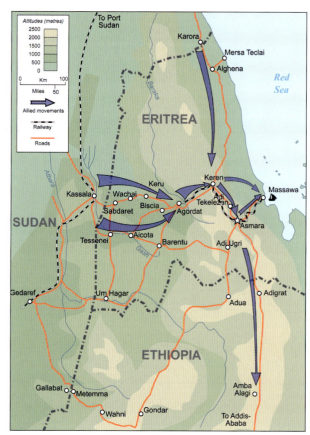

Map of the Eritrean campaign.

View of the Cima Forcuta, or Brig's Peak, reconquered by the Alpini on February 11, 1941. *Museo Nazionale Storico degli Alpini*

Sudan, and Moyale, in northern Kenya. However, in January 1941 the British took the initiative, set to remove the potential threat of the Italian colony and open the Red Sea to the ships that needed to reach Egypt, and attacked both from the south, toward Italian Somaliland, and from the north, invading Eritrea. On this latter front, a first Italian attempt to put up a resistance near the town of Agordat failed; therefore, all the resources of the northern front were concentrated near the town of Keren, only 70 kilometers northwest of Asmara, capital of the colony of Eritrea, and about 100 kilometers east of the port of Massaua, on the Red Sea, as the crow flies. Keren was in a position that was almost impossible to bypass, and it dominated the only road that led to the Eritrean Plateau. The town itself lies at 1,400 meters (4,593 feet) above MSL, and it is surrounded on three sides by high peaks and ridges with steep slopes; the only way to reach the town was the narrow Dongolaas Gorge, closed to the west by Mount Sanchil and to the east by Mount Dologorodoc, where both the road and the railway passed. In this theater that recalled more the Great War than the swift advances of mechanized units seen so far in Europe and North Africa, the commander of the Eritrean sector, General Luigi Frusci, gathered the troops that were retreating from Agordat and the reserves he had at his disposal and put them under the command of General Nicola Carnimeo. The battle lasted from February 2 to March 27, and can be subdivided into three main phases:

- February 2 to 13: the British forces tried to make the most of their momentum and force their way through the Italian defenses that were still improvised, but they were stopped and forced to take a pause
- February 14 to March 14: both parties engaged in patrol activities, trying to gain better positions while they built up their forces. The Italian and Eritrean troops were shelled daily by enemy artillery and bombed by the RAF
- March 15 to 27: the British launched their final offensive and got the better of the Italian defenses

Within the units stationed in East Africa there was, as previously mentioned, the Battaglione Alpini *Uork Amba*. At the beginning of the war, it was deployed to the southeast of the capital city, Addis Ababa, but at the beginning of February 1941, it was moved first to Asmara and then to Keren, where it arrived on the tenth. The following day, the *Alpini* were already entrusted with the task to retake an important position that had been conquered a few hours before by the Indians of the Fourth Division, the Brig's Peak (Cima Forcuta, for the Italians) on the left side of Mount Sanchil, which threatened the integrity of the whole Italian line. The Alpini moved out of their shelters at 10:30 p.m. with scarce knowledge of the territory, since there had been no time for an effective reconnaissance. After four hours of furious fighting, they managed to drive the Indians away from the peak, with the loss of about eighty men. After this action, the battalion was moved farther north, in the Mount Amba area, where it

was given two Eritrean battalions as support; these forces repelled every enemy attempt to penetrate the lines during the following month. On March 15, the decisive phase of the battle started, and on the seventeenth the British managed to conquer the key position of the Mount Dologorodoc. The Alpini were immediately called in and charged to launch a counterattack to retake the mountain. The first attempt was carried out on the night of the seventeenth: at 10:00 p.m., the battalion started its movement, and after thirty minutes, it seemed that the action might be successful since the Alpini were very close to the enemy positions and about to dislodge them. Unfortunately, a second attack on the right flank of the Indians, entrusted to an Eritrean unit, failed, and furthermore, the Italians were shelled by some short rounds of their own artillery; therefore, the *Uork Amba* was forced to withdraw having suffered the loss of almost half of its men. Other assaults launched on the eighteenth and the nineteenth were likewise unsuccessful. On March 25, Mount Sanchil fell as well; thus, the British were able to open the Dongolaas Gorge for the passage of the armored vehicles. Keren was clearly doomed; thus, the Italian command ordered the withdrawal of its forces. The *Uork Amba,* reduced to some hundred men, managed to avoid capture, and reached Massaua, where, however, it surrendered on April 8, when the port fell into British hands. During the two months of operations, the battalion had suffered 800 losses, out of an initial force of 900 men.

THE ALPINI IN MONTENEGRO AND THE BATTLE OF PLJEVJA

After the defeat of Yugoslavia, the kingdom was dismantled. To the north, the Kingdom of Croatia was formed, which also included part of Bosnia, having a member of the Savoia Italian royal family, Aimone di Savoia-Aosta, as the new king; he took the name "Tomislav II," although he never set foot in his kingdom. To the south, the Kingdom of Montenegro was restored under

A unit of the Divisione *Pusteria* marches through a village in Montenegro; the 75/13 howitzer is towed by a mule instead of being carried by a pack mule, possibly because of a lack of a suitable number of animals. *Storia Militare*

The Kingdom of Montenegro during World War II

An oversized portrait of Stalin, probably the work of some Yugoslavian partisans captured by a unit of Alpini. *Storia Militare*

Montenegro. A messenger on ski delivers a note containing some operations orders. *Storia Militare*

A mule train marching along a difficult track in the Montenegrin mountains. *Storia Militare*

Alpini with a Yugoslavian partisan taken prisoner, burdened with some captured rifles. *Storia Militare*

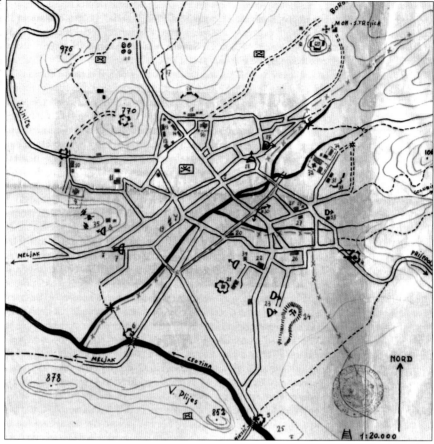

Map of the Montenegrin town of Plijevlja, where the three defensive sectors and the main Italian strongholds are indicated, as well as the position of the artillery, contained in a report written by the Headquarters of the 11° Reggimento. *Storia Militare*

the regency of the King of Italy Vittorio Emanuele III, whose wife, Elena, was the daughter of the former king of Montenegro. Furthermore, Italy directly annexed part of Slovenia, the whole of Dalmatia, and the area around the town of Kotor, on the Adriatic Sea. Germany occupied the remaining part of Slovenia and the greatest part of Serbia, while other portions of the territory went to Bulgaria and Hungary, which had taken part in the operations. Even Albania, now an Italian satellite, managed to slice off some pieces of the country for itself. Although the discontent of most of the population was at its highest in many areas of the country, and there were still thousands of former Yugoslavian army soldiers at large, and large quantities of weapons available everywhere, the Italian units stationed in Montenegro were taken completely by surprise when the uprising in July 1941 exploded. This was probably because the Italian political authorities had thought that the recent independence of the state had been welcomed. In a few days, the small Italian garrisons, scattered over the territory, mainly composed of infantrymen of the *Messina* Division and a few *Reali Carabinieri*, remained completely isolated, with little to no capability to effectively react. The Regio Esercito immediately sent no fewer than six divisions and other troops to Montenegro. Among them, the 2° Gruppo Alpini *Valle*, with the Battaglioni *Val Leogra*, *Val Pescara*, and the Gruppo *Valle Isonzo* of Alpine artillery arrived at Podgorica, the capital city, in mid-July; followed from July 17 by the Alpine division *Pusteria*, concentrated for a while in the area around Podgorica as well; and the 1° Gruppo Alpini *Valle*, with the Battaglioni *val Tagliamento*, *Val Natisone*, *Val Fella*, and the Gruppo *Val Tagliamento* of Alpine artillery arrived a little later, toward the end of the month. In December, the 4° Gruppo Alpini *Valle*, consisting of the Battaglioni *Val Chisone* and *Val d'Orco*, reinforced with the Battaglione *Susa* and the Gruppo *Val d'Adige* of Alpine artillery also arrived in Montenegro, disembarking in Kotor.

The next summer and autumn were spent—in an exhausting counterguerrilla activity for which the Italian divisions were not specifically trained—combing the territory to search for partisans, opening the roads to reach isolated garrisons, moving frenetically from one threatened area to another, and suffering dozens of small firefights and ambushes that caused an endless stream of deaths. The winter season, with the drop of the temperature that made it hard for the partisans to operate in open territory, brought a bit of quiet; therefore, the Italian units started to move to the areas assigned to spend the winter season. On November 30, the 1° Gruppo Alpini *Valle* was concentrated in the area of Visegrad; the 2° Gruppo *Valle* was in Podgorica, while the *Pusteria* was stationed in several locations in northern Montenegro. The greatest part of the division was concentrated in the town of Pljevlja, some 100 kilometers north of the capital, as the crow flies; here, there were the divisional headquarters and the headquarters of the 11° Reggimento; the Battaglione *Trento*; a company of the *Belluno*; the V Battaglione genio; and two artillery batteries, one of the Gruppo *Lanzo* and the other of the Gruppo *Belluno*. In the nearby town of Prijepolje, 25 kilometers to the east, were the headquarters of the 7° Reggimento, two companies of the Battaglione *Belluno* and two of the Battaglione *Pieve di Cadore*, with a battery of the Gruppo *Lanzo*. Other smaller units, of company strength, sometimes with a howitzer battery, were assigned to other smaller villages.

The partisans, however, had not been completely defeated and planned to exact their revenge during the winter months, when it was least expected, with an action carried out by as many units as possible against Pljevlja itself. The fall of such an important center, manned by hundreds of men, might be important from both the military and the political point of view, echoing throughout the whole of occupied Europe.

An Italian pillbox, part of a greater stronghold. *Storia Militare*

Second, it would leave the smaller garrisons completely isolated, easy to attack and annihilate; or, on the contrary, it might induce the Italians to withdraw these smaller garrisons from the area. On the other hand, the partisan activity had not gone unnoticed by the Italians, and the plan was, by and large, known by the headquarters of the *Pusteria*, which took its countermeasures. The garrison of Pljevlja could count on about 1,800 men, for the most part Alpini, but also a few *Reali Carabinieri* and *Guardia di Finanza*, a sort of custom guards, which could also depend on eight 75/13 howitzers. The defenses were divided into three sectors, each hinged on a series of strongholds that were able to resist even if surrounded, most of them located on some hills surrounding the town center; the most important was the fortino (small fort), many of which were in the remains of an ancient Ottoman fortification and the Orthodox monastery of Sveta Trojka, manned by two companies of the Battaglione *Trento*. The artillery was concentrated on another hill and positioned in a way that would enable it to shell every point of the defensive perimeter.

During the night of December 1, about 4,000 partisans attacked Pljevlja from three different directions; two columns were repelled, but the third managed to conquer the important position of the fortino, where it was able to threaten the Alpine artillery. The assault on the howitzers was driven off by the artillerymen with two volleys of grapeshot and hand grenades. The assailants gave up but remained, dangerously, close to the town perimeter. The morning of December 1 the situation seemed in a balance: the partisans had in some points dangerously penetrated the defenses, on the other hand many strongholds

had withstood the assaults and, with the light coming and the lack of the surprise effect, the Italians could take advantage of their better armament. During the early morning the partisans renewed their attacks, without obtaining any result, but the Alpini were reorganizing and started to counterattack. At 9:00 a.m. some platoons supported by mortars and machine guns retook the fortino, closing the gap in the defenses. Later, they started to deal with the squads of partisans that were still inside the town, eliminating them one by one. The fighting went on the whole day and the following night, but on December 2, the battle was over, although at the price of about 250 casualties for the defenders. Undoubtedly, the battle had been a significant victory for the Italians but a serious setback for the partisans of Montenegro, who took several months to recover. On the other hand, on December 1, a column of the Battaglione *Belluno* that been sent from Pijepolje to Pljevlja had been ambushed on its way there, suffering about one hundred casualties, including around forty Alpini, who had surrendered and been executed by the partisans.

The *Pusteria* remained in Montenegro, fighting against the partisans, until August 1942.

Beginning in March 1942, the 2° and 4° Gruppo Alpini *Valle* were temporarily grouped to form a new division, called *Alpi Graie*. In August 1942, the *Pusteria*, the 1° Gruppo Alpini *Valle*, and the 4° Gruppo Alpini *Valle*, with the command of the *Alpi Graie*, were repatriated, while the 2° Gruppo Alpini *Valle*, detached from the *Alpi Graie* itself, was sent to northern Greece. To replace these units, in Montenegro arrived the Divisione *Taurinense*.

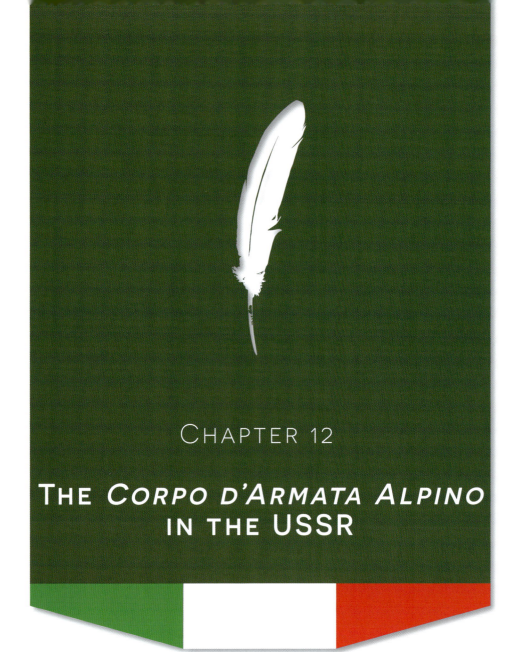

CHAPTER 12

THE *CORPO D'ARMATA ALPINO* IN THE USSR

Italian Participation in Operation Barbarossa, 1941

On June 22, 1941, Operation Barbarossa, the great German offensive against Soviet Union, began. The German führer addressed a personal letter to the Italian dictator only after the offensive had already started, as had become usual practice, although preparations were too obvious for Mussolini to ignore the German intentions. On this point, the information sent from the Italian embassy in Berlin was rather precise; thus, one cannot say that the news was a complete surprise. Mussolini, although again resentful with the Germans for what he considered a serious lack of respect, immediately offered a substantial Italian contribution in the form of an expeditionary corps, which the German ally accepted only after a degree of insistence both because it was positively convinced that German forces alone were enough for the task and, on the other hand, because it considered the Italian forces to be more useful in the African war theater. In the summer of 1941, the Italian Supreme Command organized an army corps consisting of three divisions, *Torino*, *Pasubio*, and *Principe Amedeo Duca d'Aosta*, the legion *Tagliamento* of the Black Shirts, and support units, designated the *Corpo di Spedizione Italiano in Russia*, or *CSIR* (Italian Expeditionary Corps) *in Russia*, about 62,000 men strong. The CSIR was defined by the Italian military authorities as a "transportable unit," meaning that part of its support equipment could be transported on trucks, and all its artillery was adapted to mechanical traction, instead of being packed on mules, as was usual in the Italian infantry divisions. On the other hand, most of the soldiers still moved on foot. What happened, then, was that to be able to follow the swift advance of the German forces, most of the vehicles were generally concentrated on one of the three divisions, which would therefore be able to keep up with the Germans, while the other two trailed behind. However, the Italian soldiers fought well during the summer and during the defensive battles of the winter of 1941–42.

In the spring of 1942, the Duce decided that the Italian presence on the Eastern Front needed to be increased significantly to enhance the Italian contribution to the struggle against Bolshevism, and this time, the Germans, who had lost thousands of men during the winter and needed new units to deploy on the long front, willingly accepted. The supreme command, therefore, set to work organizing two new army corps to be added to the CSIR, to form the Eighth Army, also called *Armata Italiana in Russia*, or *ARMIR* (Italian Army in Russia). The German plan for 1942 entailed a great advance on the southern stretch of the front, with the goal of occupying all of Ukraine and advance to the Caucasus Mountain range, capture the important oil fields of Baku and, eventually, invade Asia from that direction. For this reason, the Eighth Army, besides the new infantry divisions *Sforzesca*, *Cosseria*, *Ravenna*, and *Vicenza*, also included three Alpine divisions, the *Tridentina*, the *Julia*, and the *Cuneense*. The new army had a total force of some 230,000 men.

However, it must be mentioned that the presence of Alpini on the Eastern Front preceded the three divisions by some months since, in February 1942, the Battaglione sciatori *Monte Cervino* had reached the Ukraine, replenished after the heavy losses it had suffered in Greece. It was a small unit, consisting of a headquarters platoon with fifty men and two companies of 110 men each, with a few Breda mod. 30 light machine guns. As soon as it arrived, the unit was assigned to the CSIR headquarters as army corps reserve. The battalion had its baptism of fire at the end of March, when it took part in the action launched by the CSIR against the village of Olkovatka, in the lower basin of the Donetz River. Their aim was to pin down Russian forces and prevent their movement to the north, where the Germans and the Russians were fighting in the area

Russia, a battery of 75 mm guns, part of the Horse Artillery Regiment, attached in the summer of 1941 to the Divisione *Principe Amedeo Duca d'Aosta*

A battery of mechanically towed 75 mm guns. The tractor is a modern TL37, while the guns still have the original World War I wooden wheels. Hence, to be towed at the required speed, they had to be placed onto a specifically designed, two-wheeled bogie arrangement.

Alpini of the Battaglione *Monte Cervino* in action on the Eastern Front in the summer of 1942. *David Zambon*

of Izyum. The plan required that two columns converge at the village, engage the Russian defenses and then be withdrawn; the first column consisted of two battalions of the *Pasubio* Division and the *Monte Cervino*, supported by a mortar company; the second consisted of a battalion of the *Torino* Division reinforced with mortars and 47 mm guns. The Italian soldiers moved at 5:00 a.m., when the temperature was about -30° Celsius, and soon reached the Soviet lines, surprising the defenses in the area. After some hours of firefight and since their mission had been achieved, the attackers withdrew and went back to their lines, having suffered light casualties.

A few weeks later, the *Monte Cervino*, reinforced with two heavy machine gun platoons, was attached to a special Italian task force formed to cooperate with the Germans in their offensive against the salient of Izyum. The operations started on May 17, and the following day, the Italians were ordered to conquer the village of Klynovoy and the heights immediately beyond. The action was successful, notwithstanding stiff enemy resistance. But the village could not be defended effectively against a Soviet counterattack; thus, the Italian troops, including the Alpini, were forced to retreat with heavy losses. The Izyum salient was nevertheless eliminated; thus, the *Monte Cervino* was sent to the rear for a period of rest that lasted until July.

THE *CORPO D'ARMATA ALPINO* ARRIVES IN UKRAINE

While the *Monte Cervino* was fighting in Ukraine, the *Tridentina*, *Julia*, and *Cuneense* Divisions, repatriated not many months before from Greece, were preparing for their transfer to the Eastern Front. For the coming campaign, the divisions were reinforced with additional units and weapons; thus, the new organization chart was the following:

Divisione *Tridentina* consisting of
5° Reggimento, with the Battaglioni *Morbegno, Tirano,* and *Edolo*
6° Reggimento, with the Battaglioni *Vestone, Verona,* and *Val Chiese*
2° Reggimento of Alpine artillery, with the Gruppi *Bergamo, Vicenza,* and *Val Camonica*
II Battaglione genio.
Divisione *Julia*, consisting of
8° Reggimento, with the Battaglioni *Tolmezzo, Gemona,* and *Cividale*
9° Reggimento, with the Battaglioni *Vicenza, L'Aquila,* and *Val Cismon*

The Headquarters of the Corpo d'Armata Alpino leave the town of Trento, in northern Italy, on July 14, 1942, with Nowo Gorlovka as its destination; it would arrive on July 27. *Museo Storico Nazionale degli Alpini*

Several moments of the march of the Alpini toward the Don. A little rest, maybe in the hope of getting a lift on the trucks, although the mules still remain the alpino's best friend. During the march, the Alpini meet their German allies; passing through a Ukrainian village, the Alpini collect some foodstuffs to vary the rations. *Davis Zambon*

3° Reggimento of Alpine artillery, with the Gruppi *Conegliano, Udine,* and *Val Piave*

III Battaglione genio

Divisione *Cuneense,* consisting of

1° Reggimento, with the Battaglioni *Ceva, Pieve di Teco,* and *Mondovì*

2° Reggimento, with the Battaglioni *Borgo San Dalmazzo, Dronero,* and *Saluzzo*

4° Reggimento of Alpine artillery, with the Gruppi *Pinerolo, Mondovì,* and *Val Po*

IV Battaglione genio

The newly assigned *Valle* artillery battalions were equipped not with the usual 73/13 howitzer, but with two batteries of the more powerful war-booty French 105 mm mountain howitzer, which could be carried by a pack mule and, although its range was no more than 8 kilometers, represented an enhancement in firepower; furthermore, the artillery regiments were assigned two batteries consisting of eight pieces each of the 20 mm Breda antiaircraft guns. Each division was also equipped with two companies of 47 mm antitank guns, consisting of eight pieces each. Finally, once it reached the River Don, they received an antitank battery consisting of six 75 mm pieces from the Germans.

In addition, the army corps was furnished an artillery regiment, the Eleventh, with three battalions consisting of three batteries of four 105 mm guns each, and a battalion consisting of three batteries of four 149 mm howitzers each, with two more batteries of 20 mm Breda antiaircraft guns, eight pieces each. All in all, the army corps had 274 pieces of artillery, among which sixty-four were 20 mm Breda guns, forty-eight were 47 mm guns, seventy-two were the Alpine artillery 75/13, eighteen were 75 mm antitank guns, twenty-four were 105 mm mule pack howitzers, thirty-six were 105 mm guns, and twelve were 149 mm howitzers.

The movement to the Eastern Front started in June, when the Eleventh Artillery Regiment left Italy, arriving at its destination after almost a month. In mid-July, the headquarters of the army corps were moved to the town of Gorlovka, in the basin of the River Donetz, where it arrived between July 28 and August 4. Later, it moved to the town of Rykovo, where it started to function on August 18. The first division to leave Italy was the *Tridentina,* which started to move on July 17 and gathered in the area of Gorlovka between August 3 and 17. The *Cuneense* followed beginning on July 27, reaching Ukraine between August 8 and 21, partly at Rykovo and partly near Izyum. The *Julia* was the last to leave, on August 8, and reached the area of Izyum between August 17 and September 2.

As has been mentioned, when the army corps had been formed in Italy, it had been established that its destination would be the Caucasus mountain range, attached to the German Seventeenth Army. Therefore, the *Tridentina* started to move south as soon as it arrived, marching on foot. On the nineteenth, however, the plans changed, and the Alpini were assigned to the Eighth Army, to be deployed in the Don River area. The division went back to the area of Millerovo, while the other two divisions were sent directly to the Don River. Here, they replaced some German units, deploying along the western banks of the river, to the north of the point where the River Don receives its tributary, River Kalitva.

THE FIRST DEFENSIVE BATTLE OF THE DON RIVER

On August 20, a Soviet offensive hit the lines of the Italian divisions that garrisoned the banks of the Don River, the first of a series of events known in Italy by the name "*Prima battaglia difensiva del Don*" (First Defensive Battle of the River Don). The Soviets planned to break through the long flank of the German advance toward Stalingrad and the Volga River, relieving the pressure of the German Sixth Army on the city. After probing several stretches of the front, the Soviet command assessed that the weakest point was the one defended by the XXXV Italian Army Corps and attacked that point with all of its forces. The blow was parried for the most part by the *Pasubio* and *Sforzesca* Divisions, which, after an initial withdrawal, managed to contain the Soviet attack. Thanks also go to the reserves sent in by the army corps command, such as the Battaglione *Monte Cervino,* which took part in the furious battle around the stronghold of Jagodny at the end of August. However, on August 28, the army corps, which had remained without further reserves, arranged to have the *Tridentina* Division assigned as well, with a view to use its units to mount a counteroffensive as soon as the momentum of the Soviet

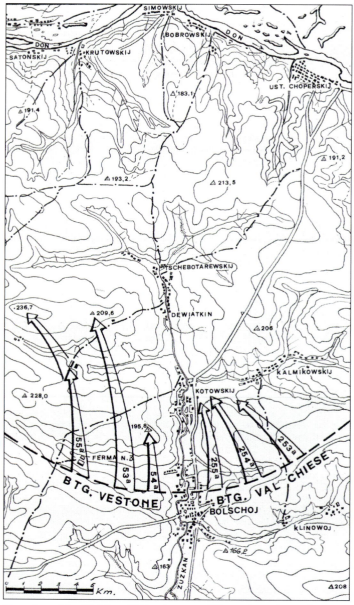

The action of the Divisione *Tridentina* toward Kotowskij in September 1942

Alpini posing near a destroyed T-34 Soviet tank in the summer of 1941. *David Zambon*

attack weakened. The action was launched on September 1, entrusted to the Battaglioni *Val Chiese* and *Vestone* supported by some twenty Italian light tanks of the LXVII *bersaglieri* armored battalion that were charged with the advance toward the village of Kotowskij and some hills beyond, some kilometers to the south of the Don River; at the same time, a German unit was assigned to attack another village to the right of the Alpini to protect the flank of the Italian action. The aim was to eliminate a dangerous wedge between the lines of the XXXV Army Corps and the adjoining German XVII Army Corps and, in the most favorable case, reach and reoccupy the southern bank of the river. The attack started at 5:30 a.m., and although the resistance had been stiff, by midmorning the Alpini had performed their task, even capturing a 76 mm gun battery. However, the Germans failed to show up on the right flank; therefore, the Italians remained to face the Soviet counterattack alone and were not able to hold the recently conquered positions. The Battaglione *Val Chiese* withdrew toward Kotowskij by the end of the morning, while the *Vestone* needed the whole afternoon to be able to disengage from the enemy and withdraw in good order. At 8:00 p.m. the small-scale action was over, with the Italian units back behind their lines. The casualties had been severe: more than 500 Alpini were lost, and with no positive result of the action; however, the Soviets had paid a great toll as well, so were therefore forced to interrupt their attacks and take a more defensive attitude.

Near a village not far from the Don River, an officer of the Alpini stands near a German soldier who is probably in charge of directing traffic. *David Zambon*

THE SECOND DEFENSIVE BATTLE OF THE DON RIVER

The *Tridentina* was stationed in the area of Kotowskij that coincided with the extreme right of the Italian line for the whole month of September and was able to join its army corps only at the beginning of October, replaced by a Romanian division. The Alpini, partly on foot and partly by train, gathered at Podgornoje and then moved north to deploy to extreme left of the Corpo d'Armata Alpino, with the right flank leaning on the left of the *Julia*, replacing a Hungarian division. On the eve of the new series of defensive battles that goes by the name "*Seconda battaglia difensiva del Don*" (Second Defensive Battle of the Don River), the Italian Eighth Army, with its 230,000 men, manned a line of no less than 270 kilometers, which stretched for the most part along the western bank of the river itself, where, however, the Soviets held two bridgeheads. The Italian army joined with the Hungarian Second Army on its left, with the Romanian Third Army on its right. The lineup, *from left to right*, was the following:

Corpo d'Armata Alpino, with *Tridentina*, *Julia*, and *Cuneense*, which had to their rear the *Vicenza* Infantry Division, a light unit with rear area duties

A column of light trucks of the Autocarretta OM type, largely used by the Alpini on the Eastern Front, is driving over muddy terrain in Ukraine. *David Zambon*

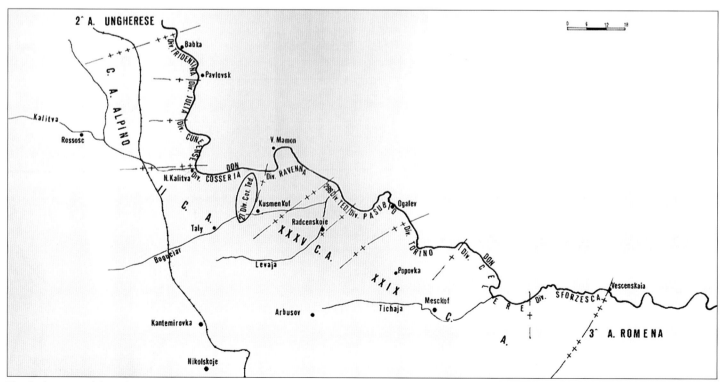

The deployment of the Italian Eighth Army along the banks of the Don River at the beginning of December 1942

II Army Corps, with *Cosseria, Ravenna,* and Black Shirts Raggruppamento *23 Marzo*

XXXV Army Corps, with 298th German Infantry Division, *Pasubio,* and Black Shirts Raggruppamento *3 Gennaio;*

XXIX German Army Corps, with *Torino, Principe Amedeo Duca d'Aosta,* and *Sforzesca*[1]

The Corpo d'Armata Alpino, whose headquarters was in the town of Rossosch, defended about 70 kilometers of front and was reinforced with the Battaglione sciatori *Monte Cervino,* a horse drawn artillery regiment, consisting of twenty-four 75 mm guns, and two heavy artillery battalions detached from the Eighth Army artillery regiment.

Autumn passed more or less uneventfully for the Italian divisions, who took advantage of this quiet period of time to dig their defenses against the Soviets and their shelters against winter. In these months, war consisted mainly of actions carried out by patrols, aimed at the reconnaissance of the terrain and the capture of enemy soldiers for information; snipers tried to make enemy life difficult, recalling to a certain extent the western front during the Great War. Both parties were too engaged in the great battle that was raging at Stalingrad to be able to mount major actions on this part of the front. But while the Germans were weakening other areas to send reinforcements

Alpini of the Battaglione *Val Chiese* of the Divisione *Tridentina* in their trenches in January 1943, a few days before the beginning of the retreat. The variety of the equipment adopted to protect the men from the extreme cold can be seen. *David Zambon*

to the besieged city, the Soviets were building up their forces. In mid-December, the Soviet command decided the moment had arrived to launch the great offensive, called Little Saturn, aimed at reconquering the wide area between the Don River and the Donetz River, which was now rather weakly manned by Axis forces. The stretch of the front chosen for the breakthrough was where the River Don changes its course and bends due east; the most fragile point was the one defended by the II Army Corps, between the villages of Novo Kalitva and Verhnij Mamon. Preparatory actions started on December 11 to find the weakest points, wear out the defenses, and call in the Italian reserves; thus, when the offensive was launched

on the sixteenth, the Soviet troops found little difficulty in overwhelming the Italian first line and Soviet armored units were able to spread in the rear, heading west and south, where there was little to oppose them.

The first Alpine unit to be involved in the fighting was the Battaglione sciatori *Monte Cervino*, which was sent from its headquarters in Rossosch to reinforce the II Army Corps on December 14. At first it was stationed in the village of Golubaja Krinitza, south of the Kalitva River, as reserve of the Corps. Later, on the sixteenth, it was advanced to occupy some heights a little south of Novo Kalitva, but soon it was hastily moved again some few kilometers south to the town of Ivanovka, where it arrived on December 17. Here, the battalion found a chaotic situation with hundreds of infantrymen of the *Cosseria* Division, who withdrew in disorder before the advancing Soviet vanguards: the division had almost completely collapsed and did not exist anymore as an organized fighting unit. That evening, the *Monte Cervino* was joined by a German unit, equipped with *Nebelwerfer*,[2] which made it possible to set up a very thin defensive line. On the sixteenth, a company of the Battaglione *Saluzzo*, of the nearby *Cuneense* Division, was also sent to Novo Kalitva, which was being attacked by the Soviets and was involved in hard fighting against overwhelming forces supported by tanks on the eighteenth and nineteenth.

In the afternoon of this fateful December 16, the Corpo d'Armata Alpino ordered the *Julia* to prepare a task force, consisting of the Battaglione *L'Aquila*, a battery each from the Gruppi *Conegliano* and *Udine*, and a few 20 mm Breda antiaircraft guns, to be sent south. The artillery moved that same afternoon, transported on trucks, onto which even the mules were loaded. After a journey of

A patrol of the Battaglione sciatori *Monte Cervino* is examining a map. The Alpini of the *Monte Cervino* had special equipment, like this white camouflage suit and the white cover for the helmet. *David Zambon*

A unit of Alpini is marching in the snow of the Russian winter.

Alpine artillerymen of the Gruppo *Valpiave* of the Divisione *Julia* are queuing up for their rations.

two days in temperatures regularly reaching below 30° Celsius, it arrived on the evening of the eighteenth at the village of Ivanovka, where it joined the Battaglione *Monte Cervino* and deployed its pieces in open ground. The Battaglione *L'Aquila* moved instead during the seventeenth, originally directed to Ivanovka as well, but then diverted to the location of Seleny Jar, a road junction a few kilometers west of it, under the command of the German 385th Division. On December 19, the arrival of the Battaglione *L'Aquila*, in the area of Seleny Jar, allowed a defensive line to be set up. Here, the forces that disengaged from Ivanovka were meanwhile able to gather under the protection of the Alpini of the *Monte Cervino*, which took the rearguard. For several days, these units stoically resisted the Soviet infantry and tank attacks.

The situation, however, was deteriorating very fast; therefore, in the same evening of December 16, the *Julia* was ordered to prepare another task force for departure. The task force consisted of the Battaglione *Tolmezzo*, the divisional antitank 47 mm gun battery, and a 20 mm antiaircraft Breda gun battery. On the afternoon of the seventeenth, the motorized column with the task force left, heading toward the town of Mitrofanovka, 25 kilometers south of Rossosch, as the crow flies. It was the seat of command for the II Army Corps, where it arrived on the morning of the eighteenth; from there, it was sent to the village of Krinitschnaja to join the German 385th Division. The task force only managed to reach the location on the night of December 19, after more than a day traveling on roads jammed with Italian and German units that retreated in disorder and were constantly threatened by Soviet aircraft. One company lost contact and only managed to rejoin the Battaglione *Tolmezzo* on the twenty-second. The Alpini and their guns took position on the right of the River Kalitva, having the Battaglione *Saluzzo* on the left and a German unit on the right.

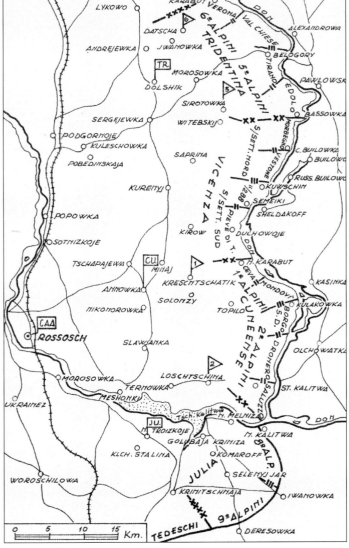

January 1943, the Divisione *Julia* has been redeployed to the south of the Kalitva River, and the *Vicenza* infantry division has replaced it on the frontline.

Soon, anyway, the whole *Julia* division received the order to move south to assist the II Army Corps, replaced in its positions by the poorly equipped *Vicenza* Infantry Division. The Alpine division started to move on the eighteenth, partly on trucks but partly marching on foot, a sort of tragic preview of what would happen a few weeks later, and was assigned to the German XXIV Armored Army Corps, which was, unfortunately, armored only on paper. It was immediately sent south of the Kalitva River to strengthen that stretch of the front that had so far been defended only by the Battaglione *Tolmezzo* and a few other scattered units: between December 23 and 24, the deployment of the entire *Julia* division was completed, giving the defenses adequate strength. The exhausted Battaglioni *L'Aquila* and *Monte Cervino* were temporarily withdrawn from the line; the survivors of the *Monte Cervino*, a handful of men, were sent back to Rossosch, reassigned to the Corpo d'Armata Alpino. On the new improvised positions, with environmental conditions that can certainly be defined as prohibitive, with almost no shelter and reinforced with a few German antitank vehicles, the Alpini managed to resist for a month, repelling Soviet infantry and tanks at a high price, and preventing a breakthrough. The fighting was particularly fierce until the end of the month, then lightened slightly in January. The Soviets had suffered very high losses as well, and gave up that stretch of the front, concentrating their efforts on other sectors, where their armored columns had been able to penetrate hundreds of kilometers behind Axis lines.

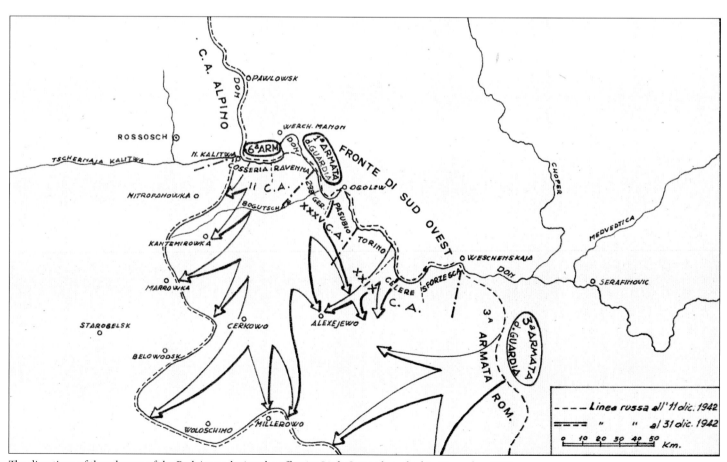

A patrol of Alpini on the Eastern Front, wearing a different kind of winter camouflage. *Antonio Tallillo*

The directions of the advance of the Red Army during the offensive Little Saturn launched in December 1942

THE LONG RETREAT OF THE *CORPO D'ARMATA ALPINO*

January 18, 1943, Alpini of the Divisione *Tridentina* gathered in Podgornoje, first stage of the long march toward the German lines. *David Zambon*

While the fighting was raging at the bend of the River Don, to the north of the junction with the Kalitva River, the situation was rather calm, and the Soviet units opposite the Corpo d'Armata Alpino and the Hungarian divisions showed little aggressiveness. However, things were about to change very soon. On January 13, the Soviets launched a new offensive, called *Ostrogosz-Rossosch*, which aimed to surround the Hungarian Second Army and what remained of the Italian Eighth Army. The Hungarians were attacked first, and in a few hours, they were forced back several kilometers, leaving the left flank of the *Tridentina* Division completely open. On January 14, Soviet armored units overwhelmed the few remaining armored vehicles of the German XXIV Armored Army Corps and made their way behind the Alpini. On the night of the fifteenth, Soviet infantry, supported by some twenty tanks, attacked Rossosch, headquarters of the Corpo d'Armata Alpino, by complete surprise. The fighting flared up street by street and house by house, and involved what remained of the Battaglione sciatori *Monte Cervino*—the only Italian combat-ready unit stationed in town. It also involved men drawn from all kinds of headquarters, offices, and duties, supported by a handful of German self-propelled guns and a few German Stukas. After some hours, the attack was repelled with the destruction of a dozen tanks, but the toll had been very high. The following day, the command decided to move the headquarters to the town of Podgornoje, thinking it was safer. Along the Don River, attacks hit the Battaglioni *Edolo* and *Vestone*, which held out doggedly while, to the south, the *Julia* was slowly being pushed toward the northern shore of the Kalitva

January 20, 1943, the headquarters of the 5° Reggimento leaves the town of Skororyb and heads west toward Postojalyi. *David Zambon*

Postojalyi, the last trucks that remained without fuel are sabotaged and abandoned: from now on, the retreat will be on foot. *David Zambon*

January 21, 1943, the long column of the Divisione *Tridentina* marches toward Sceljakino. The march was interrupted by a blizzard and by temperatures that had dropped to -40° Celsius. *David Zambon*

River. On January 16, Rossosch was attacked again, and this time the town fell into Soviet hands, although the *Monte Cervino* fought bravely: only about a hundred Alpini managed to disengage and retreat to the west. It was clear that the position of the Corpo d'Armata Alpino was extremely precarious, but the order to retreat, which had been requested of the Germans by the headquarters of the Italian Eighth Army several times, did not arrive until the morning of January 17, when the Soviets were already dozens of kilometers to the rear of the Alpini. The retreat started in the afternoon of that same day, with the *Tridentina* and the 276th Regiment of the *Vicenza*,[3] which moved toward Podgornoje while the 277th Regiment of the same division, the *Cuneense* and the *Julia*, headed instead toward the town of

Popovka. The final destination of the retreat was the village of Valuijki, controlled by the Germans, some 130 kilometers from the Don River, as the crow flies, but in the end, the distance would be much longer, and most of the men would not make it. The units moved in good order, taking all their equipment, under the cover of a few men that were charged to conceal the retreat from the Soviets as long as possible and move away the following night. The northern column arrived in Podgornoje during the eighteenth, while the southern columns, which had more distance to cover, completed the gathering at Popovka a day later. It was discovered, however, that the Soviets already occupied the town of Postojalyi, some 15 kilometers west, and had closed that path of retreat for the army corps.

The long lines of the retreating Alpini that meander, divide, intersect, and merge again, following the topography of the terrain. *David Zambon*

JANUARY 19

On the morning of December 19, the vanguard of the *Tridentina*, consisting of the Battaglione *Verona* and a battery of the Gruppo *Bergamo*, engaged the defenses of Postojalyi but was repelled by the prompt reaction of the enemy. The rest of the division, the headquarters of the army corps and the headquarters of the German XXIV Army Corps, were some kilometers behind, near the village of Opit, which was crowded with some thousands of disbanded Hungarian soldiers as well. The two regiments of the *Vicenza* Division met at the village of Samojlenkov, ready to join the new attack on Postojalyi that was planned for the following day. The *Julia* was concentrated at Popovka, but in the morning, the 8° Reggimento, along with the Gruppo *Conegliano*, moved toward Novo Postojalovka, which was already occupied by Soviet forces supported by tanks. The fighting raged the whole day, but the Italians did not manage to break through. In the morning, the 1° Reggimento of the *Cuneense* also arrived at Popovka, while the 2° Reggimento arrived in the afternoon. The *Cuneense* continued toward Novo Postojalovka that evening, while the 9° Reggimento of the *Julia*, along with the Gruppi *Udine* and *Val Piave*, headed toward Kopanki, a village that was 7 kilometers west of Popovka.

JANUARY 20

January 20 was a day of furious and bloody fighting and started in the early morning with an attack by Soviet armored units against Opit, which was still crowded with Italian, German, and Hungarian soldiers, many of them unarmed. During the battle, the II Battaglione genio stood out, losing, however, more than half of its men. Unfortunately, much equipment was destroyed in the attack. This included vital communications equipment; so, from that moment on, the army corps headquarters were

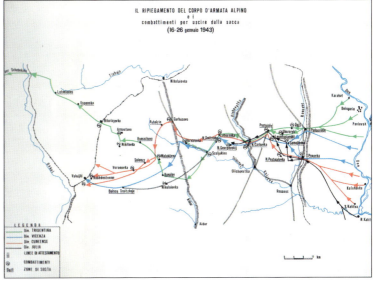

The routes followed by the three Alpine divisions and by the *Vicenza* infantry division in their attempt to escape being surrounded

not able to communicate with the subordinate units anymore. Meanwhile, farther west, the *Tridentina* was organizing the attack on Postojalyi, which was to be launched by the Battaglioni *Val Chiese* and *Vestone* with the support of the guns of the Gruppi *Vicenza* and *Bergamo*, a German gun battery, a German *Nebelwerfer* battery, and four German self-propelled guns. The Battaglione *Verona*, instead, was deployed to the north to protect the right flank of the attack against enemy actions, reinforced with three companies of 47 mm guns and two 75 mm antitank guns. This time, the attack was successful; hence, part of the column was able to proceed toward Novo Charcovka, which was conquered, clearing it of the Soviet forces that occupied it. However, the headquarters of the army corps remained at Postojalyi for the whole day, waiting for the arrival of the other subordinate units and trying unsuccessfully to establish contact with them. The *Vicenza* continued its march that day, dislodging some enemy forces from the village of Lesnitscianskji, then reaching Postojalyi and Novo Charcovka, where it joined the *Tridentina*.

To the south, at dawn of the twentieth, after a terrible night spent on the open ground with freezing temperature, units of the *Cunenese* and the 8° Reggimento of the *Julia* attacked Novo Postojalovka again. At first, the action was entrusted to the Battalione *Ceva*, supported by the artillery of the Gruppi *Conegliano* and *Mondovì*, but it was unsuccessful; thus, the attack was renewed at 10:30 with the participation of all units available: the Battaglioni *Cividale* and *Gemona*; the remnants of the *Tolmezzo*, *Ceva*, and *Mondovì*, with the howitzers of the Gruppi *Conegliano*; *Mondovì*, and a newly arrived battery of the *Val Po*. The fighting went on the whole day, bolstered in the afternoon by the arrival of the *Borgo San Dalmazzo*, *Saluzzo*, and the artillery of the Gruppo *Pinerolo*. In the evening, however, the village was still in enemy hands; therefore, the headquarters of the divisions decided that it was better to disengage and head north in the night, toward Samojlenkov and Postojalyi. During the assaults of December 19 and 20, the Battaglioni *Cividale*, *Gemona*, and *Tolmezzo* of the *Julia* had virtually ceased to exist as combat units, as had the Battaglioni *Ceva*, *Mondovì*, *Borgo San Dalmazzo*, and *Saluzzo* of the *Cuneense*. The Gruppi of the Alpine artillery had either lost or left behind all their pieces, apart from five howitzers of the *Conegliano*, which had no more than a handful of shells. The only unit that was still sufficiently operational was the Battaglione *Dronero*, which acted as rearguard.

The 9° Reggimento of the *Julia*, on the other hand, fought at Kopanki on the twentieth, trying to clear its way. But in the evening, it was forced to break contact and head north to Samojlenkov, after having suffered heavy losses.

JANUARY 21: THE ANNIHILATION OF THE 9° REGGIMENTO OF THE *JULIA*

January 21 was a day of exhausting marches in blizzards and snow that was dotted with fighting. The *Tridentina*, which now acted as vanguard of the army corps, advanced westward, occupying some villages east of Sceljakino. However, it was not possible to proceed farther and reach Sceljakino itself; that was the target of the day because the blizzard worsened and the temperature dropped to -40° Celsius. The *Vicenza*, which reached the same villages, trailed right behind the *Tridentina*. Meanwhile, the *Cuneense* and the 8° Reggimento of the *Julia* and the Gruppo *Conegliano*, always trying to shorten the distance with the vanguard, reached Postojalyi, which had been occupied again by light enemy forces that had to be cleared away, and proceeded to Novo Charcovka and Novo Georgevskij, respectively. The 9° Reggimento, instead, was further behind and reached Lesnitscianskji; in this village, the Alpini were attacked by overwhelming Soviet forces, supported by tanks, and annihilated after a short but bloody fight. The Battaglioni *L'Aquila*, *Vicenza*, *Val Cismon*, and the Gruppi *Udine* and *Val Piave* simply ceased to exist, and only small groups of Alpini and artillerymen were able to escape the enemy and resume their march westward. January 21 is also the day that marks the end of the Battaglione *Monte Cervino*; the Battaglione, having escaped from Rossosch after days of marching in the snow and firefights with partisans, consisted of only five skiers, who were captured by partisans not far from the German lines.

The Alpini advance, bent in the snow, covered head to toe with whatever they managed to find; in the sledges, the last boxes of ammunition and equipment, soon to be replaced by ill and wounded men. In the background, some men are riding horses, possibly artillerymen of the Horse Artillery Regiment, assigned to the Corpo d'Armata Alpino as reinforcement. *David Zambon*

That evening, the headquarters of the army corps received the news that Valuijki, the original destination of the divisions, was not in German hands anymore but was occupied by substantial enemy forces. The new target was farther north, at Nikolaijevka. Unfortunately, since there was no connection between the divisions anymore, the army corps only managed to communicate with the *Tridentina*, which marched with it, but it did not reach the other columns, which continued straight on to their destiny.

JANUARY 22: THE 8° REGGIMENTO OF THE *JULIA* MEETS ITS DESTINY

On the dawn of January 22, the *Tridentina* barely re-formed its exhausted units, hindered in this supposedly simple operation by the presence of thousands of disbanded soldiers of several nationalities, and moved to Sceljakino, escorted by the few remaining German armored vehicles. It was clear that the way westward was again closed by the presence of enemy troops in the village; therefore, a hasty attack was mounted at midmorning, entrusted to the Battaglioni *Val Chiese*, *Vestone*, and to the few remaining engineers, supported by the residual Italian and German pieces of artillery. Later, the Battaglioni *Edolo* and *Tirano* supported the action with outflanking maneuvers. The battle was won, and a counterattack by Soviet tanks was beaten back, thanks to a few 75 mm antitank guns and German self-propelled guns. Thus, the column was able to proceed some kilometers farther and halt at a group of villages to the west of Sceljakino. However, the Battaglione *Morbegno*, with a battery of the Gruppo *Bergamo*, became intermixed with the disbanded troops and set off northwest to Varvarovka by mistake.

The *Vicenza* spent the day in the izbas that the Alpini of the *Tridentina* had vacated in the morning and resumed its march in the evening. Meanwhile, the remains of the *Cuneense* were passing not far to the north and halted for the night, some at Lymarevka and some at Novo Dmitrovka, after clearing away the enemy forces that were already stationed there.

On December 22, the 8° Reggimento of the *Julia* met its end. The village of Novo Georgevskij was attacked in the morning by Soviet armored units, and the surviving Alpini surrendered after a short fight. Of the Battaglioni *Cividale*, *Gemona*, *Tolmezzo*, and the Gruppo *Conegliano*, only a few men were able to escape death or captivity.

JANUARY 23

On January 23, the *Tridentina* marched the whole day without being disturbed by enemy action and halted for the night at Kovalev. A little after midnight, the Battaglione *Morbegno* stumbled into an enemy stronghold put up at Varvarovka and was crushed in the following fight: it was yet another battalion that would not find its way to the Axis line. The *Vicenza* reached Sceljakino after a night of marching, found it occupied by Soviet forces, and was forced to fight to open its way; then it proceeded toward Varvarovka. By the end of the morning, the division was close to Varvarovka, where signs of the fighting that had involved the Battaglione *Morbegno* a few hours before were still visible. The infantrymen tried to assault the stronghold but, having realized that it was impossible to pass that way, diverted their march toward the southwest and went on to avoid the pursuers for the whole night. The *Cuneense* gathered its units at Novo Dmitrovka in the morning and split them into two columns, corresponding more or less to its two regiments; then, avoiding both Sceljakino and Varvarovka, it reached the villages of Garbusovo and Rybalzin without any encounters with enemy regular units.

JANUARY 24

On January 24, the *Tridentina* reached Malakijeva, which was occupied by an enemy garrison. The Battaglioni *Val Chiese* and *Vestone*, supported by a few remaining Italian and German pieces of artillery and by a handful of German self-propelled guns, assaulted the village and cleared the way. The columns went on until late afternoon, when the exhausted Alpini were able to have some rest at the village of Romachovo. The *Vicenza*, after a short pause, resumed its march until noon, stopping to rest as soon as

The vanguard of the 5° Reggimento of the Divisione *Tridentina*, with one of the last operating German Sturmgeschutz III assault guns. *Davis Zambon*

the men found shelter in some izbas. The 1° Reggimento of the *Cuneense* was attacked at Garbusovo in the morning, and many Alpini did not make it out of the village; only some of the men managed to escape west and join the other column at Rybalzin. A severe blizzard forced the 2° Reggimento to stay at Rybalzin the whole day and the following night, preventing enemy attacks.

JANUARY 25

January 25 was a day relatively eventless for the retreating forces, which did not have to face serious fighting. The *Tridentina* advanced from Romachovo to Nikitovka, which had to be taken from a weak enemy garrison where the 5° Reggimento halted for the rest of the day, and to Arnautovo, which sheltered the 6° Reggimento. During the day, the headquarters of the army corps was warned by a German reconnaissance plane that had landed near the column that the locality of Nikolajevka, some kilometers northwest of Nikitovka, was strongly guarded by Soviet troops and that it would be necessary to conquer it; however, that would be the last battle since, not far away, the Alpini would reach the German lines. Unfortunately, the *Vicenza* and the *Cuneense* had definitively lost contact with the army corps and were pursuing their march to Valujiki, still unaware of the changed orders. In the late evening, the *Vicenza* pushed forward to the southwest, reaching a village not more than 20 kilometers from Valujiki itself, engaging in some firefights with partisans. The *Cuneense* followed a parallel path. During the night, the 2° Reggimento, with the divisional headquarters, halted at Malakijeva, where the *Tridentina* had passed the previous day, while the 1° Reggimento went farther southwest to Solonzy.

During the night between January 25 and 26, Soviet units attacked Arnautovo, but the Alpini of the *Tridentina* still had operational capability and a few artillery pieces in working order; therefore, they were able to repel the attackers. During the same night, Nikitovka was shelled but not attacked.

JANUARY 26: THE BREAKTHROUGH OF THE *TRIDENTINA* AND THE SURRENDER OF THE *VICENZA*

At dawn of January 26, the depleted battalions of the *Tridentina* started to deploy for the action against Nikolajevka. The town lay to the west of a railway running on an embankment about 2 meters (6.5 feet) high, dominated by the bulky building of the railway station. The embankment would be the first target for the attacking Alpini, who needed to cross several hundred meters of open ground, covered in high snow, to reach it; the next step would be to break into the town by crossing a tunnel under the railway, to the left of the railway station. The attack was entrusted to the Battaglioni *Verona*, *Vestone*, and *Val Chiese*, supported by six 47 mm guns, a battery of the Gruppo *Bergamo*, and the last three German self-propelled guns; during the fighting, other units continued to arrive and were able to join the action. The attack started at 9:30 a.m., and notwithstanding the artillery and machine gun barrage, the Alpini managed to reach the embankment, force the tunnel, and penetrate into the eastern

sector of the town, engaging in a street by street, house by house fighting. However, the momentum slowly faded away; the action could not be immediately sustained without fresh troops, and the supply of ammunition was extremely difficult to ensure. Thus, the Soviets were able to take the initiative, repelling the Italians beyond the embankment. One of the self-propelled guns was hit by an antitank gun and destroyed; therefore, the other two vehicles withdrew to a safer position. Around midday, the highly anticipated 5° Reggimento, which had been slowed down in its approach march, arrived with some of Gruppo *Vicenza*'s howitzers and a few German guns that were immediately deployed to shell the enemy positions in Nikolajevka. The 150 Alpini that remained in the Battaglione *Tirano* and the headquarters company of the regiment joined the battle and gave renewed strength to the attack. Last but not least, in the late afternoon, the Battaglioni *Edolo* and the Gruppo *Val Camonica*, which were in the rearguard, arrived and were immediately thrown into the fray. Apart from the few units that still maintained their organization, many isolated Alpini and artillerymen spontaneously moved to the frontline to give their support to the attackers. Nonetheless, the situation in Nikolajevka remained very critical and the balance was still on the Soviet side.

When it seemed clear that the breakthrough was not possible, General Reverberi, commander of the *Tridentina*, made a gesture that has gone down in history: he climbed onto a German self-propelled gun and, standing on it, gave the order to move toward the town, launching the famous call "Tridentina, Avanti!" (Forward, Tridentina). This move gave new strength to the Alpini but, more importantly, set in motion the whole column of the disbanded soldiers who were helplessly watching the battle: thousands of men started to advance toward Nikolajevka, heedless of the losses, while the Soviets, seeing this great mass of men appearing all of a sudden, wavered and then hastily withdrew. The battle was won, although at a high price, and the *Tridentina* were free. The other divisions would not make it.

While these events were happening, to the south, the *Vicenza* resumed its march in the early morning of the twenty-sixth, heading toward Valuijki, with the Alpini of the *Pieve di Teco* as vanguard; around noon it reached the outskirts of the town, only to realize that it was heavily guarded by enemy troops. After a short battle, the remnants of the division, reduced to some 3,000 men, found themselves hopelessly surrounded by tanks and cavalry; thus, the command agreed to surrender at 4:00 p.m..

JANUARY 27–28: THE END OF THE *CUNEENSE*

The *Cuneense* marched, divided into two columns toward its doom, which it met between January 27 and 28. During the twenty-sixth, the division pressed southwest, occasionally attacked by small enemy units or groups of partisans. At dawn of the twenty-seventh, the column of the 2° Reggimento reached the northern side of Valuijki, and found it guarded by the Soviets instead of the Germans, as had been hoped for. The Alpini tried to bypass the village, crossing the railway and divided into small groups, but they were spotted and attacked; after brief resistance, the 2° Reggimento gave in and surrendered. The 1° Reggimento reached the southern outskirts of Valujiki in the evening of the same day instead; it tried as well to cross the railway but did not manage to do it undetected. What remained of the regiment surrendered at dawn on January 28. As the last unit to reach Valujiki, the depleted Battaglione *Mondovì*, which acted as a rearguard, arrived on the afternoon of the twenty-eighth: attacked by strong Soviet units, it refused to surrender and was annihilated in short time.

The sole division that was able to break through had been the *Tridentina*, which had collected a few small groups of the other divisions when the columns sporadically intersected. However, the march was not over yet. Over the following three days, the column pressed on, still sometimes harassed by small units of Soviet troops or partisans but not in danger anymore, until on January 30, around 3:00 p.m., the vanguards met the German lines and finally had some rest and a meal after many days. The following day, the whole column, disbanded men included, safely proceeded to the town of Scebekino, where the Alpini were able to halt for a few days, while the wounded and those with frostbite were moved to Charkov. Here, a first attempt to reorganize the units was carried out, intended to restore a certain order in the mass of the disbanded men as well. On February 2, the Alpini were forced to resume their march, because the Soviets were attacking again and the frontline was rapidly moving westward. They reached Belgorod, where some 3,000 lightly wounded and ill men could find places on a train and some trucks to be moved to the hospitals in the rear. Those who were still considered fit had to march farther west on foot for 140 more kilometers, reaching their destination on February 10. From there, the movement continued by train to Gomel, where all the survivors of the Italian Eighth Army were assembled before being repatriated. The trains with the surviving Alpini left the USSR between March 6 and 15.

The thoughtless employment of the Alpine divisions in the USSR and, furthermore, their deployment in an environment completely different from the one they were trained and equipped for, had cost the Italian army three of its best divisions. Of about 57,000 Alpini that had left Italy, roughly 20,000 did not come back. The numbers change from one source to another, but those collected by the Army Historical Office say

More and more wounded are loaded onto the sledges, towed by the few remaining mules: many Alpini owe their lives to the sturdy animals. *David Zambon*

The Alpini, finally out of the pocket, are approaching the town of Belgorod, still marching on foot.

that the *Tridentina* suffered 4,923 losses; the *Julia*, 7,280; and the *Cuneense*, 9,261. Units directly subordinate to the army corps headquarters suffered another 530 casualties.

Many units were awarded with Gold Medals: all the Regiments, both Alpini and Alpine artillery, the Army Corps Artillery Regiment, and the Battaglione sciatori *Monte Cervino*. The Silver Medal was awarded to the three engineer battalions and the Bronze Medal to the Battaglione *Vestone*. Many medals were also awarded to single Alpini and artillerymen.

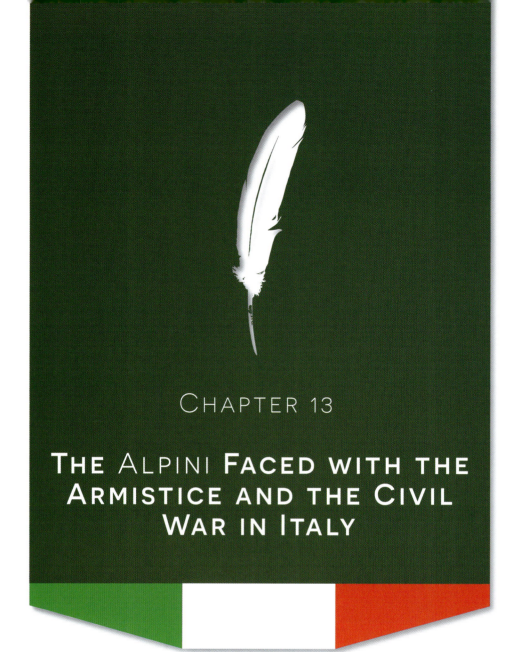

CHAPTER 13

THE ALPINI FACED WITH THE ARMISTICE AND THE CIVIL WAR IN ITALY

A column of Alpini, possibly in a southern French town. Some of them carry on their backpack an old Great War helmet, which might indicate a second-line unit. *Antonio Tallillo*

ORGANIZATIONAL CHANGES AND DEPLOYMENT OF THE ALPINE UNITS IN THE LAST MONTHS BEFORE THE ARMISTICE

In November 1942, the Allies launched *Torch*, the operation aimed at landing huge forces in Morocco and Algeria. The immediate reaction of Germany and Italy was to occupy Tunisia and southern France, and this latter operation saw the participation of Alpine troops as well.

The *Pusteria* Division had been repatriated from Montenegro during the summer of 1942 and had been stationed in Piedmont afterward. After the occupation of France, it was sent to guard a wide strip of French territory west of the Alps, with headquarters at Grenoble and garrisons at Gap and Digne, where it remained until September 1943.

In the summer of 1942, the *Alpi Graie* Alpine division had also been repatriated from Montenegro but only with its 4° Gruppo Alpini *Valle* since, as mentioned, the 2° Gruppo Alpini *Valle* was detached from the division and sent to Greece. In Italy, the division had instead assigned the 1° Gruppo Alpini *Valle*, but the two Gruppi were deployed very far apart from each other: the 4° Gruppo, along with the divisional headquarters, was stationed in Liguria, while the

1° Gruppo was sent first to Valle d'Aosta and then, in November 1942, moved into French territory occupying an area between Bourg St. Maurice and Albertville, in the Savoie. In July 1943, the 1° Gruppo was detached from the *Alpi Graie* again and sent to Friuli, to be transformed into the new 8° Reggimento of the restored *Julia* Division.

The 3° Gruppo Alpini *Valle*, stationed in the upper Maurienne Valley, extended the occupation of the valley as far as the town of Saint Jean de Maurienne in November 1942. In December, it changed designation and became the *XX Raggruppamento Sciatori* (XX Skier Group); thus, its Battaglioni *Val Toce* and *Val Cenischia* changed their names to "*Monte Cervino*," replacing the battalion annihilated in Russia, and *Moncenisio*, respectively; furthermore, it received the Battaglione *Monte Rosa*. The artillery, though, remained the Gruppo *Val d'Orco*. A new 3° Gruppo Alpini *Valle* was formed in the summer of 1943, with the Battaglioni *Val Pellice*, *Val Dora*, *Val Fassa*, and the Gruppo *Val d'Adige* of Alpine artillery and was assigned to the *Alpi Graie* Division, replacing the 1° Gruppo (see above).

Between December 1942 and February 1943, some new Alpine regiments were formed, called *Reggimenti Alpini costieri* (coastal Alpine regiments), and *Reggimenti Alpini territoriali mobili* (mobile territorial Alpine regiments), consisting of men drawn from older classes and charged with the defense of stretches of the seacoast, which is characterized by the presence of mountains. In the summer of 1943, the battalions subordinated to these regiments were named after the Italian mountains. The organization chart was as follows:

165° Reggimento Alpini costiero, consisting of the Battaglioni *Monte Marmolada*, *Monte Canin*, and *Monte Clapier*, assigned to the 224th Coastal Division

166° Reggimento Alpini costiero, consisting of the Battaglioni *Monte Spluga*, *Monte Pavione*, *Monte Arvenis*, and *Monte Stelvio*, assigned to the 223rd Coastal Division

167° Reggimento Alpini costiero, consisting of the Battaglioni *Monte Levanna*, *Monte Suello*, and *Monte Berico*, assigned to the *Legnano* Infantry Division until August 1943 and later to the 223rd Coastal Division

168° Reggimento Alpini costiero, consisting of the Battaglione *Monte Maiella*, assigned to the *Taro* Infantry Division

All the above units were stationed in southern France, subject to Italian occupation.

175° Reggimento Alpini territoriale mobile, consisting of the Battaglioni *Mongioje*, *Monte Albergian*, *Monte Bicocca*, *Monte Mercatour*, *Monte Granero*, and *Monte Baldo*, stationed in Corsica, subordinated to the VII Army Corps

176° Reggimento alpino territoriale mobile, consisting of the Battaglioni *Monte Adamello*, *Monte Antelao*, and *Monte Nero*, operating in Friuli-Venezia Giulia, in the areas of Fiume, Trieste, and Gorizia, subordinated to the Eighth Army, under reconstruction after the disaster in the USSR

The three Alpine divisions that had returned from the Eastern Front were slowly being rebuilt. The *Julia* was in Friuli, while the *Tridentina* and the *Cuneense* were in Trentino-Alto Adige. The *Taurinense* Division remained in the Balkans, in Montenegro, while the 2° Gruppo Alpini *Valle* was stationed in Greece between Epirus and Thessaly.

THE ALPINI IN FRANCE AND ITALY

Two Alpini peacefully strolling, unaware of the storm which is mounting. In the background: a German soldier. *David Zambon*

France, a unit of Alpini is climbing the slopes of a mountain a few days after the armistice.

The Alpine units stationed in France were subordinated to the Fourth Army, which in mid-August received the order to withdraw its forces to Italy, leaving its positions to the Germans, except for the area of Nice. Therefore, the *Pusteria* and the XX Raggruppamento Sciatori started their preparations for departure at the beginning of September, loaded their equipment and supplies on trains, and assembled their units in order to repatriate. In this precarious situation, they learned of the armistice. At Grenoble, the Germans soon captured the headquarters of the *Pusteria*, and when some Alpini of the Battaglione *Trento* tried to free them, they were stopped by an Italian officer, who ordered them to cease fire. The Battaglioni *Bassano* and *Bolzano* were gathered at Gap; they refused to surrender and fought until the morning of the tenth, but then new German forces arrived, and the headquarters of the 11° Reggimento were ordered to lay down their arms. The battalions of the 7° Reggimento were on their way to Italy, on foot as usual, and scattered in various locations. Once it reached the town of Menton, the headquarters of the regiment was ordered to reach the Col de Tende; therefore, it assembled its battalions *Feltre*, *Pieve di Cadore*, and *Belluno* and the batteries of the Gruppo *Belluno*, and on the tenth, the units were deployed as ordered. However, on September 12, it became tragically clear that the whole Fourth Army had melted away, therefore the

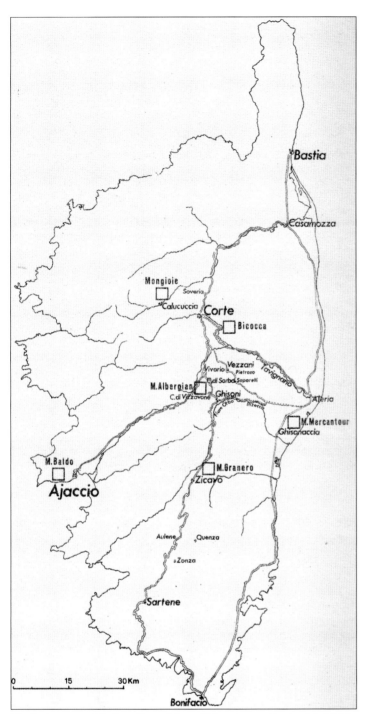

The deployment of the battalions of the 175° Reggimento Territoriale Mobile in Corsica, in September 1943

Susa, but it realized that another German column was advancing along the valley coming from Turin, blocking the path of retreat. The commander decided, therefore, to disband the battalions and leave the men free to find safety.

In Corsica, the armistice found the battalions of the 175° Reggimento territoriale mobile scattered in several garrisons that were very far apart from each other. In a short space of time, however, the units were able to assemble in the mountainous center of the island and effectively block the movement of the Germans along the road that traversed it. The Battaglione *Monte Granero*, supported by a battery of 100 mm howitzers carried out an action against the German garrison at the town of Quenza on September 15, overwhelming and capturing it. In the beginning of October, the operations to free Corsica from the Germans went on with the help of French troops who had landed on the island, until all enemy units had left. Then, the regiment was transferred to Sardinia, and, in August 1944, the battalions were disbanded except for the *Monte Granero*, which was attached instead to the *Corpo Italiano di Liberazione* (see below).

At the beginning of September 1943, the *Alpi Graie* Division was redeploying in the mountains around the port of La Spezia, headquarters of the bulk of the Italian fleet, facing east and northeast along the Magra River; some of its units were still on their way. On September 8, the Alpini were able to stop the Germans that attempted to capture the Italian vessels at the port, buying enough time for the fleet to lift its anchors and head to Malta. Once La Spezia was occupied by forces coming from Genoa, the Alpini tried to withdraw, but in the chaos of those days, all resistance by regular units had become impossible and ceased completely on the thirteenth.

Very critical was the position of the three divisions that had returned from Russia. They were under complete reconstruction, with units to replenish, men to train, and equipment to repair. The *Cuneense* had its headquarters at Appiano, not far from Bolzano, in Alto Adige. It had most of its battalions and batteries scattered more than 60 kilometers along the Adige River and the Isarco River, while a strong reserve consisting of five companies of the Battaglioni *Mondovì* and *Borgo San Dalmazzo*, with two batteries of the Gruppo *Pinerolo*, was in the mountains above Appiano, around the Mendola Pass. During the summer, German forces had cleverly deployed between the Alpini units; therefore, they were able to overwhelm many of them, one by one, once the armistice was announced. The divisional headquarters moved to join its reserves at the Mendola Pass instead and, in this stronger position, delayed the surrender, giving the Alpini gathered there time to escape captivity.

The battalions and batteries of the *Tridentina* were stationed along the Isarco River Valley, north of the *Cuneense* and up to the Brenner Pass, at the border with the German Reich. The presence of German troops in this area was high, being of paramount importance for the communications between Italy and Germany; therefore, the Alpini here had no opportunity to put up any kind of resistance and were disarmed and captured a few hours after the armistice.

The *Julia*, which had already been in a state of alarm since the end of August, was able to perform somewhat better. On August 26, in fact, a German column had entered Italy via the

commander of the regiment ordered the units to disband; most of the Alpini were captured once they descended to the plain anyway, but some of them took refuge in the mountains and became the first Italian partisans, starting the struggle against the Germans.

A similar fate was met by the XX Raggruppamento Sciatori. On September 8, the Battaglione *Monte Rosa* was at Grenoble, waiting to move to Italy, and was captured by the Germans. The headquarters of the Raggruppamento, though, managed to leave Chambery during the night between September 8 and 9, collect the Battaglione *Monte Cervino*, and join the Battaglione *Moncenisio*; the units were deployed to defend Mont Cenis. Over the following two days, the Alpini effectively held their positions against a German column that was trying to enter Italy crossing the Susa Valley, inflicting heavy casualties. On September 10, the Raggruppamento withdrew to the town of

Val Fella without previous agreement of the Italian authorities. Immediately, the Battaglione *Tolmezzo* and the Gruppo *Val Piave* had been sent to bar the way, joined a little later by the Battaglione *Gemona* and the Gruppo *Conegliano*. Italians and Germans remained in a stalled status for days, even after the announcement of the armistice, until on September 12, a German motorized unit reached Udine coming from the west, de facto surrounding the Alpini. The following day, once it was realized that there was no help to be expected, the units disbanded, and most of the men managed to reach their nearby homes and avoid capture.

THE *TAURINENSE* DIVISION IN MONTENEGRO

In the Balkans, the 2° Gruppo Alpini *Valle* was stationed in Greece, and the *Taurinense* Division, in Montenegro. In Greece, the Italian Eleventh Army was in a very weak position, surrounded by numerous German divisions that had a strong presence in the area; furthermore, a few weeks before the armistice, the Eleventh Army had been subordinated to the German Heeresgruppe E, which took advantage of its position. The result was that the units dissolved in a few hours, and the Italian troops were captured by the Germans, except for the few soldiers that managed to join the Greek partisans.

The situation of the *Taurinense* Division in Montenegro was different since, during the weeks that preceded the armistice, it had redeployed its units around the town of Kotor, maintaining a certain degree of concentration. The divisional headquarters, the 4° Reggimento, consisting of the Battaglioni *Ivrea*, *Intra*, *Aosta*, the Gruppo *Aosta* of Alpine artillery with a battery of

Montenegro, machine gunners of the Battaglione *Exilles* take care of their Breda mod. 37 weapons in order to be ready for the coming action.

Frame, a bit blurred, from a film made in Montenegro, likely by Major Ravnich, head of the Gruppo *Aosta* of mountain artillery of the Divisione *Taurinense*, showing a unit of the Gruppo crossing a river in 1943. The film belongs to S. Pelosin and is filed at the Archivio del Cinema di Impresa of Ivrea.

the Gruppo *Susa* attached, and the I Battaglione genio were stationed in and around the town of Nikšić, 40 kilometers northeast of Kotor. The 3° Reggimento, consisting of the Battaglioni *Pinerolo, Fenestrelle, Exilles,* and the remaining batteries of the Gruppo *Susa,* was in the area around the villages of Viluse and Grahovo, about 30 kilometers southwest of Nikšić. The division was subordinate to the XIV Army Corps, which also had as subordinate units the *Venezia, Ferrara,* and *Emilia* infantry divisions, the latter charged with the direct defense of Kotor. The Germans opposed these forces with the 118th *Jäger* Division, about 18,000 men strong, well armed and well equipped, and, above all, with clear orders to execute. As soon as the armistice had been announced, the Alpini got ready to defend their positions against their former ally, who many were sure would act very soon, and against the partisans, who had reorganized their ranks during the summer and saw, owing to confusion among the Italians, the possibility to capture precious weapons and equipment.

On the morning of September 9, the Sixth Battery of the Gruppo *Aosta,* which had a howitzer of the Gruppo *Susa* attached, while defending the road leading to Nikšić from the north, fired a warning volley against a German column, forcing it to stop: this is the first registered episode of open resistance by the *Taurinense.* The following days were characterized by much confusion on the Italian side, which did not help the effectiveness of the reaction by the Italian divisions in general and of the *Taurinense* in particular. On September 9, part of the 3° Reggimento was temporarily detached from

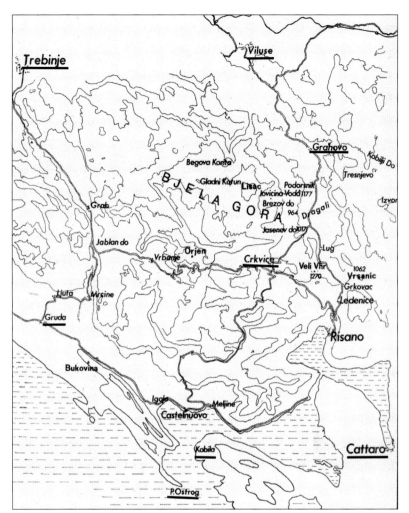

The area of Montenegro around the town of Cattaro, today's Kotor, which had been an Italian province since 1941 and was where the Divisione *Taurinense* fought the Germans in the weeks that followed the armistice

Alpini of the Divisione *Taurinense* parade in a village of Montenegro in the autumn of 1943, followed by partisan units. *L. Manes*

Yugoslavian partisans and Alpini of the Divisione *Taurinense* in October 1943. *L. Manes*

October 1943, the head of the II Korpus of the Yugoslavian partisans meets with the Divisione *Taurinense* al Kolasin. *Luigi Manes*

November 1943, Alpini are ferried over the Tara River in northern Montenegro.

A Yugoslavian partisan armed with a Czechoslovakian ZB vz. 26 light machine gun. *Storia Militare*

Major Carlo Ravnich, head of the Gruppo *Aosta* of mountain artillery; later, head of one of the brigades of the Divisione *Garibaldi* composed mainly of former mountain artillerymen and finally, from July 2, 1944, until March 1945, the last commander of the division itself. *Luigi Manes*

the division and subordinated to the *Emilia* Division; the Battaglioni *Exilles* and *Fenestrelle* with a battery of the Gruppo *Susa* were sent south of Grahovo to guard the route that led to Kotor, but then it was moved farther south to Crkvice. The Battaglione *Pinerolo*, with the last battery of the *Susa*, was sent to Trebinje, 30 kilometers northeast of Grahovo, into Bosnia, to support the *Marche* Infantry Division that was dealing with the Waffen-SS *Prinz Eugen* Division. The battalion and the battery were deployed to the north of the town, but suddenly, it received the order on the following day to go back to Montenegro and take positions at Crkvice as well. On the thirteenth, another counterorder moved the *Pinerolo* and the battery to Gruda, about 20 kilometers west, to take part in an action aimed at recapturing the local airfield, occupied by the

Germans, along with two battalions of the *Emilia* Division. The attack started at 5:00 a.m. on September 14, with a two-and-a-half-hour-long barrage by the Italian artillery; at 7:30 a.m., the Italian infantrymen moved against the German defenses, while the Alpini, hindered by the terrain, only managed to join the action at about midday. The attack seemed to be successful at first, but the sudden arrival of some Stuka dive bombers forced the attackers to break off the action and look for shelter. Meanwhile, the defenders received reinforcements that gave them the advantage over the Italians. At 4:30 p.m., the attack was called off, and the units started to withdraw. The Alpini and artillerymen that had been forced to abandon the howitzers headed east through the mountains and joined the 3° Reggimento at Crkvice on the sixteenth.

A SM81 Italian transport carries supplies for the Divisione *Garibaldi*. Luigi Manes

His Majesty the Prince Umberto visits the veterans of the Divisione *Garibaldi* repatriated from Montenegro in Apulia in the spring of 1945.

The 3° Reggimento seemed to be unable to keep its battalions together, since the *Fenestrelle* and a battery of the *Susa* were sent down to Kotor on the fourteenth and, a little later, were ordered to move to Gruda to support the action against the airfield; finally, they were stopped in Herceg-Novi, when news came that the attack had already failed. The Battaglione *Exilles*, on the other hand, with another battery of the *Susa*, were sent to Herceg-Novi and then a few kilometers farther west to Igalo, to take part in a rather difficult task: to open the Bay of Kotor to the traffic of Italian vessels by recapturing the old Great War fortifications built by the Austro-Hungarians on the northern promontory, Fort Ostra, and on the southern one, Fort Kobila, now occupied by the Germans. While a company of the battalion blocked the road leading to Fort Ostra, preventing any movement to and from the fort, the other two companies with the howitzer battery marched south to take part in the assault to Fort Kobila, which they reached at 6:00 p.m. on September 14. The action of the Alpini started the following day, in the early afternoon, with the support of the Alpine artillery battery and some batteries of the *Emilia* Division. A howitzer was brought very close to the fort and started to fire directly into the loopholes until, at 6:00 p.m., the garrison surrendered. The vessels that transported the bulk of the *Emilia* were able to cross the strait and sail to Bari, but the Alpini were left ashore, apart from a small group of 150 men. On September 16, a German motorized column reached the area of Kotor and found the Alpini of the Battaglioni *Exilles* and *Fenestrelle* exhausted and with very low morale, so the Alpini did not offer any real resistance to disarmament and capture. What remained of the 3° Reggimento was still in the area of Crkvice: the *Pinerolo*; a handful of men of the *Fenestrelle* that had escaped from the Germans; some infantrymen of the *Emilia* who had been left behind and had assembled in an improvised battalion named "*Bijela Gora*"; and some artillerymen of the Gruppo *Susa* without pieces of artillery.

The headquarters of the *Taurinense*, the headquarters of the 4° Reggimento with two of its battalions, *Ivrea* and *Aosta*; the Gruppo *Aosta* of Alpine artillery; and the remaining battery of the Gruppo *Susa* had instead been concentrated in the area of Danilovgrad since September 12, while the *Intra* had been left at Nikšić as a rearguard. On September 12, the Italian XIV Army Corps had ordered its subordinate divisions to deliver their heavy equipment to the Germans, who had promised to repatriate the Italian soldiers in return, thus the artillerymen of the *Aosta* and *Susa* also handed in their howitzers. On the fifteenth, however, the Germans arrested the commander of the army corps in Podgorica with all its officers. Therefore, the *Taurinense* decided to move its men to Kotor, dividing its forces into two columns. The first column consisted of the Battaglione *Ivrea*; the artillerymen of the *Aosta*, who had managed to recover two of their howitzers; the I Battaglione genio; and the mule train of the 4° Reggimento. The second column consisted of the Battaglione *Aosta* and the regimental headquarters. On September 17, the first column ran into some roadblocks put up by the Germans and was not able to break through: the way to the Adriatic Sea was definitively blocked and there was no way to reach the port of Kotor, which had been in German hands since the day before. The headquarters of the *Taurinense* decided, therefore, to head the columns toward Crkvice and join what remained of the 3° Reggimento, which had still not moved. The Battaglione *Intra* also arrived in the area; they had left Nikšić along with other Italian units. The second column, however, was not able to move from Danilovgrad before the nineteenth, since their road to Crkvice was blocked by the Germans and by the presence of several hundred disbanded Italian soldiers in town, who could not be left behind. The commander of the regiment decided, therefore, to head to the town of Berane, about 60 kilometers to the northeast, where the *Venezia* Infantry Division was stationed and still under arms. The march was interrupted quite soon by the partisans, who tried to get their hands on the weapons and equipment of the Alpini and managed to capture some of the mules; the Battaglione *Aosta* then managed to reach an area controlled by Chetnik combatants, fierce enemies of the communist partisans, and tried to establish cooperation with them. But finally, isolated and unsure of the intentions of the Chetniks, they decided that the best option was to surrender to the Germans at the beginning of October.

What remained of the *Taurinense*, and remnants of other units, among which were the infantrymen of the *Bijela Gora*, remained instead at Crkvice with two 75/13 howitzers of the Gruppo *Susa* and a couple of 47 mm guns. The headquarters deployed the units for the defense of the stronghold, including the *Bijela Gora* in the town; the *Ivrea* and a platoon of the *Pinerolo* defending the accesses from Kotor at a bottleneck of the road; the *Pinerolo*, watching the western approaches; the artillerymen of the *Aosta*, who, having lost their artillery pieces, were now fighting as an assault group; and the *Intra* as a reserve. The

Germans did not intervene at first, needing some days to deal with more important targets and to gather their forces. But on September 23, two German trucks that were driving on the road north of Kotor were attacked by a squad of the *Ivrea*; thus, the Germans decided that the time had arrived to get rid of the Alpini. On the twenty-seventh, they attacked the *Ivrea* with artillery and *Stukas*, forcing the battalion to slowly withdraw; however, the Alpini were able to maneuver in the mountains and inflict severe losses with their light weapons and mortars. On the twenty-ninth, the Germans suspended the action to reorganize their ranks; thus, the *Intra* managed to replace the *Ivrea*. This attack, however, had demonstrated beyond any doubt that the *Taurinense* could not hope to remain in its positions and defend them as in a regular war, since it was now seriously outnumbered and outgunned. The headquarters of the division assessed the options and finally decided to negotiate with the partisans to fight together against the new enemy. The agreement, which was in the best interest of both parties, was finally reached, and they prepared to disengage from the Germans and join the Third Partisan Division in the area of Gornje Polje, north of Nikšić, at least 50 kilometers from Crkvice, as the crow flies, in a country now controlled by the Germans. The units started to move on October 3, starting with the heavy column with the mule train, supplies, and ammunition, which were all protected at the rear by the Battaglione *Intra* and at the right flank by the *Pinerolo*, while the town of Crkvice was defended by the *Bijela Gora* infantry battalion. On the fifth, Crkvice was heavily attacked, shelled by artillery, and bombed by Stukas; thus, after a brief fight, the *Bjiela Gora* battalion surrendered. The Battaglioni *Intra* and *Pinerolo* remained irremediably distanced from the main column, pushed more and more westward, and hit constantly by Stukas. On October 7, the commanders of the two battalions decided to surrender to the Germans. About two hundred Alpini of the two battalions chose instead to continue to fight, and they managed to join the Twenty-Seventh Partisan Division, under the name "Battaglione *Taurinense*."

The main column had temporarily succeeded in disengaging and shaking off its pursuers, but on October 6, it met with the major road that connected Nikšić with the west of the country, which was heavily guarded by the Germans. The Alpini, divided into groups, tried to cross the road, but the Battaglione *Ivrea* was spotted and surrounded by enemy forces; in the following fight, the unit was destroyed; only about 200 men managed to escape and meet the partisans. Of the engineer battalion, only 120 men reached Gornje Polje. The Gruppo d'Assalto *Aosta* had better luck, managing to pass undetected, and it arrived at its destination on the seventh with 2,000 men and 500 mules. From that moment on, the process of the transformation of the Alpine units into partisan units began, to become organized for guerrilla warfare. The first unit to be transformed was the Gruppo d'Assalto *Aosta*, which formed the 1ª Brigata Alpina *Aosta* (First Alpine Brigade *Aosta*), about 1,150 men strong, divided into four battalions. The other survivors were moved farther into the interior of the country and, on October 15, reached the town of Kolasin, where the fittest Alpini, numbering about 700, were organized into the 2ª Brigata Alpina *Taurinense* (Second Alpine Brigade *Taurinense*), which consisted of three battalions. The others were divided into labor companies. The engineers, who were highly appreciated by the partisans, were grouped into a special engineer battalion subordinated directly to the II Korpus of the partisan army. At Kolasin, the Alpini met the other Italian unit that was still in arms, the *Venezia* Infantry Division, which had chosen to join the Yugoslav resistance and fight the Germans. In the course of the following autumn , this latter division was also completely reorganized into brigades similar to the partisan brigades, to respond to the specific needs of the kind of war it would fight from that moment on. Finally, in November 1943, with the brigades of the *Venezia* and those of the *Taurinense*, the Divisione Italiana Partigiana *Garibaldi* (*Garibaldi* Italian Partisan Division) was formed; it was a large unit that was entirely Italian and subordinate to II Yugoslav Korpus. The new division consisted of four brigades, each about 1,300 men strong, selected from among the fittest and more motivated men.[1] The I Brigade was composed exclusively of Alpini. In March 1944, the brigade was reinforced with the survivors of the Battaglione *Taurinense*, who had fought the whole winter with another partisan division (see above) and were now able to join their fellow Alpini.

The feats of the *Garibaldi* Division are beyond the scope of this book; let it suffice to say that it battled alongside the partisans until March 1945, when those who had survived the hardship of a year and half of war in the mountains were repatriated. The Alpini of the *Taurinense* received no fewer than 1,138 rewards for valor for the actions carried out after the armistice.

THE ALPINI IN THE ITALIAN COBELLIGERENT ARMY

After the armistice, the Italian king Vittorio Emanuele III, and the government, still presided over by Marshal Pietro Badoglio, reached southern Italy, which was now in the hands of the Anglo-American troops, and settled temporarily in the town of Brindisi, in Apulia. Here, they established a (difficult) relationship with their former enemies, a relationship which also entailed the declaration of war against Germany on October 13, 1943 and the participation of Italian army, navy, and air force units in the war in Italy. The army units became known as the *Esercito Cobelligerante Italiano* (Italian Cobelligerent Army), a rather byzantine definition for an army formed by a nation that was not an enemy anymore, but that could not immediately be called an ally. The Cobelligerent Army, for the most part, consisted of former *Regio Esercito* units that had not disbanded during the difficult days that had followed the armistice.

The reconstruction of the Alpine component of the *Esercito Cobelligerante Italiano* started with a small number of Alpini and artillerymen of the *Taurinense* Division, about 420 men, who were stationed in the beginning of September at a holding area near Bari, either bound for Montenegro or coming from it to enjoy leave at home. They did not take part in the battle that broke out between Italians and Germans at the harbor of Bari on September 9, but the following day, some of them were able to deploy to the north of the port and contribute to frustrating a German counterattack. Once the British troops had occupied Bari, they used the men as workers at the port to unload ships at first, but soon the Italian army staff requested them and mobilized them as its directly subordinate unit on October 28, with the new designation of *Reparto Esplorante Alpino* (Alpine reconnaissance unit). The Alpini were moved near the village of Alberobello, some 50 kilometers southeast of Bari, for a period of training. Meanwhile, in a camp near Lecce, in Apulia, other Alpini had been gathered, either coming from the Balkans like the 150 men of the Battaglione *Fenestrelle* that had escaped from Kotor (see above), or coming from the part of Italy that was under German control. In December, a battalion was formed of these men and the men of the *Reparto Esplorante*. It was called "Battaglione *Taurinense*" since most of the Alpini came from that division. The new unit numbered 27 officers, 43 NCOs, 764 Alpini, and consisted of a headquarters company and three Alpine companies, which in turn consisted of a headquarters platoon, two rifle platoons, and a machine gun platoon. The headquarters was established first at Nardò, near Lecce and then, beginning in January 1944, at Cisternino, between Bari and Brindisi. At Cisternino, the battalion received a battery of the 75/13 howitzers normally assigned to the Alpine artillery, and the mule train was increased significantly. The conditions of the unit were improving by the day, both from the equipment point of view, as the equipment had been completely repaired by this time, and from the operations point of view, with its intense training program. On February 10, the battalion's name changed and became the "Battaglione *Piemonte*."

THE BATTAGLIONE *PIEMONTE* WITHIN THE *I RAGGRUPAMENTO*

View of the Mainarde massif, with Monte Marrone on the right

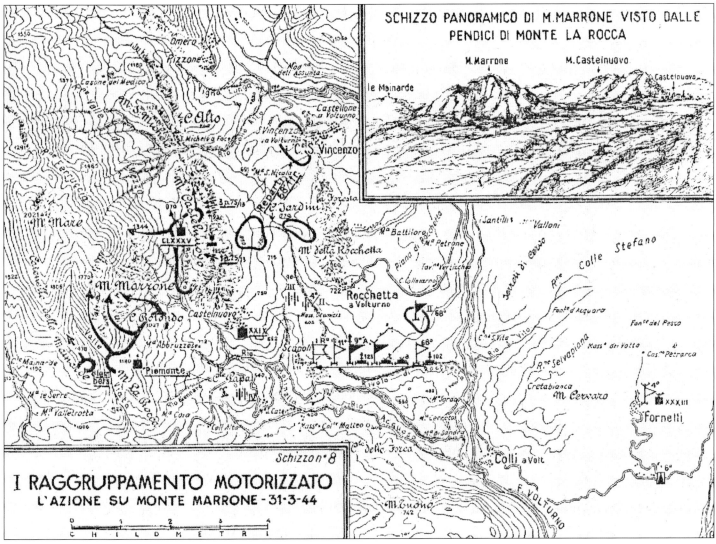

Scheme of the action of the Battaglione *Piemonte* against Monte Marrone on March 31, 1944

Alpine artillerymen of the Battaglione *Piemonte* tenaciously hoist a 75/13 howitzer on top of Monte Marrone and put it in firing position. *Luigi Manes*

MOTORIZZATO

Meanwhile, a large Italian unit called *I Raggruppamento Motorizzato* (first motorized combat group), had been formed in the month of November 1943, and had started to fight alongside the Anglo-American forces, directly subordinate to the II Army Corps of the American Fifth Army. Its baptism by fire had been in December with two attacks, the first on the eighth and the second on the sixteenth, against Monte Lungo, a peak about 16 kilometers southeast of Cassino, a German stronghold on the Gustav Line. The first action had been unsuccessful due, in part, to bad coordination with flanking American units, but the following attack seized the position from German hands, making a good impression on the Allied military authorities. After a period of rest, at the beginning of February 1944, the Raggruppamento was attached to the French expeditionary corps and deployed on the Mainarde massif, between Lazio and Molise, about 20 kilometers northeast of Cassino. The area was then transferred to the British Eighth Army; thus, the Italians came under the command of the Polish army corps. On March 19, the Battaglione *Piemonte* was assigned to the I Raggruppamento Motorizzato and, a few days later, was entrusted with the assault aimed at the conquest of Monte Marrone, a ridge about 1 kilometer long, with a maximum height of 1,770 meters (5,807 feet) above MSL, overlooking the valley below.[2] During the winter months, the mountain had not been occupied, but with the beginning of the military operations in spring, it would be a perfect observation point on the upper Volturno River Valley and on the Mainarde massif. And at the same time, it would deprive the Germans of a good position from which to view Allied lines. The Alpini were to occupy the ridge and establish a series of strongholds to resist the German counterattack, while the *bersaglieri* on the left of the mountain and the paratroopers on the right carried out supporting actions. The artillery support was provided by the Alpine battery of the *Piemonte* itself, by the other pieces of artillery of the Raggruppamento and, if needed, by some batteries of the Polish army corps. The attack was launched at 3:30 a.m. on March 31 and took the Germans completely by surprise. The Alpini moved to the ridge in three columns, preceded by small reconnaissance groups that reached their targets between 5:50 a.m. and 6:15 a.m., while the main columns arrived at 7:15 a.m. Once Monte Marrone had been conquered, the Alpini immediately started to dig their strongholds, while carrying barbed wire and other material for trenches and shelters. On April 6, a 75/13 mountain howitzer was even positioned on top, transported on the backs of the artillerymen themselves since there was no track for the mules. The German reaction began on April 2 with the sending of patrols whose mission was to test the Italian defenses, looking for a weak point, but the counterattack was launched on the tenth, a heavy artillery having been prepared. The fighting lasted more than two hours and hit the positions of the First Company hard, but nowhere did the line give way; thus, the attackers were forced to retreat. On May 7, the Alpini left Monte Marrone, replaced by a *bersaglieri* unit, but the howitzer remained on top and their mortars were left behind.

ALPINI IN ACTION WITH THE CORPO ITALIANO DI LIBERAZIONE . . .

In April 1944, the I Raggruppamento Motorizzato changed its name to "*Corpo Italiano di Liberazione*" (Italian Liberation Corps), or CIL. The unit, though, remained deployed in the same area. On May 12, the major Anglo-American offensive against the Gustav Line began, and the Italian troops maintained a highly aggressive attitude, with continuous patrol activity, to pin down as many German troops as possible. The order to advance arrived to the CIL on May 26, and operations started the following day at 7:00 a.m. The Alpini in particular advanced toward the northwest from Monte Marrone to Monte Mare and then to the Colle dell'Altare Ridge, slowed down both by the strong German rearguards and by the difficult terrain.

Alpini of the Battaglione *Piemonte* ascend the slopes of an Italian mountain, carrying a Breda mod. 37 machine gun and Beretta MAB38 submachine guns as individual weapons, to mark a certain enhancement in the equipment compared to the Regio Esercito. *Luigi Manes*

Alpini in the town of Jesi, recently evacuated by the German army. *Luigi Manes*

On the twenty-eighth, the Battaglione *Piemonte* was given the task of crossing the Canneto Valley and taking the town of Opi, on the Abruzzo Apennines, to cut off a possible path of retreat for the enemy. The Alpini advanced along the only mule track in the valley, and on the morning of the twenty-ninth, they engaged the German units that held the road, which were crossed within those hours by retreating enemy columns. The fighting went on between the twenty-ninth and the thirtieth, but the Italians, supported only by their artillery battery, did not break through. On the evening of May 30, the Alpini were exhausted, but while they prepared for resuming the attacks the following day, the order came to go back to their base, since the CIL was being transferred from the mountains to an area near the Adriatic coast. Between June 1 and 3, the Italian units reached the area of Lanciano, 30 kilometers south of Pescara, in Abruzzo, and came under the command of the British V Army Corps. At Lanciano, the CIL was reinforced with new units—the *Nembo* paratroop division and the Battaglione *Bafile* of marine infantry. The offensive on the Adriatic side of the front started on June 8 and the Italian units advanced rapidly, liberating many towns in Abruzzo, such as the capital L'Aquila, where part of the CIL paraded on June 22. On July 1, the Battaglione *Monte Granero*, coming from Sardinia[3] with a battery of Alpine artillery, joined the Italian Liberation Corps, thereby joining it with the Battaglione *Piemonte*. It then became possible to form a new Alpine regiment that was attached to the newly formed I Brigade.[4] The new unit was stationed for a few days in the area of Chieti, in Abruzzo, for the men to rest and organize themselves. It was then sent north, where the CIL, now attached to the Polish army corps, was progressing on the liberation of the Marche region. On July

9, the *Piemonte* was deployed on the northern bank of the Fiumicello River, one of the numerous small rivers that run from the Apennines to the Adriatic Sea. The river was used by the Germans to slow down the Allied advance, and it was reached two days later by the *Monte Granero*, which remained in support on the southern bank. Over the following days, the Alpini were engaged in an intense patrol and coups de main activity to improve their positions and weaken the Germans. On July 17, the battle for the liberation of the port of Ancona by the Polish army corps began, with the forcing of the Musone River. During these operations, the Italians were able to advance steadily, engaged by the German rearguards that protected the general retreat to the next obstacle, the Esino River, but during the night of the twentieth, the Alpini succeeded in forcing this river and set foot in the town of Jesi, on the northern bank, and they established an important bridgehead. After a few more days of pause, the advance was resumed on July 26 and was continuing to struggle against the German rearguards, which strongly contested the terrain, while retreating toward the Gothic Line. From August 17 onward, the Italian units were gradually withdrawn from the front after many weeks of uninterrupted advancing and fighting, the *Monte Granero* being one of the last to leave the line. They were concentrated in the area of Benevento, in Campania, to be completely reorganized.

ALPINI IN ACTION WITHIN THE *GRUPPI DI COMBATTIMENTO*

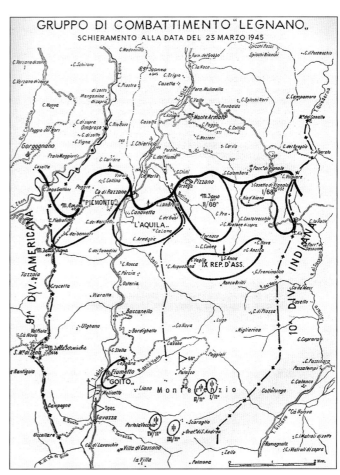

The deployment of the Battaglioni *L'Aquila* and *Piemonte* of the Gruppo di Combattimento *Legnano* on the Gothic Line, a little south of Bologna, at the end of March 1945

Picket of Alpini of the Gruppo di Combattimento *Legnano* lined up; the uniform and individual weapons are supplied by the British army, but they do not give up the beloved felt cap with the feather. *Luigi Manes*

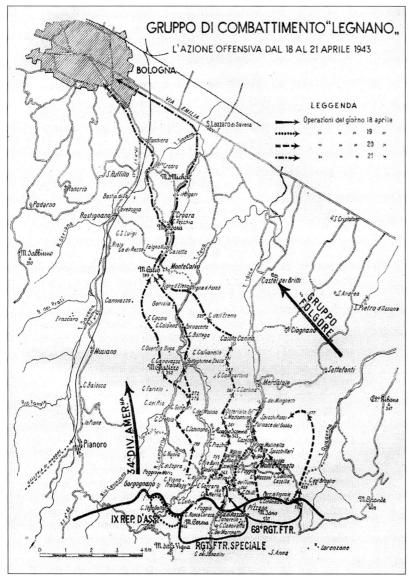

The advance of the Gruppo di Combattimento *Legnano* toward Bologna in April 1945

At the end of July 1944, during a meeting between high-ranking Italian and Allied officers, it had been decided to enhance the Italian participation in the war effort, agreeing on the creation of some divisions consisting of two regiments, although not called "divisions" but *Gruppi di Combattimento* (combat groups). These units were to be equipped and armed by the British Eighth Army. The first two Groups to be formed were the *Cremona* and the *Friuli*, with personnel drawn from the divisions of the same name, the *Regio Esercito*; later, the *Legnano* and the *Folgore* were formed, while the *Mantova* and the *Piceno* arrived too late to take part in any action.

In this context, it was decided that the Battaglione *Monte Granero* would transfer its youngest and fittest men to the *Piemonte*, who in turn would cede its older Alpini to its fellow battalion; thus, the *Piemonte* was incorporated into the new Gruppo di Combattimento *Legnano*, replacing its Alpine artillery battery with British 3-inch mortars and 6-pounder antitank guns, while the *Monte Granero* was sent to Sicily with public order duties. To replace it, a completely new battalion was levied in Abruzzo with new recruits and Alpini that had fought with the partisans on the Apennines; at first, it had been named "Battaglione *Abruzzi*," and was soon renamed "Battaglione *L'Aquila*." The two Alpine battalions, with a *bersaglieri* battalion, formed the Reggimento Fanteria Speciale (Special Infantry Regiment) of the Gruppo di Combattimento *Legnano*.[5] The combat group was deployed to the southeast of Bologna, across the Idice River Valley, between March 18 and 23, subordinate to the American II Army Corps, at an extremely fragile point to the extreme right of the Fifth Army, in contact with the left wing of the British Eighth Army. After a few days spent in patrol activity and reconnaissance, beginning on April 16, when the American Fifth Army started its offensive, the *Legnano* was engaged in secondary attacks to pin down enemy forces. But soon, on April 19, the group started its advance. On that same day, the Battaglione *Piemonte* conquered the important German position known as Hill 363, with a skillful action that saw the Alpini advance under the barrage fire of their artillery up to a few dozen meters from the enemy positions and then break in while the Germans were still in their shelters. At the same time, the Battaglione *L'Aquila* advanced on the right flank of the *Piemonte*, reaching Jano Creek. During the following days, the *Legnano* pressed on, facing lessening resistance ever since the strong German positions in the Idice River Valley had been overwhelmed. On April 21, the group entered Bologna and were evacuated by the Germans and the troops of the Repubblica Sociale Italiana (see below), along with American and British units and the Gruppo *Friuli*. The Gothic Line had been shattered; thus, the following operations consisted of pursuing enemy units in full retreat, if not in flight, carried out by task forces. The Alpini of the Battaglione *L'Aquila*, with *bersaglieri* and an artillery battalion, reached

The Gruppo di Combattimento *Legnano* enters Bologna on April 21, 1945. The Alpini of the Battaglione *Piemonte* are on the first Dodge truck. *Luigi Manes*

Bergamo on April 30, and one of its companies and a half battery was sent to Pavia to cooperate with an American unit the following day. Once any last resistance from the Germans had been overcome, the unit followed the American motorized unit and reached Torino on May 2. Other Alpine units arrived in Como and on the Tonale Pass, between Lombardy and Trentino. On May 2, the news of the surrender of the German units and those of the Repubblica Sociale was broadcast, putting an end to the war in Italy.

ALPINE DIVISIONS AND INDEPENDENT ALPINE UNITS IN THE *REPUBBLICA SOCIALE ITALIANA*

THE FIRST VOLUNTEER ALPINI UNITS

In the southern part of Italy, under Allied control, the King continued to reign and appoint the government, though with rather restricted powers; in the northern part of the country, under German control, a new state was established, under the control of the occupiers and presided over by Benito Mussolini itself. He had been freed from his imprisonment in a hotel on the Gran Sasso massif, in the Abruzzo Apennines, by German

Alpini of the Reggimento *Tagliamento* during a patrol. *Archives of the Veterans of the Reggimento Tagliamento via Carlo Cucut*

Pillbox, being part of the fortifications of the town of Coritenza, today Koritnica in Slovenia, in the upper Isonzo valley, garrisoned by the Reggimento *Tagliamento*. *Archives of the Veterans of the Reggimento Tagliamento via Carlo Cucut*

The Battaglione *Cadore* parades in Venezia on March 18, 1944. *Achives of the Divisione Monterosa via Carlo Cucut*

paratroopers and transferred to Germany; then, after a meeting with his fellow dictator, had gone back to Italy to proclaim the cancellation of the monarchy and the birth of a republic, calling it the "*Repubblica Sociale Italiana*" (Italian Social Republic), or RSI. He appointed a government and pressed on to recruit an army to continue the war alongside the Germans. It is a given that the army of the RSI would have had its own Alpine units.

However, the creation of the first Alpine unit that had been formed with pursuing the war with the Germans in mind, the Reggimento Alpini *Tagliamento*, even predates the birth of the RSI. In mid-September, a very few days after the armistice, a group of volunteers gathered at the barracks of the 8° Reggimento Alpini at Udine, in Friuli, at the initiative of a former Black

Shirts officer. Very soon, the unit assumed the size of a company and, in the following weeks, reached 1,400 men. The regiment adopted its definitive organization chart and designation in April 1944, with a headquarters company; the Battaglioni *Isonzo*, *Vipacco*, and *Natisone*, the latter with a mixed composition of Alpini and *bersaglieri*; and a battle group named "*Montenero*," which was formed to intervene quickly in support of garrisons in danger. During its eighteen months of activity, the regiment operated on the Italian eastern borders, fighting against the Yugoslav partisans, with operational headquarters at Tolmino, Trieste, and Canale d'Isonzo and dozens of smaller garrisons near roads, railways, bridges, and any kind of important facility. The *Tagliamento* was disbanded on April 30, 1945.

A few weeks after the *Tagliamento*, at Conegliano Veneto, about 50 kilometers north of Venice, in the Veneto Plain, the Battaglione Alpini *Pieve di Cadore* was also formed; at that time, it was simply known as Battaglione *Cadore*. The battalion operated constantly against the Italian partisans, first as an independent unit, then subordinated to the Centro Addestramento Reparti Speciali, which deployed it in Emilia in the spring of 1944 and, finally, within the *Cacciatori degli Appennini*[6] in Piedmont from August 1944. In January 1945, the battalion was included in the ranks of the Divisione alpina *Monterosa* (see below) but employed again against the partisans to secure the rear of the division that was deployed in the western Alps, on the border with France. Although its organization and numbers varied over time, the Battaglione *Cadore* consisted of a headquarters and supply company, three Alpine companies, and a support weapons company. The unit was disbanded at Venaria Reale, near Torino, on April 27, 1945.

Another battalion of Alpini was attached to the *Raggruppamento Anti Partigiani* (antipartisans' group), a counterguerrilla unit active in Piedmont between 1944 and 1945.

THE MOUNTAIN TROOPS OF THE *ESERCITO NAZIONALE REPUBBLICANO*

In the late autumn of 1943, the newly born Repubblica Sociale Italiana decided, in agreement with its ubiquitous German ally, to form a regular army, the *Esercito Nazionale Repubblicano* (National Republican Army), with divisions consisting both of volunteers recruited from among the thousands of Italian soldiers taken prisoner by the Germans after the armistice and of new recruits levied in Italy. These divisions were to be trained in Germany by German instructors. In the following months, four divisions were formed: the *San Marco* marines division, the *Monterosa* Alpini division, the *Littorio* grenadier division, which however consisted of a grenadier regiment and an Alpini regiment, and the *Italia bersaglieri* division.

The Divisione alpina *Monterosa* was officially established on January 1, 1944, and consisted of

1° Reggimento Alpini, with the Battaglioni *Aosta*, *Bassano*, *Intra*, with five companies each, and the 101st antitank company
2° Reggimento Alpini, with the Battaglioni *Brescia*, *Morbegno*, *Tirano*, with five companies each, and the 102nd antitank company
1° Reggimento artiglieria da montagna, with the Gruppi *Aosta*, *Bergamo*, *Verona*, the latter later renamed "*Vicenza*," equipped with three batteries of 75/13 howitzers each, and the Gruppo *Mantova*, equipped instead with three batteries of 100 mm howitzers, later replaced by German 10.5 cm FH18 field howitzers
I Gruppo esplorante (Reconaissance group), with three squadrons, formed, however, with *bersaglieri*, armed with twenty German PaK40 antitank guns, later replaced with thirty-six more handy Panzerschreck,[7] and German infantry howitzers 7.5 cm IG18
Battaglione pionieri (engineer battalion), with headquarters company and three companies
Divisional antitank company

Signals battalion
Light column
Supply unit

In January 1945, as mentioned, the Battaglione *Cadore* joined the division.

The units were formed and trained in Germany at the Heuberg, Feldstetten, and Münsingen training fields, and in July 1944, the division received its war banner and started to move to Italy to be deployed first in Liguria, on the Levante Riviera, where a landing operation by the Anglo-American troops aiming to isolate the German troops in central Italy was expected. However, after the Allies had instead landed in Provence, the danger against Liguria became negligible; therefore, many units of the division were redeployed. Unfortunately, the battalions and batteries were scattered into different directions, losing any link between them. The Battaglioni *Bassano* and *Tirano* moved first: the *Bassano*, to guard the area between the Varaita Valley and the Maira Valley, to the northwest of the town of Cuneo, in Piedmont; the *Tirano*, toward the Colle di Monginevro, not far from Sestriére, in today's France. Here, they were engaged in patrol and counterguerrilla activities. The Gruppo *Vicenza* was transferred to the Stura Valley, southwest of Cuneo, and attached to the *Littorio* Division. The divisional headquarters, the Battaglioni *Intra*, *Brescia*, and a company of the *Aosta*, along with the Gruppi *Bergamo* and

Units of the Divisione *Monterosa* back in Italy after their training in Germany, in the summer of 1944. *Achives of the Divisione Monterosa via Carlo Cucut*

The Battaglione *Aosta* of the Divisione *Monterosa* parades in Torino. *Achives of the Divisione Monterosa via Carlo Cucut*

Mantova and the reconnaissance group, moved to the Garfagnana, an area in the northern Tuscany, on the Apennines north of the town of Lucca, where they fought against the advancing American forces in October. The most relevant action carried out in this area was the *Offensiva di Natale* (Christmas Offensive), or *Wintergewitter* for the Germans, which, between December 26 and 28, brought great turmoil to the American lines. A joint Italo-German task force, with a total of nine battalions, among which were the Battaglioni *Intra* and *Brescia*, the reconnaissance group of the *Monterosa*, and a battalion of the *San Marco* Division, supported by mountain artillery and German guns, broke through the lines of the American Ninety-Second Buffalo Division in the Serchio River Valley. They captured many prisoners and war booty in abundance, forcing the Americans to send in substantial reinforcements taken from the forces assigned to the offensive against Bologna, which had to be postponed until the next spring. Once they had achieved this important result, the attacking forces were withdrawn behind their starting lines.

The following spring, many units were withdrawn from the Garfagnana and sent back to Liguria, to be partly redeployed on the western Alps. The Battaglione *Aosta* gathered its companies and moved to the Stura Valley; the *Morbegno*, to the Viù Valley, northwest of Turin; and the *Brescia*, farther north to the Locana Valley. The Gruppo *Mantova* sent two of its batteries—one in the Susa Valley, west of Turin, and one to the Aosta Valley, near La Thuile—to support the defenders of the Little St. Bernard Pass. All these units remained in their positions until the very end of the war at the end of April 1945, only leaving the mountains to surrender to the Americans and sometimes to the partisans. Meanwhile, the battery of the *Mantova* near La Thuile, along with other units, joined the resistance against the French troops that tried to reach Aosta, until after the city had been occupied by the Americans on May 8. The Gruppo *Aosta* and the Reconnaissance Group were instead stationed in Liguria until the end of the war and surrendered to the Americans on April 27, as had the Battaglioni *Intra* and *Bergamo* and the engineer battalion that had remained in Garfagnana. The Gruppo *Vicenza*, attached to the *Littorio* Division, descended to Ivrea at the beginning of May with the other units of that division after sabotaging its guns.

Garfagnana, autumn of 1944. Alpini prepare barbed-wire obstacles to defend their positions. *Achives of the Divisione Monterosa via Carlo Cucut*

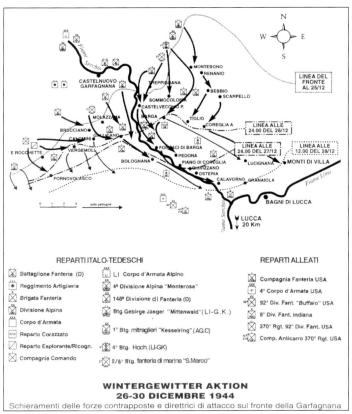

The development of the *Offensiva di Natale* in the Garfagnana, December 26–30, 1944

A German 10.5 cm FH18 of the Gruppo *Mantova* on the Garfagnana front

The Divisione *Littorio* at Sennelager just before it packs up to return to Italy, in the autumn of 1944. *Galliani Archives via Carlo Cucut*

A unit of Alpini of the Battaglione *Bergamo* of the Divisione *Littorio* in the Western Alps, near the Col de la Seigne, in the winter of 1944–45. *Quaquaro Archives via Carlo Cucut*

The *Littorio* grenadier division was formed on April 7, 1944, with two grenadier regiments and an artillery regiment, at first. However, most of the men expected that the 4° Reggimento that arrived from Italy would come from the disbanded 5° Reggimento Alpini; thus, they demanded—and were allowed to keep—the hat with the feather and change the regiment from grenadiers to Alpini. The same was true for the artillerymen of the Gruppo *Gran Sasso*, who came from the Alpine artillery. The *Littorio*, at the end of its training in the camps of Sennelager and Münsingen, was composed as follows:

3° Reggimento *granatieri*, with three battalions and the 103rd Antitank Company

4° Reggimento Alpini, with the Battaglioni *Varese*, *Bergamo*, *Edolo*, and the 104th Antitank Company

2° Reggimento artiglieria, with the three Gruppi of mountain artillery; *Gran Sasso*, consisting of two batteries of 75/13 and one of 75/18 model 35 howitzers; *Romagna*, consisting of two batteries of 75/13 and one of German 7.5 cm Gebirgsgeschutz 36, renamed "75/21," howitzers; *Verona*, consisting of three batteries of 75/13 howitzers; and a further battalion of field artillery with 149 mm howitzers

Battaglione esplorante (reconnaissance battalion)

Battaglione pionieri (engineer battalion), with headquarters company and three companies

Divisional antitank company

Signals battalion

Light column

Supply unit

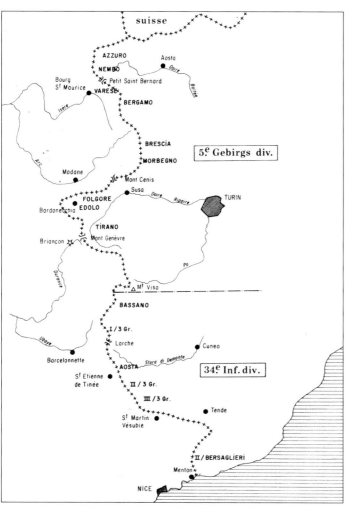

The deployment of the armed forces of the RSI in the Western Alps. *Achives of the Divisione Monterosa via Carlo Cucut*

The 4° Reggimento completed its training and moved to Italy in October 1944, but like the *Monterosa* Division, its units were dispersed along various stretches of the front. The regimental headquarters settled at La Thuile, the Battaglione *Varese* was deployed at the Little St. Bernard, and the Battaglione *Bergamo* saw its companies positioned at the two flanks of the *Varese*; in the rear of the battalions, the *Gran Sasso* provided its artillery fire support. The Battaglione *Edolo* was moved 75 kilometers south, in the area of Bardonecchia, west of Turin, where it was stationed for the rest of the war. Additionally, the regiment had, as subordinated units, a battery of the Gruppo *Mantova*, of the *Monterosa* Division (see above); two paratroop battalions; and a few German units. Furthermore, it also controlled two strongholds with fixed position artillery: one with four 75 mm guns and another with two 149 mm old, rigidly mounted guns. The activity was, for the most part, limited to patrolling the borders and preventing the infiltration of enemy patrols; however, the Battaglione *Varese* was involved in the offensive launched by the French-American forces at the end of March 1945 against the Col de Traversette. The attack started on March 25 and was called off six days later without reaching any result. On April 29, however, the *Alpini* received the order to abandon their positions and descend to the valley below, and the units were disbanded at Aosta on May 4.

Alpini of the machine gun company of the Battaglione *Bergamo*, Divisione *Littorio*, with a German MG42 machine gun used as an antiaircraft weapon on the shoulders of a machine gunner. *Quaquaro Archives via Carlo Cucut*

Moments of camaraderie between Italian Alpini and German *Gebirgsjäger* in the Western Alps. On their sleeves, the German soldiers wear the ribbon of their participation in Operation *Merkur* on Crete in 1941. *Antonio Tallillo*

The *Decima MAS* Division

After the armistice, the *Decima MAS* Division was gradually made a marine infantry unit, derived from the glorious *X*ᵃ *Flottiglia MAS*, a special navy assault unit to which is attributed, among others, the famous raid against Alexandria of December 1941, where a handful of divers sank two British battleships. Among its troops, however, the division also counted an Alpine sapper battalion, the Battaglione *Valanga*, which consisted of the headquarters company, the Compagnia *Aquila*, the Compagnia *Uragano*, and a support weapons company; at the end of 1944, a new company was added: the *Serenissima*. The

battalion was formed in Pavia where, starting on September 21, 1943, the former commander of the Third Engineer Regiment called for volunteers. The unit trained first along the Ticino River, and in January 1944, it was planned to send it to Germany for further training and to be attached to one of the new divisions of the RSI army. The Alpini's request to join the *Decima* instead was granted. The battalion was moved to Jesolo, near Venice, to complete its training and receive the equipment. Here, the Alpini were momentarily forced to become marines and give up their hat with the feather; the name of the unit was changed to "Battaglione *Tarigo*" as well. In mid-August, the *Tarigo* was sent to Piedmont, where the men took part in

The antitank platoon of the Battaglione *Valanga* of the Xᵃ MAS, near the town of Vittorio Veneto, tow a 47/32 gun. *Roberto Archives via Carlo Cucut*

an intense antiguerrilla activity at the rear of the front of the western Alps; at the end of these operations, the Alpini were authorized to reclaim their former hat and name. In October, the *Valanga* moved to Vittorio Veneto, and at the end of the year, two companies were sent to Friuli and took part in the Battle of Tarnova (now Trnovo) a village about 10 kilometers east of Gorizia in Slovenia. Here, the marines of another battalion of the *Decima*, the *Fulmine*, were attacked on January 19, 1945, by overwhelming forces of Yugoslavian partisans. After two days of fighting, part of the battalion managed to disengage and withdraw, while the rest was liberated with a counterattack launched by other *Decima* units, the Battaglione *Valanga* among them, and some German units. The battalion disbanded on April 28, at Marostica, in Veneto; a handful of Alpini decided to take refuge in Trentino but surrendered anyway to the Americans on May 2.

ALPINI IN THE RSI COASTAL DEFENSE

The Repubblica Sociale formed sixteen battalions destined to the defense and fortification of its long coasts, among them were three that included Alpini. The IX Battaglione was born in Treviso in November 1943 and entrusted with the defense of a stretch of the Adriatic Coast near the delta of the Po River. It was, however, disbanded in August 1944 due to the high number of deserters, and the remaining personnel were transferred to perform antiaircraft defense duties. The X Battaglione was formed in Padua in December 1943 and sent to the Marche, where it was stationed until the arrival of the British troops in August 1944; in the spring of 1945, one finds the unit disarmed and used as a labor battalion north of Bologna. The XVI Battalion was born in the autumn of 1943, assembling preexisting companies that were formed in Gorizia

Alpini of the X Battaglione Difesa Costiera. *Acta Archives via Cucut*

and Udine; in the spring of 1944, it left two companies in these towns and moved the rest of its forces to Fiume, which is today Rijeka in Croatia, where it also took part in some counterguerrilla activities. In April 1944, the Germans disarmed and imprisoned many members of the unit, who were suspected of cooperating secretly with the partisans, but some Alpini remained in Rjieka and defended the town against the Yugoslav partisans until May 2. The story of the 37ᵃ Batteria *Julia* is peculiar, as it was created from the 163rd antiaircraft battery of the *Julia* Division, which was being reorganized after the Russian campaign with veterans of the 3° Reggimento Artiglieria Alpina of that division. When the armistice was announced, the unit did not disband, but remained at Gorizia, taking part in the defense of the town against the Yugoslav partisans. When the Germans took hold of the town, the battery was reequipped with 100 mm howitzers

and attached to the German 171st Artillery Regiment until, in October, it was sent to Fiume; beginning in January 1944, it was subordinated to the XII Gruppo and deployed on a height near the town. The battery left Fiume on April 29 and was disbanded the day after at Trieste.

One last unit of note is the *I Compagnia Protezione Impianti* (First Infrastructure Protection Company), formed at Bassano del Grappa, in Veneto, to ensure the protection of some important infrastructures and factories in the area of Vicenza in September 1943.

The changing of the guard by the XVI Battaglione Difesa Costiera at the stronghold of S. Caterina, at Fiume. *Comin Archives via Carlo Cucut*

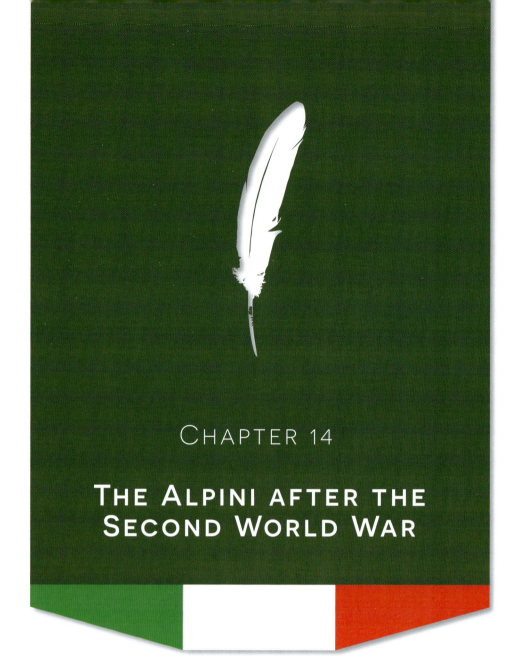

CHAPTER 14

THE ALPINI AFTER THE SECOND WORLD WAR

An old 73/13 howitzer of the newly re-formed artiglieria da montagna on the Tofane massif at the beginning of the 1950s. *Museo Nazionale Storico degli Alpini*

THE RECONSTRUCTION OF THE ALPINE UNITS AFTER THE WAR

At the end of the war, the Italian army was represented by the six Gruppi di Combattimento, two of which, however, had not taken part in any action. The reconstruction of the army, navy, and air force was understandably a very delicate topic to be discussed with the Allied authorities, who had decision-making powers on every detail of the administration of Italy. In 1945, the limits imposed were very strict: the army could have at most 140,000 soldiers and 65,000 *Carabinieri*; that meant that about 90,000 men were available to form the new operational units. This resulted in five divisions with two regiments each, direct heirs of the Gruppi di Combattimento, three divisions with solely internal security duties and ten independent regiments. The organization of the new army, called *Esercito di Transizione* (transitional army), entered into force in the spring of 1946.

Concerning the Alpini, there were only two operational battalions at the end of the war, *Piemonte* and *L'Aquila*. However, it was decided that three out of the ten independent regiments would be formed with Alpini: the 1° Reggimento, stationed in Piedmont; the 4° Reggimento; stationed in Alto Adige; and the 5° Reggimento, stationed in Veneto. They soon changed their number to Fourth, Sixth, and Eighth, respectively, to carry on the traditions of the most decorated Alpine units. As a consequence, the Battaglione *Piemonte* was transferred to the 4° Reggimento, changing its name to "*Aosta*," while the Battaglione *L'Aquila* moved to the 8° Reggimento. In the spring of 1946 the organization chart of the three regiments was the following:

- 4° Reggimento, with headquarters in Piedmont, consisting of the Battaglioni *Aosta*, *Saluzzo*, and *Susa*
- 6° Reggimento, with headquarters in Alto Adige, consisting of the Battaglioni *Bolzano*, *Trento*, and *Edolo*
- 8° Reggimento, with headquarters in Veneto, consisting of the Battaglioni *L'Aquila*, *Feltre*, and *Tolmezzo*, joined in 1948 by the *Cividale*

Starting from 1948, the mountain artillery was concentrated into two Gruppi that were not assigned to the regiments but to the newly established *Comandi Militari Territoriali*, or CMT, which were nonoperational commands responsible for the military organization of a specific area of the Italian territory. The Gruppo *Bergamo* was assigned to the CMT of Bolzano; the Gruppo *Belluno*, to the CMT of Padua. They consisted of three batteries of the veteran former Austro-Hungarian 75 mm mountain howitzer.

Things changed drastically in April 1949, when the North Atlantic Treaty was signed in Washington, DC, forming the alliance known as the North Atlantic Treaty Organization (NATO).[1] All restrictions to the reconstruction of the Italian armed forces were removed, and the other members of the organization, beginning with the USA, started to put pressure on the Italian government to strengthen its military apparatus, to be able to ensure an effective defense of a fragile stretch of the new frontier between the European Western and the Eastern Bloc, also known as the Iron Curtain. The USA provided Italy with significant financing and equipment that enabled the country to significantly enlarge its armed forces.

A series of evocative images of the new battaglioni and gruppi, taken during excursions in the mountains: Alpini of the 5° Reggimento of the Divisione *Orobica* on the Col Visentin, in the Prealps near Belluno; two moments of the ascent of the same 5° Reggimento in the deep snow of the Crocetta Pass; a patrol of the 6° Reggimento marches just under the Tre Cime di Lavaredo. *Museo Nazionale Storico degli Alpini*

THE NEW ALPINI BRIGADES

As a consequence, in October 1949, the first Alpine brigade was formed, named "*Julia*," which changed its organization chart several times over the years. It consisted first of the 8° Reggimento Alpini, with the Battaglione *Feltre*, which changed its name to "Gemona" in 1956. As its artillery component, it had at first assigned the Gruppo *Belluno* and one battalion with British 6-pounder antitank guns. In 1951, these units were grouped into the new 3° Reggimento artiglieria da montagna, which was soon reinforced with a battalion of 100 mm howitzers, named "*Conegliano*," and a battalion of 40 mm Bofors antiaircraft guns. Very soon, the antitank battalion was removed but was replaced by a new Gruppo, the *Gemona*, later renamed "*Udine*," which was equipped with heavy American M30 107 mm mortars. In 1961, a further Gruppo, the *Osoppo*, was composed, and they were equipped following the new guidelines (see below) and also joined the Reggimento artiglieria. A signals company, a sapper company, and a paratrooper platoon were also subordinate to the brigade.

In 1951, the Brigata *Tridentina* was formed, which, taking into consideration the experience acquired with the *Julia*, consisted of:

- 6° Reggimento Alpini, to which a new battalion was added, named "*Bassano*"
- 2° Reggimento artiglieria da montagna, consisting of the Gruppo *Bergamo*, later renamed "*Vicenza*," and Gruppo *Verona*, with three batteries of 100 mm howitzers, a 6-pounder antitank battalion, and a 40 mm Bofors antiaircraft battalion. As with the *Julia*, the anti-tank battalion was soon removed and replaced by the Gruppo *Asiago* with heavy American M30 107 mm mortars
- Signals company
- Sapper company
- Paratrooper platoon

In the few months between April 1952 and July 1953, three more brigades were formed.

Brigata *Taurinense*, consisting of
- 4° Reggimento Alpini, which added the Battaglione *Mondovì* in 1953
- 1° Reggimento artiglieria da montagna, with Gruppo *Aosta*, three batteries of 75 mm howitzers, Gruppo *Susa*, three batteries of 100 mm howitzers, Gruppo *Pinerolo*, three batteries of 107 mm mortars, and 40 mm Bofors antiaircraft gun battalion
- Signals company
- Sapper company
- Paratrooper platoon

The brigade had its Battaglione *Mondovì* and its Gruppo *Pinerolo* transferred to the *Julia* in 1962; a new Gruppo *Mondovì* was formed in 1970

Brigata *Orobica*, consisting of
- 5° Reggimento Alpini, with Battaglioni *Edolo*, coming from the 6° Reggimento, *Tirano*, and from 1956, *Morbegno*
- 5° Reggimento artiglieria da montagna, with a newly formed Gruppo *Bergamo*, three batteries of 75 mm howitzers, Gruppo *Sondrio*, three batteries of 100 mm howitzers, Gruppo *Vestone*, three batteries of 107 mm mortars, and 40 mm Bofors antiaircraft gun battalion
- Signals company
- Sapper company
- Paratrooper platoon

Brigata *Cadore*, consisting of
- 7° Reggimento Alpini, with Battaglioni *Pieve di Cadore*, *Belluno*, and, from 1956, *Feltre*
- 6° Reggimento artiglieria da montagna, with Gruppo *Lanzo*, three batteries of 75 mm howitzers, Gruppo *Pieve di Cadore*, three batteries of 100 mm howitzers, Gruppo *Agordo*, three batteries of 107 mm mortars, and 40 mm Bofors antiaircraft gun battalion
- Signals company
- Sapper company
- Paratrooper platoon

During the 1959s and the 1960s, the organization of the Alpine brigades underwent several minor changes, although the general structure was maintained intact. In particular, the antiaircraft battalion was taken away from the Alpine brigades in the mid-1950s, while the paratrooper platoons were removed as well in mid-1960s and assembled in an independent company, attached to the IV Army Corps. This latter unit was formed in Bolzano in 1952, originating from the Comando Militare Territoriale (see above) and progressively extended its responsibility to all the Alpine brigades, the last being the *Taurinense* in 1973; it changed its designation therefore to IV Alpine Army Corps.

Starting from 1959, the regiments of mountain artillery started to replace their guns, which by now were obsolete, with the remarkable 105 mm howitzer, or 105/14, produced by the Italian firm, OTO Melara. Furthermore, the artillery battalions were organized as being multicaliber, with two batteries of the new howitzer and a battery of the American HM50 120 mm heavy mortar.

Artillerymen of the Gruppo Bergamo hoist a howitzer on the Ortles Massif. *Museo Nazionale Storico degli Alpini*

A unit of Alpini of the Divisione *Tridentina* during a training session in the mountains in 1965; in the foreground, there is still a veteran Breda mod. 37 machine gun, while a recoilless gun appears in the background, both of them transported on sledges towed by the men. *Museo Nazionale Storico degli Alpini*

Alpini disembark from a helicopter on a snowy landing zone. *Museo Nazionale Storico degli Alpini*

Alpini paratroopers in the UK in 1967, with a British officer. *Luigi Manes*

Some images of NATO exercise Winter Express, conducted in the area of Tromsø, Norway, in 1966, which saw the participation of units of the Divisione *Taurinense*. The scope of the exercise was the opposition to a hypothetical Soviet invasion of northern Norway in an extremely difficult environment and temperatures below 30° Celsius. *Museo Nazionale Storico degli Alpini*

THE ALPINI D'ARRESTO

In 1952, the defense of the long eastern and northeastern border of Italy against threats coming from the East was entrusted to new units created for that purpose. They were named *"Raggruppamenti di Frontiera"* (border groups), consisting of subunits called *barriers* and *groups of barriers*. They were static units, charged to halt the infiltration of enemies relying on fixed fortifications, with the following organizational chart:

XI Raggruppamento di Frontiera, with headquarters at Tolmezzo, consisting of three groups of barriers, responsible for the defense of the Canale Valley and Fella Valley, in the northeastern Friuli

XII Raggruppamento di Frontiera, with headquarters at Paluzza, responsible for the But River Valley, to the northwest of the previous Raggruppamento; this unit, however, would be disbanded the following year, and the responsibility for the area transferred to the *Cadore* Brigade

XXI Raggruppamento di Frontiera, with headquarters at Dobbiaco, consisting of three groups of barriers, responsible for the Puster Valley, in eastern Alto Adige

XXII Raggruppamento di Frontiera, with headquarters at Merano, consisting of two groups of barriers, responsible for the high Isarco River Valley and Venosta Valley, in northern and western Alto Adige

In 1957, the Raggruppamenti di Frontiera changed their name to *"Raggruppamenti Alpini da posizione,"* (Alpine fixed-position groups), and the groups of barriers and the individual barriers became battalions and companies, respectively. Between 1962 and 1963, these units changed designation again to *Raggruppamenti Alpini d'arresto*, "arresto" meaning the act of stopping the enemy, and the subordinated battalions took the name of the Alpine *Valle* battalions:

11° Raggruppamento Alpini d'arresto, consisting of the Battaglioni *Val Tagliamento*, *Val Fella*, and *Val Natisone*

21° Raggruppamento Alpini d'arresto, consisting of the Battaglioni *Val Brenta*, *Val d'Adige*, and *Val Leogra*

22° Raggruppamento Alpini d'arresto, consisting of the Battaglioni *Val Chiese* and *Val Camonica*

Battaglione *Val Cismon*, directly subordinate to the *Cadore* Brigade

In 1964, the Alpini *d'arresto* were completely reorganized again: the 21° and 22° Raggruppamento were disbanded, as well as the Battaglioni *Val Natisone*, *Val d'Adige*, *Val Leogra*, and *Val Camonica*. The remaining units were assigned as follows:

11° Raggruppamento Alpini d'arresto, with the Battaglioni *Val Fella* and *Val Tagliamento*, subordinate to the *Comando Truppe Carnia-Cadore*[2]

Battaglione *Val Cismon*, subordinate to the *Cadore* Brigade

Battaglione *Val Brenta*, subordinate to the *Tridentina* Brigade

Battaglione *Val Chiese*, subordinate to the *Orobica* Brigade

FROM THE REORGANIZATION OF THE ITALIAN ARMY IN 1975 TO PRESENT DAY

A helicopter landing exercise by Alpini paratroopers in the mountains of the Alto Adige. *Museo Nazionale Storico degli Alpini*

Mountain artillery with the 105/14 OTO Melara howitzer during a winter exercise

At the beginning of the 1970s, the army staff became aware that a complete reorganization of the army was necessary, in order to make it more flexible and modern. Furthermore, the budget of the state needed to cut the expenses to a certain degree. What resulted was a reorganization that left a smaller but more efficient army. The reform did not affect the Alpine troops as much as other units, due to this specific duty, of paramount importance, which was entrusted to them in the framework of the defense

A BV206 tracked vehicle towing a 105/14 OTO Melara howitzer

of the northeastern part of Italy. However, due also to the elimination of the regiments, the structure of the units was revised and some of them were disbanded.

After the reform, the Alpine brigades, twenty years after their formation, were organized as follows:

Brigata alpina *Julia*, consisting of
Headquarters and signals unit
Battaglioni *Tolmezzo, Gemona, Cividale, L'Aquila*, each one with a headquarters company, three Alpine companies, and a mortar company
Battaglione *Alpini d'arresto Val Tagliamento*
Training battalion *Vicenza*
Gruppi *Belluno, Conegliano*, and *Udine* of mountain artillery, each one with three 105/14 howitzer batteries
Logistic Battalion
Engineer company
Antitank company
Brigata alpina *Tridentina*, consisting of
Headquarters and signals unit
Battaglioni *Trento* and *Bassano*
Battaglione *Alpini d'arresto Val Brenta*
Gruppi *Vicenza* and *Asiago* of mountain artillery
Logistic Battalion
Engineer company
Antitank company
Brigata alpina *Taurinense*, consisting of
Headquarters and signals unit
Battaglioni *Susa* and *Saluzzo*
Training battalion *Mondovì*
Gruppi *Aosta* and *Pinerolo* of mountain artillery
Logistic Battalion
Engineer company
Antitank company
Brigata alpina *Orobica*, consisting of
Headquarters and signals unit
Battaglioni *Morbegno* and *Tirano*
Battaglione *Alpini d'arresto Val Chiese*

Training battalion *Edolo*
Gruppi *Bergamo* and *Sondrio* of mountain artillery
Logistic Battalion
Engineer company
Antitank company
Brigata alpina *Cadore*, consisting of
Headquarters and signals unit
Battaglioni *Feltre* and *Pieve di Cadore*
Training battalion *Belluno*
Gruppi *Lanzo* and *Agordo* of mountain artillery
Logistic Battalion
Engineer company
Antitank company

In 1976, the *4° Raggruppamento Aviazione Leggera Esercito* ALTAIR (Light Army Air Force Group) was added; it reunited all the helicopter units that had so far been subordinate to each brigade, and it was now transferred to the IV Alpine Army Corps.

In 1990, the paratrooper company was named "*Monte Cervino*" and, in 1996, was upgraded to a battalion—a new *Monte Cervino* battalion—to commemorate the actions of the sky battalion in the Second World War.

This structure had remained unchanged for about fifteen years until the political upheaval in Eastern Europe caused the fall of the USSR and the dissolution of the Warsaw Pact, ending the Cold War. The priorities assigned to the Italian army changed dramatically, revealing that what was needed now was a smaller force, but one that was highly trained, highly specialized, very well equipped, and able to operate at great distances from its bases, in close cooperation with units of foreign armies. This has caused a decrease of the staff, even greater than that of 1975, which has involved the Alpini as well. In 1991, the Brigata *Orobica* was disbanded, followed by the *Cadore* in 1995 and the *Tridentina* in 2002. In 1992, the Battaglioni d'arresto were disbanded as well, abandoning the fixed defenses, since the threat at the northeastern borders had, to a great extent, decreased. At Bolzano in 1997, the IV Alpine Army Corps was reorganized as *Comando Truppe Alpine* (Alpine troops headquarters), or COMALP. Ever since 2016, COMALP has been directly subordinate to the army chief of staff. The units under its command are

Brigata *Julia*, with headquarters at Udine, consisting of
Headquarters and tactical support unit
5° Reggimento Alpini, with the Battaglione *Morbegno*
7° Reggimento Alpini, with the Battaglione *Feltre*
8° Reggimento Alpini, with the Battaglione *Tolmezzo*
3° Reggimento of mountain artillery with the Gruppo *Conegliano*, with mechanically towed pieces of artillery
2° Reggimento *Piemonte Cavalleria* of mechanized cavalry
2° Reggimento of Alpine engineers
Logistic regiment *Julia*
Brigata *Taurinense*, with headquarters at Torino, consisting of
Headquarters and tactical support unit

2° Reggimento Alpini, with the Battaglione *Saluzzo*

3° Reggimento Alpini, with the Battaglione *Susa*

9° Reggimento Alpini, with the Battaglione *L'Aquila*

1° Reggimento of mountain artillery with the Gruppo *Aosta*

1° Reggimento *Nizza Cavalleria* of mechanized cavalry

32° Reggimento of Alpine engineers

Logistic regiment *Taurinense*

Alpine Training Centre, in Valle d'Aosta

The COMALP has the potential to become a divisional command itself, able to form the Divisione *Tridentina*, having brigades as subordinate units to the Reparto Comando e Supporti Tattici *Tridentina* (Headquarters and Tactical Support Unit *Tridentina)* and have other units assigned as needed. They would be based at Bolzano but also capable of operating abroad.

THE ACTIVITY OF THE ALPINI IN THE POSTWAR PERIOD: CIVIL PROTECTION AND PEACEKEEPING

From 1945 onward, the Alpini have fortunately not been called upon to fight, but they have not been completely inactive either: very often, they have been called on to aid people affected by natural disasters or to take part in peacekeeping missions abroad, within multinational units.

During the days that followed the disaster of the Vajont, the Alpini of the Brigata *Cadore* did their utmost to find survivors and bring food and medicines to the population. *Museo Nazionale Storico degli Alpini*

In 1963, the Brigata *Cadore* performed the sad duty to reach the area of Longarone, roughly 16 kilometers north of Belluno, in Veneto. The area had been hit by a wave of water and mud that destroyed the town almost completely, affecting around 2,000 victims. The cause of the disaster had been a landslide that had cascaded down into the Vajont Dam, causing the overflow of millions of cubic meters of water. The *Cadore* was the first to arrive on the scene, followed by other units of the 7° Reggimento and later by other Alpini; in the end, more than 10,000 men were involved in the effort to find survivors, provide shelter to the homeless, and feed them. For this valuable work, the Brigata *Cadore* was awarded the Medaglia d'Oro al Valore Civile (Gold Medal for Civil Valor). Only three years later, the *Cadore* sent its Alpini to the areas of the Province of Belluno that had been hit by a flood.

In 1976, during the evening of May 6, a huge 6.5 magnitude earthquake razed a vast area of Friuli, with its epicenter near the town of Gemona, resulting in dozens of victims. The Alpini of the *Julia* Brigade, which in Gemona itself had lost twenty-eight of its own soldiers in the disaster, were the first to intervene, along with the infantrymen of the *Mantova* Division and the tankers of the *Ariete* Division. In the following days thousands of soldiers cooperated in the sad task of digging in the rubble to look for survivors and extract the corpses, but also to give shelter and food to the civilian population. The *Julia* was then rewarded with the Medaglia d'Oro al Valore Civile as well. Similar activities have been carried out by Alpini units following other earthquakes, which periodically and violently shake the Italian territory: in Irpinia, an area of Campania, in 1980; and in Abruzzo 2009, in central Italy between Marche and Lazio, in 2016; in these recent cases in cooperation with the Civil Protection agency.

Encampment built by the Alpine engineers in a location hit by the Friuli earthquake in 1976. *Luigi Carretta*

Additionally, in 1991, just after the Gulf War, Alpini participation in peacekeeping missions began. The medical unit of the *Taurinense* Brigade was attached to the Italian peacekeeping force, called *Airone*, entrusted with the assistance of Kurdish refugees in northern Iraq. The mission lasted from May to July, and when the Alpini repatriated, the hospital and the equipment remained in Iraq, left to local personnel. At the beginning of 1993, a UN force called ONUMOZ was sent to Mozambique to enforce the peace agreement recently signed in Rome by the factions that had been fighting in the country for years. Among the UN troops, there were some hundreds of Alpini of the *Taurinense*, replaced in October by the *Julia* and Alpine paratroopers of the *Monte Cervino*, who in turn remained until May 1994. After that date, the elections in Mozambique seemed to presage a period of peace for the country; thus, the UN mission was reduced to a minimum. The following years have demonstrated that it was only an illusion.

Wreckage and ruins left behind by the earthquake in Irpinia in 1980. *Luigi Carretta*

2010, Alpini of the 2° Reggimento Genio unload supplies from the ship *Cavour* for the population of Haiti, which had been hit by an earthquake, as part of the humanitarian mission *White Crane*. *Luigi Carretta*

IVECO armored cars of the Battaglione *Susa* in Mozambique during the UN mission ONUMOZ. *Museo Nazionale Storico degli Alpini*

Bosnia, an alpino is guarding an area that is still mined, as evidenced by the sign behind him. *Museo Nazionle Storico degli Alpini*

Sarajevo, two Alpini in completely different contexts; the first, in combat gear patrolling duty; the second, in a moment of relaxation with the local population. *Museo Nazionale Storico degli Alpini*

The end of 1990s saw an increasing engagement of the Esercito Italiano in peacekeeping missions mounted by the UN, and Alpine units have, of course, participated in these missions. Between 1995 and 2014, Alpini of the *Taurinense* had been alternating with those of the *Julia* in Bosnia, first within the *Implementation Force* (IFOR), aimed at enforcing the peace agreements signed at Dayton, and then within the *Stabilization Force* (SFOR), aimed at enhancing the political stability of the area. In 1999, the mission of the UN *Kosovo Force* (KFOR) began in Kosovo, with the arduous task of providing a buffer between the Serbian army and the Kosovar independentists. The mission, which involves military personnel from about thirty countries, is still ongoing and, within the Italian units, the Alpini have been part of the rotation.

In 2003, Italian troops took part in the most dangerous military actions since World War II, in the framework of the operation *Enduring Freedom*, launched in 2001 by some twenty countries led by the United States against Afghanistan and its Taliban rulers, as a consequence of the terrorist attack of September 11, 2001. The Italian force, called "*NIBBIO*" (kite), deployed about one thousand Alpini of the *Taurinense* from March 15 to June 15, 2003, followed by paratroopers of the *Folgore* Division, who remained until September 15 and performed duties toward control of the territory and enhancement of the security in the Afghan province of Paktia, near the border with Pakistan. Furthermore, from August 2001 until December 2014, Italian troops took part in the *International Security Assitance Force* (IFOR), aimed at supporting the Afghan government that had been established after the defeat of the Taliban. The mission has been led by NATO since 2003, and Italy has participated with units that rotate every six months. Among them are units of the *Taurinense* and the *Julia*, which have also suffered some casualties. More recently, in June 2021, the mission *Resolute Support* came to an end. The mission began in January 2015 and was aimed particularly at training and assisting the Afghan military forces; they had seen

Italian troops, Alpini among them, engaged. Since 2006, Italian forces have been deployed in southern Lebanon as well, within the United Nations Interim Force in Lebanon (UNIFIL), with units that include Alpini and rotate every six months.

The Alpini, in cooperation with the civil authorities, have participated in missions in Italian territory to enhance the control of the state in some areas of the country, as other units of the Esercito Italiano have done. The first mission of this kind was organized in Sardinia in 1992, called *Forza Paris*; it lasted only two months (July and August), and Alpini of the *Taurinense* took part in it. The most famous, however, is the *Vespri Siciliani* mission, launched in the same year, after the bomb attack in Sicily, near Palermo, which killed two judges, Giovanni Falcone and Paolo Borsellino, who were highly engaged against the Mafia. The mission lasted almost seven years and, between 1992 and 1993, 2,000 men of the *Julia* were stationed on the island, patrolling vast areas in cooperation with the police and carabinieri. Between March and June 1994, units of the *Taurinense* carried out these duties as well. The *Julia* also took part in a similar mission in Calabria, called "*Riace*," that lasted from 1994 to 1995, sending three battalions in November 1994.

Three images that are testament to the engagement of the Alpini in Afghanistan: a view of the Forward Operating Base Tobruk of Bala Baluk, in the east of the country, opened by the 2° Reggimento Genio in February 2009, and delivered to Afghan forces in 2013; the building of a bridge over a river; the distribution of supplies at a newly built school. *Luigi Carretta*

Alpine units have regularly been, and still are, members of multilateral forces. The *Taurinense*, between 1963 and 2002, has provided a battalion and a battery of mountain artillery, followed later by an airborne medical unit and a logistic battalion, to the *Allied Command Europe Mobile Force-Land* (AMF-L), an extremely rapid-response unit established by NATO to intervene anywhere in case of crisis within forty-eight hours. This unit was replaced by the *NATO Response Force* (NFR) in 2002.

The brigades are also involved with other multilateral units. Since 2001, the *Julia* has provided the framework for the *Multinational Land Force*, which also includes a Hungarian battalion and a Slovene battalion. The unit, having the force of a brigade itself, can be deployed in peacekeeping missions by the European Union, NATO, the UN, and the OSCE, and has seen action in Kosovo, Afghanistan, and Lebanon. Likewise, since 2015, the *Taurinense* and the French *27ᵉ Brigade d'Infantrie de Montagne* formed a mixed unit called *Not Standing Bi-National Brigade Command* (NSBNBC), coming from a project first conceived in 2009 for stricter cooperation between the Italian and French armies for facing international crises.

The *Vespri Siciliani* mission has seen units of the Esercito Italiano engaged in Sicily for about seven years; the Alpini took part in the mission between 1992 and 1993. *Luigi Carretta*

CONCLUSION

The year 2022 is the 150th anniversary of the foundation of the Alpini. Throughout its long history, this corps has undergone several metamorphoses: from the handful of men charged to slow down enemies in the Italian mountains until the arrival of the army, as it was at first, to the flexible brigades engaged in peacekeeping missions in many parts of the world. Their journey from where they began to where they are today has been a long one. Strangely enough, in spite of the initial concept of the Alpini, they have fought more often on the attack outside Italy's borders than in the defense of these same borders: from the colonial wars to the Great War; from the Greco-Italian War to the Russian Campaign during the Second World War. However, the Alpini have always demonstrated a high degree of flexibility, adapting to different roles in different environments, in war and in peace. In their successes as well as in their bloody defeats, they have always brought the toughness—but also the humanity—of the mountain men. This is why the Alpini have been, and still are, so popular in Italy.

The long history of the Alpini is now exhibited in the *Museo Nazionale Storico degli Alpini*, founded in 1958 in the town of Trento, in northeastern Italy. The museum has been completely renovated and expanded in recent years. Its duty is to keep alive the memory of the feats of generations of Alpini, in war and in peace.

The logo of the *Museo Nazionale Storico degli Alpini* of Trento

The recently refurbished site of the *Museo Nazionale Storico degli Alpini* of Trento

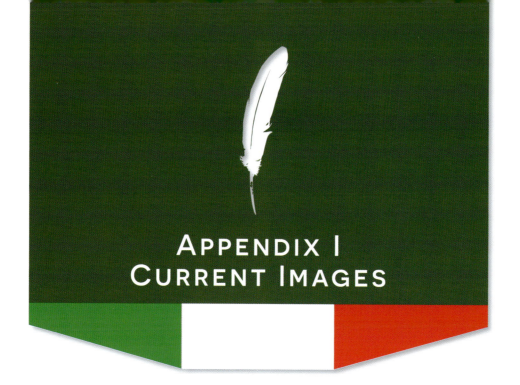

APPENDIX I
CURRENT IMAGES

A position in the upper Madre Valley, in the Orobic Prealps, in the northeast of Lombardia, part of the fortified "*Linea Cadorna*" (Cadorna line), a defensive line that runs along the Italian-Swiss border. Implemented starting from 1915, after the development of an older 1882 project, the line had the purpose of protecting Italy from an invasion by Austro-German troops through Switzerland. In the postwar years, it became part of a greater defensive line, called the "*Vallo Alpino del Littorio.*"

A glimpse of the Pasubio massif seen from the famous "*Strada delle 52 Gallerie*" (the 52-tunnel path), built by Italian engineers between February and November 1917 to protect the supply lines from Austro-Hungarian artillery. It is 6.5 by 2.3 kilometers long.

Pasubio massif, the Dente Italiano, and the Dente Austriaco. The two positions were a mere 50 meters apart, separated by a small fork, and were bloodily contended for by the opposite armies from summer 1916 to the end of the war. Their outline has been marked by heavy artillery fire and by the mines exploded by both Italians and Austro-Hungarians.

A stretch of the "*Sentieri dei Fiori*" (the flowers' path), and is now equipped with modern walkways for excursionists, built on the Adamello massif from Punta del Castellaccio and Punta Pisgana to link the Italian posts positioned over 3,000 meters (9,840 feet) above MSL

Monte Fior, on the Melette, where Italians and Austro-Hungarians fought fiercely in the summer of 1916 and then again in the following summer of 1917

Trenches on the Monte Ortigara and the outline of the Ortigara as seen from the Italians' former positions. One can only imagine the hardships met by the opposing combatants on this inhospitable, stony ground, although it is now covered by new forest.

The impressive outline of the Monte Nero, conquered by the *Alpini* in 1915. Seeing the steep and barren slopes of the mountain, one can only imagine the difficulties met by the Italian soldiers and admire their valor.

The church of Javorka, on Mount Polog, in the upper Isonzo Valley, now part of Slovenia, built by the Austro-Hungarians to commemorate over 2,800 fellow soldiers fallen on that stretch of the front

Austro-Hungarian entrenchments on the Ravelnik Hills, a little east of the town of Plezzo, now an open museum of the Great War

The Italian Shrine of Caporetto, built in the 1930s, where over 7,000 bodies of Italian soldiers, 1,748 of them unknown, have their final resting place

Italian and Austro-Hungarian positions in the area of the upper Dolomites

Remains of walkways near the Alpe Mattina Pass

Rinbon Valley, to the back of the Tre Cime di Lavaredo, with remains of barbed wire and a loophole through which one can see the Torre degli Scarperi, the Croda dei Rondoi, and the Monte Rudo

A tunnel excavated in the deep of Monte Paterno, bloodily contended for by the two armies

A simple monument on the Monte Piana where, over the course of two years of fighting, over 14,000 men fell

Remains of a barrack in a seemingly impossible position on the slopes of Monte Cristallo

A view of the Forcella Sarauta; today, a national monument area. The building is the modern hut, located at 2,950 meters (9,678 feet) above MSL, that displays dozens of finds coming from the Marmolada, making it the museum with the highest elevation in Europe.

The southern side of the Forcella a "V," on the Marmolada massif

The Monte Pal Piccolo, conquered by the Alpini with a surprise action at the very beginning of the war, but lost and conquered several times by the opposing armies during the war

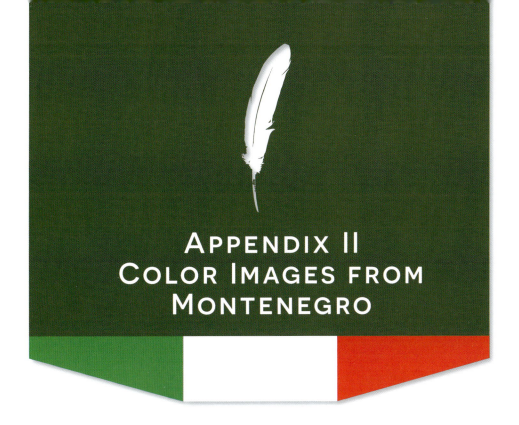

APPENDIX II
COLOR IMAGES FROM MONTENEGRO

These rare color pictures taken by an *alpino* in Montenegro have been provided by the French historian David Zambon and refer to the activity of *Alpini* units in Montenegro between 1942 and 1943.

A group of officers, NCOs, and *Alpini* in a moment of relaxation. Identifying the unit is not easy, since the number on the hat is not completely clear. However, it seems to be a "3," which would indicate the 3° Reggimento of the Divisione *Taurinense*, which arrived in Montenegro on August 1942 after operating in Croatia and Bosnia, to replace the Divisione *Pusteria*. The red *nappina* would then indicate the Battaglione *Fenestrelle*.

A mule train marching on a narrow mountain path in Montenegro. Often the mules were the only means to supply the units.

Portrait of some *Alpini* officers talking with armed militiamen who are wearing items of clothing clearly from the former Yugoslavian army. The flag belongs to the Kingdom of Montenegro, proclaimed in 1941, and might indicate that they are Chetnik fighters, who often cooperated with the Italians against Communist partisans.

A small party of *Alpini*, probably on a training shoot

Moment of relaxation for these *Alpini* who are lining up for their rations at the field kitchen. In the Regio Esercito, in peacetime as well, only the officers took their meals in a canteen, while the soldiers ate from their mess tin sitting on the ground in every weather condition.

A religious celebration in an encampment, showing a line of armed Alpini. In the background are the barren mountains of Montenegro.

An artillery officer of the *Guardia alla Frontiera*—a unit created in the mid-1930s to guard the Italian borders—posing near an old 149 mm gun. The gun is a veteran of the Great War. The *Guardia alla Frontiera* wore the same felt hat as the *Alpini* but without the feather. Some units served in Montenegro on antipartisan duties as well.

A long line of *Alpini* crossing the bed of a shallow river on a narrow walkway

A long line of armed civilians, many of them still wearing items of clothing coming from the former Yugoslavian army, near an Italian command post; on the left is the flag of the newly proclaimed Kingdom of Montenegro. Difficult to say if it is a group of chetnik combatants or one of the many militias born in the rural areas of the whole former Yugoslavia to defend the peasant villages, often supplied by the occupants.

A group of Italian officers, some *Alpini* among them, pose in the courtyard of a building that could be the seat of the headquarters of an Italian unit. Interesting to note is the variety of the trucks lined up in the background. The first truck on has been requisitioned by the military from a private firm and is covered with just a brushstroke of green paint, proof of the logistic difficulties that afflicted the Italian army throughout the entire war.

An old Fiat 3000 tank of the First Tank Company of the Guardia alla Frontiera, originally stationed at Shkodër, in Albania, but rushed to Montenegro in the summer of 1941

An Italian officer is shown talking to a Montenegrin man who wears a curious uniform mixed with items of traditional clothing; he may be a former Yugoslavian army officer who was now the head of an anti-Communist group.

APPENDIX III
DRAWINGS BY COMPAGNI

These drawings are the work of Pietro Compagni, an expert on Italian uniforms and a well-known draftsman. They have been created over the course of many years for several publications issued by Albertelli, Itineraprogetti, Mittelcultura, Club Storico Friulano, and for the Rivista Militare, edited by Stato Maggiore Esercito (Italian army staff).

March 1873
Soldier of the *Compagnie distrettuali permamenti*, which was soon to be called "*Compagnie alpine*"

1874
Alpino of the Eleventh Company, Fourth District, wearing the new bowler with the feather and the new boots that replaced the infantry shoes

1887
Corporal of the special *Alpini* battalion attached to the Italian expeditionary corps, landed in Massawa after the massacre at Dogali

1906
Alpino of what was known as the "*gray platoon,*" wearing the experimental uniform

1910
Alpino wearing the final version of the gray-green uniform adopted in 1909 and the new felt hat

1915
Corporal with the uniform and equipment of the Great War

1915
Mountain artilleryman of the Third Battery, 1° Reggimento, with his mule transporting one of the loads of the 65/17 gun

Winter 1915–16
Second lieutenant of the Battaglione *Tolmezzo* wearing the winter outfit, with knee-socks instead of the puttees, a balaclava rolled up around his head, and the snow glasses. Under the jacket he wears a wool sweater.

1917
Ardito of the *Fiamme Verdi* with the special patch on the left sleeve with the dagger, typical of the specialty. He has no feather on the hat, in order to facilitate camouflage, following the order n. 3338 of the Supreme Command, not much applied among the *Alpini* and abolished toward the end of the year.

1919
Alpino skier wearing a white uniform and snow glasses

Fiume 1919
Gabriele D'Annunzio

1934
Major wearing the newly adopted
open collar parade dress

1936
Alpino of the Battaglione *Saluzzo*, Divisione *Pusteria*, disembarks
in Eritrea wearing the kaki uniform

1938
Lieutenant of the engineer battalion
in summer field uniform

East Africa 1936–41
The very peculiar uniform of
Lieutenant E. Formento, an
officer of the *Alpini*, head of the
irregular indigenous band *Kai
Bandera* in Ethiopia

Western Alps 1940
Sergeant of the 4° Reggimento
artiglieria alpina, Divisione
Cuneense

1940
Alpino of the Divisione *Julia* on the Albanian-
Greek front

1940
Mountain artilleryman of the 3° Reggimento artiglieria alpina, Divisione *Julia*, on the Albanian-Greek front

Keren, East Africa 1941
Corporal of the machine gun company, Battaglione *Amba Uork*

Russia, winter 1942–43
Alpino of the Divisione *Tridentina*

Russia, winter 1942–43
Alpino of the *arditi* platoon, Battaglione *L'Aquila*, Divisione *Julia*

Russia, winter 1942–43
Alpino skier of the Battaglione *Monte Cervino*

1944
Sergeant major of the Gruppo *Bergamo*, 1° Reggimento artiglieria da montagna, Divisione *Monterosa*

1944–45
Alpino of the Gruppo di Combattimento *Legnano*, wearing the British battle dress

1958
Alpino of the paratrooper platoon of the Divisione *Tridentina*

1970
Corporal of the engineer company, Brigata *Julia*

Mozambique 1993–94
NCO of the Tactical Group *Susa*, Brigata *Taurinense*, with the blue UN helmet

1994
Alpino sniper, Battaglione *Bassano*, Brigata *Tridentina*

Sarajevo 1997
Sergeant major, Battaglione *Susa*, Brigata *Taurinense*, in Bosnia on the IFOR mission

2010
Observer and sniper, Battaglione *Alpini paracadutisti Monte Cervino*

ENDNOTES

Introduction

1. The Kingdom of Italy was officially proclaimed on March 17, 1861. On the following May 4, the army changed its name from "*Regia Armata Sarda*" (Royal Sardinian Army) to "*Regio Esercito*" (Royal Army).

Chapter 1

1. The war of 1866 is known in Italian history books as the Third War of Independence; the First War of Independence had been declared in 1848 and the Second in 1859. All of them had the goal to expel the Austrian Empire from Italian territory.

2. Cesare Ricotti Magnani was born in Borgolevezzaro, near Novara, in 1822. An artillery officer, he took part in the Crimean War and the wars of independence, earning the high decorations of the *Ordine Militare di Savoia* and the French *Legion d'Honneur* in 1859. From 1870 to 1876, and again from 1884 to 1887, and briefly in 1896, he was minister of war. From 1870, he was also a member of the parliament, until 1890 in the lower chamber and from 1890 onward in the senate. He died in Novara in 1917, at age ninety-five.

3. Giuseppe Domenico Perrucchetti was born in Cassano d'Adda, near Milan, in 1839. He was a university student when, in 1859, the Second War of Independence started; thus, he left Lombardy, still part of the Austrian Empire, and emigrated to enlist in the Piedmontese army. He took part in the Third War of Independence as well, when he was decorated with a Silver Medal. Between 1872 and 1885, he taught military geography at the Scuola Superiore di Guerra (war school), then during the following five years, he became tutor of Prince Emanuele Filiberto of Aosta. From 1890 to 1904, he commanded several units of the army, although he did not take part in any war. In 1912, he was appointed as member of the senate. He died at Cuorgnè, near Torino, in 1916. A curious fact about General Perrucchetti is that, although being generally considered to be the founder of the Alpini, he was never an alpino himself.

4. P.G. Franzosi, *Le origini delle truppe alpine*, Rivista Militare, 2, 1985; V. Ilari, *Giuseppe Domenico Perrucchetti e l'origine delle truppe alpine*, Rivista Militare, 3, 1990.

5. It is interesting to notice that the first tests with the new uniforms for the army were carried out by a platoon of the Battaglione *Morbegno*, and the financing was provided by an individual citizen, Luigi Brioschi, president of the Milan section of Club Alpino Italiano (Italian alpine club). For some months, the platoon wore a gray outfit with a large-brim felt hat, a sort of Boer style, and was unofficially called the "gray platoon."

6. From the 1920s onward, Italian artillery has been designated with two numbers divided by a slash. The first number represents the caliber of the gun in millimeters; the second represents the length of the barrel, obtained by multiplying it by the caliber, rounded to avoid decimals. For example, a 65/17 is a gun of 65 mm caliber and the barrel length is 1.150 mm (17.7 times the caliber, but the 0.7 is dropped).

7. Negus Johannes IV was killed by the Mahdist army in March 1889 in the battle of Gallabat; Italy would take advantage of the divisions among the Ethiopian warlords and of the need of the new Negus Menelik to win Italian support to ascend the throne.

8. Turkey, once ruler of the whole of North Africa, had already lost the greater part of it piece by piece: France had occupied Algeria in 1830, and Tunisia had been a protectorate since 1881; the United Kingdom had imposed its protectorate on Egypt and Sudan in 1882; Italy itself had taken control of Massaua and its surroundings that were still formally Ottoman.

9. The island of Rhodos, along with a dozen other islands, remained in Italian hands until 1943, as the Dodecanesos Territory.

10. The Senussiya is a politico-religious movement founded in Mecca in the 1830s by the Algerian theologian Muhammed ibn Ali as-Senussi and is deeply rooted in Cyrenaica, having its center, since the mid-1850s, at the oasis of Siwa. Under Turkish rule, the Senussiya enjoyed ample autonomy in the administration of its territory, while Italian rule had shown, from the beginning, less acceptance of its prerogatives. After a precarious truce signed in 1915, when Italy practically abandoned Libya, being involved in the war in Europe during the 1920s, the clash was resumed. Finally, the resistance of the Senussiya was rather brutally eradicated in 1930–31.

Chapter 2

1. The alliance between Germany and Austria-Hungary had been signed in 1879 and named the "Double Alliance." Italy had joined the alliance in 1882, in a period when the relations with the neighboring France were at their lowest due to the occupation of Tunisia, where Italy had substantial economic interests. It had been renewed regularly ever since, even though Italians and Austrians never fully trusted each other.

2. The Triple Entente was in fact the product of a series of bilateral agreements that joined France and Russia beginning in 1894, then France and Great Britain in 1904 and, finally, Great Britain and Russia in 1907. The main purpose of these agreements was to counteract German rearmament, which had been proceeding steadily in these years.

3. Antonio Salandra was born in Troia, near Foggia, in 1853. After his legal studies, he started to teach at the university and, at the same time, began a political career. A member of the parliament since 1886, he was minister several times and, beginning in 1914, prime minister. Being favorable to the war alongside the entente, as was his foreign affairs minister, Sonnino, he conducted the negotiations that led to the Treaty of London and the declaration of war. Dismissed in 1916, after the Austro-Hungarian spring offensive, he retired from public life and died in Rome in 1931.

4. Sidney Sonnino, born in 1847 in Pisa, Tuscany, was an Italian diplomat. He entered parliament in 1880 in the ranks of the Right Party and was minister in several governments. Favoring the war alongside the entente, he became foreign affairs minister in October 1914, and maintained the charge until June 1919. He died in Rome in 1922.

5. Giovanni Giolitti, born in 1842 in Mondovì, near Cuneo, was one of the most prominent Italian politicians. After his university studies, he started his career working for the Ministry of Grace and Justice and later for the Ministry of Finance. Member of the Chamber of Deputies since 1882, in the following years, he was minister several times and prime minister five times. He was a neutralist, convinced that by maintaining neutrality, Italy could bargain extensively with Austria-Hungary. After the war, confronted with the rising fascist movement, he supported the government formed by Benito Mussolini in the beginning, thinking that fascism could become a normal right-wing party and abandon its violent nature. When he realized his mistake, he left public life and died in Cavour in 1928.

6. The *bersaglieri*, literally "sharpshooters," are a specialty of the Italian infantry, created in 1836 as highly mobile, light units.

7. Luigi Cadorna was born in Pallanza, on the Maggiore Lake, northwest of Milan, in 1850. Encouraged by his father, who was a general of the army, to undertake the military career, he became an officer in 1868. In the following years, although he never commanded a unit in a wartime operation, he would climb the ranks until he became chief of staff of the *Regio Esercito* in 1914. He was dismissed in November 1917, a few days after the defeat at Caporetto. After the war, he had a seat in the senate, but he did not have any other assignments before he died, in 1928, in Bordighera.

8. Franz Conrad von Hötzendorf was born in Penzing, near Vienna, in 1852. From the age of eleven, he had a military career, during which time he also served in Trieste and Bolzano. Appointed chief of staff of the Royal-Imperial army in 1906, he revealed from the beginning a strong, anti-Italian attitude, because he was starting to fortify the border with the allied neighbor and proposing a preventive war against Italy, formally an ally, in 1908 and 1911. He was dismissed in March 1917 and sent to command the troops of the Trentino salient. After the war, he maintained a secluded life, until his death in 1925 at Bad Mergentheim, in Baden-Württemberg.

Chapter 3

1. From June 1915 until September 1917, the Italian army launched eleven bloody attacks trying to break through the Austro-Hungarian lines on the eastern bank of the Isonzo River; these attacks are known as the Battles of the Isonzo. The Twelfth Battle of the Isonzo, which took place in October 1917, was instead a joint counteroffensive led by Germans and Austro-Hungarians that led to the serious defeat of Caporetto, a small town where the attackers broke the Italian lines, forcing the whole front to retreat. The term "caporetto" in Italy is still synonymous with "great disaster."

2. In particular, one of the Austro-Hungarian forts on the Asiago Plateau, Forte Luserna, or Werk Lusern in German, was shelled almost without interruption between May 25 and 28 by Italian heavy artillery until the garrison raised the white flag. The Italian troops could not, however, take possession of the fort, because the Austro-Hungarian artillery started a furious barrage to prevent any advance while an infantry unit reached the position, ripped off the white flag, and arrested the commander. After that, Forte Luserna remained in Austro-Hungarian hands for the rest of the war.

3. In Roman times, the *centuria* was a basic unit of the legion, formed by hundred soldiers and commanded by a *centurione*. In this case it was used by the *Regio Esercito* to designate a small unit formed for a specific task.

Chapter 4

1. Seven other batteries were still serving in Libya.

2. This piece was an old, rigidly mounted gun, with a cast-iron barrel, weighing over 6 tons. The transport started on February 9, 1916, with the usual horse-towing; but soon, the animals could not continue due to the steepness of the path and the Alpini had to take their place. The gun was therefore disassembled and laid on sledges towed with ropes. The piece played a part in the operations of the year 1916, firing from the Venerocolo Pass and the following year was moved forward, again towed by the Alpini, to the Cresta della Croce. It is still there, declared a National Monument after the war.

3. The episode, quite common during the Great War, becomes remarkable because two officers of the Battaglione *Vicenza*, Cesare Battisti and Fabio Filzi, were in fact subjects of the Austro-Hungarian Empire, being born in Trento; Cesare Battisti, in particular, was also a renowned Socialist politician and member of the Austrian parliament. When the war in Europe broke out, he left Trento and campaigned for Italy to declare war against Austria-Hungary, convinced that the defeat of the empire was the only way to obtain the self-determination of the peoples that comprised it. He thought that it was better for the Italian minority living in ethnically Italian areas of the empire that shared the border with Italy to join the Kingdom of Italy. When Italy entered the war, Battisti, along with hundreds

of fellow citizens from Trentino, enlisted with the *Regio Esercito*. Once captured, he and Filzi were put on trial and executed in Trento a few days later as traitors. Today, the mountain where he was captured is called "Monte Corno Battisti."

Chapter 5

1. Many sources report that, among the plans put forward, there was one that proposed the use of a hot-air balloon. The balloon would have transported a small party of Alpini up along the nearly vertical slope of the mountain and land them on a small ledge not far from the top. From the ledge, they would have climbed the remaining distance and assault the enemy garrison. The plan may appear to be bizarre now, but at the time, it must have been taken into consideration given that several hydrogen cylinders arrived to the area in October and, according to other reports, there was even an air balloon.

2. Emperor Franz Josef had acceded to the throne of the empire in December 1848 and had died in November 1916, after a reign of sixty-eight years. The reign of Emperor Karl, the grandson of Franz Josef's younger brother, would not be so long-lived, since Karl lost the throne at the end of the war.

Chapter 6

1. Armando Diaz was born in 1861, in Naples. After attending the Military Academy of Torino, he became an artillery lieutenant, and from 1882 to 1895 he served with several artillery regiments. In 1895, he entered the army staff and worked for two years with the chief of staff General Tancredi Saletta and then with General Pollio. His career continued with the command of an artillery regiment and then as chief of staff of the Firenze Division, until he had an operational command in the Italo-Turkish war. After that, he joined the army staff again and worked with General Cadorna until 1916. Then, he obtained command of a division followed by command of an army corps until he was appointed supreme commander in November 1917. He left the army in 1919, held a seat in the senate, and was minister of war in the first government led by Mussolini. He left the government in 1924 due to bad health and died four years later, in 1928, in Rome.

Chapter 7

1. Royal Decree of November 21, 1919, enacted by General Alberico Albrizzi, minister of war, between April 1919 and March 1920.

2. Legislative Decree of November 20, 1920, enacted on the proposal of Ivanoe Bonomi, minister of war between March 1920 and April 1921.

3. Legislative Decree of January 7, 1923, enacted on the proposal of General Armando Diaz, minister of war until 1924 in the first government led by Benito Mussolini.

4. Law n. 396 of March 11, 1926.

5. The sources do not agree regarding the artillery equipment of the divisions. The data exposed are taken from the book by E. Faldella, *Storia delle Truppe Alpine*, p. 1008.

6. Albania had gained its independence in 1912, during the Balkan wars.

Chapter 8

1. Legislative Decree n. 1723 of October 11, 1934. The minister of war in charge was again Benito Mussolini.

2. For the defense of the national borders, a new specialty called "*Guardia alla Frontiera*" (border guard) was created from 1934 onward.

3. The 75/13 howitzer weighed 613 kilograms and could be broken down into seven pack loads, while the new howitzer, designated the 75/18, weighed 780 kilograms and could be broken down into eight pack loads, with an average 10 kilograms of weight more for each load. Although the muzzle velocity increased from 1,161 to 1,411 fps and the range increased from 9,022 yards to 10,390 yards, it was not judged to be enough to justify the higher weight.

4. Being replacement units, the two battalions were supposed to send men to the other battalions when needed, not to be used in combat situations, because they lacked the usual equipment and weapons of the combat-ready units.

5. At more or less the same time as the battle of Amba Aradam and the Second Battle of Tembien, fought between February 29 and March 2, 1935, the Battle of Shire was fought, in which the army of Ras Imru was annihilated.

Chapter 9

1. The unification of Germany and Austria was an obsession of Adolf Hitler, who was Austrian himself. Although unification had been expressly forbidden in the peace treaty, Germany made a first attempt to do so in 1934 with a coup d'état, led by the Austrian Nazi party, that caused the death of the chancellor, Engelbert Dolfuss. It had failed because of the strong reaction of Italy, which at the time was allied with Austria. In 1938, the political structure had changed significantly, and Italy praised the *Anschluss*.

2. The Sudetenland was an area of about 25,000 square kilometers on the border between Germany and Czechoslovakia, where a strong German minority resided. During a conference held in Munich in September 29 and 30, 1938, Germany, Italy, France, and the UK signed an agreement that assigned the region to the Reich, without consulting the Czechoslovakian government.

3. Although it had been accommodated in September with the Munich Agreement, Germany invaded Czechoslovakia fewer than six months later, proclaiming its protectorate over Bohemia and Moravia and recognizing the independence of Slovakia, which became a vassal state. In response, Italy annexed Albania, although the small Balkan state had already been an Italian satellite for years.

Chapter 10

1. The relationship between Italy and Yugoslavia had been affected from the beginning by the well-known Italian ambitions on the coastal area of Dalmatia; Italy's relationship with Greece had been strained since the early 1920s. In August 1923, the members of the Italian commission who had been charged to trace the borders between Greece and Albania were murdered. The Italian government had immediately placed the blame on Greece and had, in retaliation, occupied the island of Corfu, not far from the Italian coast of Puglia. After this episode, international diplomatic negotiations ordered that Greece pay compensation to Italy, but that Italy had to leave Corfu.

2. The port of Durres, the biggest port in the region, was capable of offloading an average of 1,000 tons of material per day and was the only one that had a few roads that relieved the congestion of the port by moving the material to nearby

warehouses. Vlore, which was much closer to the front and would therefore have been more suitable, had a capacity of just 250 tons per day and only poor roads to dispatch the material to the south. Even worse was the situation of the few smaller ports, such as Shëngjin, or San Giovanni di Medua, north of Durres, and Saranda, to the south of Vlore, none of which reached a capacity of 150 tons per day.

3. At the beginning of December, the entire Ninth Army was fewer than 27,000 combat-ready men strong. It was deployed on a 70-kilometer-long front, with units that were entangled and without adequate supplies. Greek forces were weary as well after weeks on the attack and were not able to take full advantage of the serious situation of the enemy.

4. The main Albanian rivers, such as the Devoll, the Vojussa, the Osum, flow roughly from southeast to northwest, while the Italian line faced southeast. Therefore, when there is a reference to a unit being to the right or to the left of a river, it is done with respect to the orientation of the Italian line and not the course of the river.

Chapter 12

1. A German army corps with only Italian divisions was a temporary anomaly, due to the frequent movements of the Italian and German units during the previous months.

2. The *Nebelwerfer*, literally "fog launcher," was a German multiple-barrel rocket launcher mounted on a two-wheel carriage.

3. The *Vicenza* was a weak infantry division equipped only for rear area duties, as mentioned; therefore, when moved to the frontline, it was reinforced with three Alpini battalions: the *Vestone* and *Morbegno* of the *Tridentina*, and the *Pieve di Teco* of the *Cuneense*. The first two battalions returned to their original division, which was already at Podgornoje, while the latter retreated with the division.

Chapter 13

1. Several work companies were formed using hundreds of other former Italian soldiers who were either judged not fit for combat service or simply not willing to fight anymore. However, in the course of these months, the exchange of men from the fighting brigades to the work companies, and vice versa, was constant.

2. At the time of the action against Monte Marrone, the I Raggruppamento Motorizzato consisted of

Sixty-Eighth Infantry Regiment, with two battalions
Fourth *bersaglieri* Regiment, with the XXIX and the XXXIII Battalions
CLXXXV *Nembo* paratrooper battalion
Piemonte Alpine battalion
Arditi assault battalion
Eleventh Artillery Regiment, with two battalions of 75 mm howitzers, a battalion of 100 mm howitzers, and a battalion of 105 mm guns
Engineer and supply units

3. As mentioned, the *Monte Granero* had been part of the 175° Reggimento Alpino Territoriale Mobile stationed in Corsica, and was the only battalion not to be disbanded after the fighting on that island.

4. With the arrival of the new units, the Corpo Italiano di Liberazione consisted now of

Nembo paratrooper division
I Brigade, with Fourth *bersaglieri* Regiment, Third Alpini Regiment, IV Gruppo of mule pack artillery
II Brigade, with Sixty-Eighth Infantry Regiment, *S. Marco* Marine Infantry Regiment, IX Assault Unit, V Gruppo of mule pack artillery
Eleventh Artillery Regiment, with I Gruppo of 105 mm guns, II Gruppo of 100 mm howitzers, III Gruppo and IV Gruppo with 75 mm howitzers, V Gruppo of 57 mm antitank guns (British 6-pounder guns), a 20 mm gun battery
Engineer and supply units

5. Apart from the Reggimento di Fanteria Speciale, the *Legnano* consisted of

Sixty-Eighth Infantry Regiment, with three battalions
Eleventh Artillery Regiment, with eight field, antitank, and antiaircraft battalions
Engineer and supply units

6. The Centro Addestramento Reparti Speciali (special units training center), was created in the spring of 1944 by the RSI authorities, in agreement with the Germans, to coordinate the several units that were already active in counterguerrilla operations in northern Italy. Later on, it was transformed into a regular unit, called *Cacciatori degli Appennini*, which was specifically assigned to antipartisan activity and consisted of four battalions, the *Cadore* being one of them.

7. The *RaketePanzerBüchse.43*, or RPzB.43, commonly known also as *Panzerschreck*, was a portable antitank rocket launcher that shot hollow-charge projectiles and was similar to the American *bazooka*; it was manufactured in Germany beginning in 1943.

Chapter 14

1. Signatories of the treaty were the United States, Canada, Great Britain, France, Denmark, Iceland, Norway, Belgium, the Netherlands, Luxembourg, Italy, and Portugal; later, Greece, Turkey, West Germany, and Spain also joined. In response, in 1955, the USSR promoted the Warsaw Pact, signed by the USSR, Poland, Czechoslovakia, Hungary, Romania, Bulgaria, East Germany, and Albania, which left in 1968. The Warsaw Pact ended in 1991, and many former adherent countries have joined NATO since then.

2. The *Comando Truppe Carnia* had first been formed in 1960 to unify the command of all the units stationed in the Carnia area, to the north of Veneto and Friuli, bordering Austria; the Brigata *Julia* was among the subordinate units. In 1969, its area of responsibility was broadened to also include the Cadore, to the west of Carnia, and, as a consequence, the Brigata *Cadore* has been subordinated to it. The *Comando* was disbanded in June 1975.

BIBLIOGRAPHY

AA.VV., *Le operazioni delle unità italiane al fronte russo (1941–1943)*, USSME, 1993.

AA.VV., *Storia dell'artiglieria italiana*, 17 volumes edited between 1934 and 1996.

Adami G., *Relazione sul ripiegamento del 5° Reggimento Alpini "Tridentina" dalla linea del Don nel periodo dal 15 al 31 gennaio 1943*, in Studi Storico-Militari, 1984, p. 357.

Andreoletti Arturo, Viazzi Luciano, *Con gli Alpini sulla Marmolada 1915–1917*, Mursia, Milano, 1982.

Anzanello Ezio, *Marmolada 1916–1917*, in Storia Militare n. 241, ottobre 2013.

Ardito Stefano, *Alpini, una grande storia di Guerra e di pace*, Corbaccio, 2019.

Barba Selene, *La resistenza dei militari italiani all'estero–Francia e Corsica*, Rivista Militare, 1995.

Boffelli Roberto, Giampiero Bonetti, Marcello Calegari, *I fratelli Calvi*, Editrice Cesare Ferrari, 1990.

Brentari Ottone, *Il tenente generale Giuseppe Perrucchetti*, Società Editrice Dante Alighieri, Milano-Roma-Napoli, 1918.

Comitato promotore perla storia del Genio Alpino, *Cronache del Genio Alpino*, Mursia, 1981.

Commissione italiana di storia militare, *L'Italia in guerra. Il quinto anno–1944*, 1995.

Corradi Egisto, *La ritirata di Russia*, Longanesi, 1965.

Crapanzano Ernesto, *Il I Raggruppamento Motorizzato italiano (1943–1945)*, USSME, 1949.

Crapanzano Ernesto, *Il Corpo Italiano di Liberazione (aprile – settembre 1944)*, USSME, 1950.

Crapanzano Ernesto, *I Gruppi di Combattimento. Cremona-Friuli-Folgore-Legnano-Mantova-Piceno (1944–1945)*, USSME, 1951.

Cravarezza Franco e Tommaso, *Il Battaglione Alpini Piemonte 1943–45: la guerra di liberazione dell'esercito italiano*, Edizioni del Capricorno, 2015.

Cucut Carlo, Crippa Paolo, *Reparti Alpini nella R.S.I.*, Soldiershop, 2019.

Cucut Carlo, *Le forze armate della RSI, 1943–1945*, GMT, 2005.

Faldella Emilio, *Storia delle truppe alpine*, Cavallotti Editori, Milano, 1972.

Fatuzzo Giacomo, *Storia della Divisione Julia nella campagna di Grecia*, Longanesi, 1970.

Finazzer Enrico, *Basti in groppa! L'artiglieria someggiata dall'Armata Sarda all'Esercito Italiano*, GMT, 2018.

Finazzer Enrico, *Le artiglierie del CTV nella guerra civile spagnola*, Notiziario Modellistico n. 3/2014.

Fontanive Giorgio, Santomaso Loris, *Appunti sul sottotenente del 7° reggimento Alpini Mario Cadorin*, in Aquile in Guerra, n.8, 2000, page 102.

Galbiati Manuel, Giorgio Seccia, *Dizionario Biografico della Grande Guerra*, Nordpress, Chiari, 2009.

Gambarotto Stefano, *Alpini–Ieri e oggi in prima linea per il prossimo*, Editrice Storica, 2017.

Gestro Stefano, *La Divisione italiana partigiana Garibaldi*, Mursia, 1981.

Grazzini Andrea Giacomo, *A difesa di Roma–Capisaldi e bunker italiani intorno alla capitale nella seconda guerra mondiale*, Youcanprint, 2021.

Ilari Virgilio, *Giuseppe Domenico Perrucchetti e l'origine delle Truppe Alpine*, in Rivista Militare, May 1990.

Martinelli Vittorio, *Guerra alpina sull'Adamello*, Antolini Centro Stampa, Tione (TN), 1996.

Massignani Alessandro, *La Stafexpedition del maggio-giugno 1916*, in Storia Militare n. 4, January 1994.

Massignani Alessandro, *La difesa dell'altopiano di Asiago dopo Caporetto*, in Storia Militare n. 21, June 1995.

Montanari Mario, *L'esercito italiano nella campagna di Grecia*, USSME, 1999.

Musizza Walter, Giovanni De Donà, *Giovanni Sala. Il capitano della Sentinella*, Edizioni DBS, 2015.

Ongaro Bruno, *La morte del generale Cantore*, ne *Il Gazzettino*, August 24, 2001.

Peduzzi Vitaliano, *La Divisione alpina Pusteria*, Mursia, 1992.

Piacentini Carlo, Formiconi Paolo, *Alpini in Montenegro*, in Storia Militare n. 243, December 2013.

Pisanò Giorgio, *Giambattista Lombi, Penna Nera, storia e battaglie degli Alpini d'Italia*, Edizioni FPE, Milano, 1968.

Rasero Aldo, *Alpini della Julia. Divisione Miracolo*, Mursia, 1977.

Rizza Mario, *I nostri battaglioni Alpini*, Manfrini Editori, Calliano (TN), 1987.

Rochat Giorgio, *La campagne italienne du juin 1949 dans les Alpes occidentales*, in Revue Historique des Armées n. 250/2008.

Rosignoli Guido, *Alpini–Uniformi, distintivi equipaggiamento ed armi dalla costituzione ai giorni nostri*, Ermanno Albertelli Editore, Parma, 2002.

Ruffo Maurizio, *L'Italia nella Triplice Alleanza–I piani operativi dello Stato Maggiore verso l'Austria-Ungheria dal 1885 al 1915*, USSME, 1998.

Scolè Pierluigi, *16 giugno 1915: gli Alpini alla conquista di Monte Nero*, Il Melograno, Bollate, 2005.

Scotoni Giorgio, *L'Armata Rossa e la disfatta italiana (1942–1943)*, Casa Editrice Panorama in cooperation with the University of Voronezh, 2007.

Viazzi Luciano, *La resistenza dei militari italiani all'estero–Montenegro, Sangiaccato, Bocche di Cattaro*, Rivista Militare, 1994.

Viazzi Luciano, *I Diavoli Bianchi. 1940–1943: Gli Alpini sciatori nella Seconda guerra mondiale. Storia del battaglione Monte Cervino*, Mursia, 1989.

Vidulich Tullio, *Storia degli Alpini*, Edizioni Panorama, Trento, 2002.

Volpato Paolo, *Ortigara calvario degli Alpini*, Itinera Progetti, Bassano del Grappa, 2006.

INDEX

Mountain artillery battalions